Advance Praise

"Dan Bloom has written a must-read for anyone in the Human Resources profession considering Six Sigma certification...Read this book - and learn from one of the best."

Christina A. Gasperino, MA
GPHR SPHR SHRM-SCP
LEAN/Six Sigma Master Black Belt

"If I had to make a single comment about Dan Bloom's new book, Achieving Human Resource Excellence through Six Sigma, *it would be, "This is Dan Bloom's best book yet!" But let me go into a bit more detail. In Chapter 4, Dan introduces the reader to what he refers to as "Dan's 10 Commandments" and believe me when I tell you, all ten are absolute gems! Being an author like Dan, my regret is that I didn't come up with these first! In addition to his 10 Commandments, Dan also provides relevant examples of how all three components of the TLS Continuum can be applied to an HR environment. The three components include, the Theory of Constraints (T), Lean (L), and Six Sigma (S). In Chapter 8, Dan presents numerous and very relevant case studies which will all be helpful in understanding the plethora of concepts and tools that Dan brings to the table.*

I could go on and on discussing everything good about Dan's book, but it would take up way too much space. In a nutshell, I highly recommend Dan's book and can't wait to get a hard copy! Great job Dan!!"

Bob Sproull, author of nine books,
including *Epiphanized, Second Edition*

"Undoubtedly one of the best books about applying Lean principles to human resource management that I have read. Dan captured the Lean foundational principles necessary to achieve organizational excellence throught strategic goal alignment, increasing value-add while delivering quantitative results day in and day out. Anyone interested in challenging the 'status quo' in a non-manufacturing business process will thoroughly enjoy the way the book transforms the reader from acquiring Lean Sigma understanding to utilizing the various tools to achieve targeted results."

William F. Mazurek BSIE, MBA, LSSBB,
SHRM-CP President Maz-tec & Associates LLC

Achieving HR Excellence through Six Sigma

Achieving HR Excellence through Six Sigma

Second Edition

Daniel T. Bloom SPHR, SSBB

Routledge
Taylor & Francis Group

A PRODUCTIVITY PRESS BOOK

First published 2019
2nd edition 2022
by Routledge
600 Broken Sound Parkway #300, Boca Raton FL, 33487

and by Routledge
2 Park Square, Milton Park, Abingdon, Oxon, OX14 4RN

Routledge is an imprint of the Taylor & Francis Group, an informa business
© 2022 Daniel T. Bloom

The right of Daniel Bloom to be identified as author of this work has been asserted by him in accordance with sections 77 and 78 of the Copyright, Designs and Patents Act 1988.

Trademark notice: Product or corporate names may be trademarks or registered trademarks, and are used only for identification and explanation without intent to infringe.

ISBN: 9781138359406 (hbk)
ISBN: 9781138359192 (pbk)
ISBN: 9780429433832 (ebk)

Typeset in Garamond
by Deanta Global Publishing Services, Chennai, India

Contents

List of Figures

Foreword to Second Edition

When Dan Bloom asked me to endorse the second edition of *Achieving HR Excellence through Six Sigma*, I enthusiastically accepted by writing a Foreword to his book. I wholeheartedly align with his thinking on approaching performance improvement through the lenses of Theory of Constraints, Lean and Six Sigma (collectively referred to as TLS Continuum) methodologies. This integrates the best-in-class thinking on continuous improvement with the belief in the importance of providing leadership to harness human talent. While the quest for productivity by harnessing human talent has been a part of our civilization history, it accelerated during the Industrial Revolution.

During the Industrial Revolution we built an economic model that was based on the exponential growth of business and human population. Historically, we found ways to increase the productivity of human beings by inventing many of the principles we use today within modern management. Setting goals, division of work, pay for performance, decentralization, resource allocation, motivating employees, controlling and coordinating human talent and developing and retaining such talent are many examples of the progress we made in our search for improved productivity and quality. The explosion of the size of organizations, resulting from mass production during the Industrial Revolution, mandated many changes with internal processes. Internal processes must be repeatable, predictable and scalable so that the resulting products are simple, reliable, durable and affordable.

There were only 18,000 miles of paved roads in the USA during 1908 when the Ford Motor Company was producing the Model T cars. Ford used light and strong steel alloy for critical parts and made the vehicle reliable and easy to maintain. To reduce the variation within the manual processes and to improve the quality, the community of practitioners invented many of the methods and processes used today for continuous improvements. Ford's innovation eventually reduced the Model T's chassis assembly line from 12.5 to 1.5 hours and in doing so precipitated a revolution in manufacturing. By 1927, Ford Motor Company sold 15 million Model Ts, making them one of the best-selling vehicles of all time. As a society, we succeeded in our quality and productivity objectives by focusing on the predictability and repeatability of processes. Unfortunately, many of the same methods also reduced the status of human beings to the level of almost programmable robots. To meet the demands of the growing economy, the role of the majority of human beings was relegated to performing repeatable, redundant and standardized work. Problem solving and creativity needed to address complex challenges that organizations faced during this time remained the hallmark only of a gifted few within the corporations.

Today our world faces an entirely different set of unprecedented challenges as we make progress on this little planet that we call home. Everything around us is changing at a rapid rate that we have not experienced before. The lifecycle of most technologies is decreasing at a higher rate than ever before. Customer expectations for better and flawless products, services and experiences are rising sharply. Barriers to entry are disappearing, and we face new competitors every day from unexpected sectors. The number of devices connected to the Internet is increasing at an exponential rate. The amount of new information we generate every year is also growing at an exponential rate. The amount of non-recyclable waste produced by human beings is increasing at an alarming rate. With more than 8 million tons of plastic entering the ocean each year, we are on a trajectory that will result in the plastics in the ocean outweighing the fish in just 30 years. It is estimated that packaging and single-use plastic make up a majority portion of marine debris. These and many other challenges that we face today put pressure on organizations and the society at large to innovate at a faster pace and frequency than ever expected. The methods and processes that we applied to create excellence with human talent during the Industrial Revolution era are no longer sufficient or valid. The role of human resources must transition from one of "semi-programmable robots" to "adaptable, agile, and innovative human beings" in order to address the challenges of today and create the future of tomorrow. Toward this end, we must find ways to harvest excellence from the creativity and problem-solving capabilities of every human being within each of our organizations.

Dan Bloom's book, *Achieving HR Excellence through Six Sigma*, rises to this challenge. He has addressed the "Excellence in Human Resources" as a broad topic and provided insights and prescriptions from a holistic perspective. He frames HR excellence in terms of (1) **CARING** more about your organization than others think is wise, (2) **RISKING** more than others consider safe to change the corporate culture, (3) **DREAMING** more than others think practical about the potential for your organization, and (4) **EXPECTING** more than others find possible from your human capital assets. Such a bold and broad perspective can enable the human talent of any organization to tackle the challenges of today, while creating a future that is fit for human beings.

Bloom addresses "HR Excellence" as an approach with dual purposes. First, it is used for motivating, engaging and optimizing human talent across the organization to meet the challenges of today, while creating the future for tomorrow for all the stakeholders. Second, it is used for optimizing the HR processes and functions within the organization. For the former, one must apply the principles elucidated in the book across the entire value chain of the organization. For the latter, one must break down the HR functions and processes within the organization and apply the principles to improve and optimize the processes.

Broadly speaking the key HR functions within a typical organization are HR Strategy and Planning, Organization Management, Employee Life Cycle Management and HR Services.

Typically, most HR process improvement projects focus on Employee Life Cycle Management processes and HR Services processes. Major life cycle management processes include recruiting, onboarding, workforce administration, learning and development, talent and succession planning, employee performance management, compensation, benefits, payroll administration and exit management. HR Services processes include data and knowledge management, reporting and analytics, employee communication and enquiry management. All these processes will benefit from Bloom's framework and vision for excellence.

The overall framework Bloom advocates in the book for process improvement is the TLS Continuum. TLS Continuum represents the "Theory of Constraints," "Lean" and "Six Sigma" methodologies, which are the best-in-class approaches for continuous process improvement. The framework is holistic in nature from a systems perspective, and he explains how it is used in tandem for improving the processes within service functions. The book explains the application of key methods, techniques and tools with the help of examples and case studies. As such, the book is practical and can be used as a reference by anyone interested in process improvements involving human resources.

Based on my experience of deploying Business Excellence approaches across organizations around the world, I wholeheartedly endorse *Achieving HR Excellence* as one of the finest books that provides a collection of the practical framework, techniques, and tools to elevate quality, productivity, and excellence involving human talent. Therefore, I expect and hope that this book will raise the bar to achieve excellence in everything we do as human beings. Greatness and excellence are within the reach of all of us when we harness the spirit of creativity and problem solving.

Philip Samuel, PhD
Managing Partner
Lean Methods Group
www.leanmethods.com

Foreword

The theme of this book is increasing HR excellence through the use of Six Sigma processes and approaches, and it could not be more relevant in today's business climate. The intense competition that firms face requires them to reduce waste and to maximize their quality, efficiency and their rate of continuous improvement. And Six Sigma is a well-established business process that contributes to each of these goals. Top firms like Toyota and GE have relied on Six Sigma as an important element in building their performance cultures. Although Six Sigma is not new to business, these processes have only been infrequently applied to the HR function. Cost reduction and control processes can be especially impactful in the area of people management simply because employee costs are themselves so high (the cost of labor can reach as high as 60% of all corporate variable costs). A lack of Six Sigma principles and tools in people management is also surprising because preventing errors and improving quality are of paramount importance in the critical people management processes of hiring, retention, appraisal and development. Looking at hiring as an example, if you hire a weak employee, they will likely begin their job by making numerous errors, which can damage the firm's products and your customer reputation. A weak new hire will also initially require a great deal of management time and training resources. And it's possible that even after all of that investment, the weak hire will continue to be a below-average performer for many years in the future. If you calculate the cost of a bad hire (including the cost of errors and customer impacts), the total cost over a few years can easily reach twice an employee's annual salary.

There are of course numerous reasons why HR leaders have avoided the full-scale implementation of Six Sigma. However, rather than dwelling on the historical reasons, I find that it is more important to look toward the future. The question that HR professionals should be asking themselves is, "Is now the opportune time to reevaluate the direction of HR, and should Six Sigma be an integral part of that new direction?"

Now Is an Opportune Time to Reassess the Direction of HR and Focus on Excellence

Every profession faces periodic major opportunities and threats. When several threats occur simultaneously, it is often called a crossroad or an "inflection point," because the decisions made at these points can impact the entire future of the function and the professions in it. Many authors, in addition to the author of this book, find that today, the HR profession is facing a major inflection point. It is a high point because HR has finally secured its desired "seat at the table," so what we do in HR is much more visible to senior executives and shareholders. But it is also a time of trouble and concern. Over the past decade, HR has faced many threats and challenges. In addition to economic turmoil, there've been many threats such as outsourcing, hiring freezes, layoffs, and changes in workers' attitudes and expectations. HR has faced the challenges of new generations of workers, the aging workforce, a more diverse workforce and the globalization of talent competition. When all of these challenges to HR and business are taken together, few would disagree that it has been a volatile decade (in fact *Time* Magazine called it the decade from hell).

However, before rethinking HR and deciding to go a new direction, professionals must decide whether this volatility is a permanent condition that will remain for the foreseeable future. Unfortunately, most forecasters now suggest that this chaotic environment has become the "new normal" not just for HR but for the business community in general. There is even a name for this new chaotic environment called VUCA, which is an acronym for an environment full of volatility, uncertainty, chaos and ambiguity. Even if the prediction of a continuing VUCA environment isn't 100% certain, it still makes sense to plan for its continuation as part of a worst-case scenario. *Achieving HR Excellence through Six Sigma* does an excellent job of explaining the two choices that are facing our profession. Should HR maintain our current traditional focus on administration and service or is it time to go in a "new direction," where HR focuses on excellence by becoming more businesslike and strategic? I call this second approach Business Impact Human Resources (BIHR) because it shifts focus away from the administration and toward using people management tools and approaches to directly and measurably increase business results. If you choose this new approach as a professional, you will find the contents of *Achieving HR Excellence through Six Sigma* extremely helpful in guiding your transition. I have found that there are four key complementary or supporting components of HR excellence. They are data-based decision-making, a focus on increasing productivity, an emphasis on increasing innovation and increased learning and sharing. Each will be discussed in greater detail in the following sections.

Metrics and Data-Supported Decision-Making Are a Critical Component for HR Excellence

One of the critical components or elements of this new direction for HR is an emphasis on quantification, metrics and data-supported decision-making. The extensive use of measures allows leaders to shift away from relying on hunches or past practices and toward making decisions supported by data. It is obvious from the title of this book that Six Sigma is expected to play an important role in any shift toward a more strategic HR. But it is important to realize that the Six Sigma approach must be supported and complemented by a complete toolkit that also includes metrics, analytics and the use of "big data" to identify and solve people management problems; if you're going to shift away from the traditional approach of HR, you need to stop relying exclusively on traditional HR metrics. Almost all HR metrics currently in use are weak because they simply report history. For example, the traditional turnover rate metric tells managers and HR professionals that a percentage of the workforce has left. But unfortunately, it reports turnover numbers in a historical context, meaning that it tells you how many people left last month or last year. The report also fails to tell you "why" these individuals left and whether any of the turnovers were preventable. Under the new HR model, your metrics need to be reported in "real time" so that managers have data that is current at the precise time that they are making the decision. An even more advanced approach that is utilized in other parts of the business involves the use of "predictive analytics." By its very name you can tell that predictive means that it tells managers what their turnover rate is likely to be next month or next year. Obviously if a manager knows in advance that they will soon have a turnover problem, where it is and why it will occur, they can take proactive actions in order to either prevent the problem or help to reduce its severity. With these advanced metrics for decision-making, people management results can improve dramatically. Another important metric-related component is the use of cost accounting techniques to quantify in dollars the impact of effective HR programs and processes. Quantifying or converting HR metrics into their dollar impact is important because the language of business is money. Once you realize that executives better understand money as a common denominator across all business functions, you will begin to convert all major HR results into their dollar impact. For example, traditional HR metrics report that you reduced turnover by 5%. But it is important to realize that the impact of reducing turnover by 5% can be better appreciated by executives if you add to that metric the fact that 5% reduction resulted in an increase in revenue of $2.5 million (over the reduced revenue that would have been reached if those 5% had left). In the sports environment, it would be obvious to everyone that if LeBron James left your basketball team, your revenue would drop by tens of millions of dollars. However, in business, HR has frequently failed to make a similar convincing argument about the tremendous revenue impact of losing your organization's top performers, leaders and innovators to your competitors. Even Six Sigma metrics become more powerful when the reported error rate is converted to dollar impacts (i.e., for each 1% reduction in our error rate, there is an increase in revenue of $1.2 million). The key lesson to be learned by HR professionals is that it takes reporting a significant dollar impact on a major business goal to get the attention of senior executives. They simply won't pay much attention to or adequately fund hiring, training, leadership development or anything in HR unless they see that failing to do it well will negatively impact corporate revenue and profit (and thus their bonus).

The New Direction of HR Requires a Focus on Increasing Workforce Productivity

A second key component of the "new direction" of HR is an emphasis on increasing productivity. For years, workforce productivity has been the primary measure of HR's impact because it is the measure of the return on investment on an organization's investment in employees. The workforce productivity formula is simply the ratio between the dollar value of the employee output compared to the dollars spent on employees and HR. For example, if you pay an average employee less than $100,000 per year but they generate $2.25 million per year in revenue, you don't have to be a CFO to see a positive side of that ratio. As important as an increase in workforce productivity is, under the traditional HR model, many functions failed even to calculate the productivity of their workforce (i.e., the total corporate revenue divided by the number of employees). And as a result, they also failed to understand and implement the positive actions that were necessary in order to increase it. Obviously, if you expect HR excellence, a primary goal must be to increase the value of the output of workers while simultaneously maintaining or reducing the labor cost required to produce those outputs.

The New Direction of HR Includes an Added Emphasis on Increasing Innovation

Let's return for a moment to our previous discussion of the rapidly changing business environment. In the past, most CEOs would have been happy to have HR continually increase workforce productivity, but during the past decade, their expectations have been raised. This is because while the economy has been down, a handful of firms have grown and prospered in this chaotic environment. For example, Apple, Google, Facebook, and Target have all thrived in this volatile environment coupled with an economic downturn. Firms like Apple thrived because they added to their traditional focus of productivity a new emphasis on producing continuous innovation. Innovation is defined as implemented practices, product features or new products that outperform the existing ones by more than 20%. Obviously in the case of Apple, they have created a series of product innovations beginning with the iPod, to iTunes, to the iPhone and eventually to the iPad. The result of continuous innovation is that not only does Apple's average revenue per employee exceed $2.2 million per year but the firm's continuous high level of profitability has raised its market capitalization to the point where Apple is now literally the most valuable company in the history of the world. Being envious of the results produced by Apple makes every CEO want to emulate their continuous innovation model. Obviously, if HR is to contribute to meeting this new expectation, it must raise its emphasis on increasing innovation to the highest level. This means that instead of simply hiring top performers, HR is now expected to modify their hiring processes so that they can successfully recruit innovators, game changers and what Google calls purple squirrels. In order to increase innovation, HR must also refocus its retention efforts on innovators and it must also improve training, assessment, and reward systems so that they have a measurable impact on increasing employee innovation. In order to increase innovation through-out the business, HR professionals must become experts on collaboration and the other tools and approaches that can dramatically increase employee innovation.

As part of the overall innovation process, it's only logical that HR itself would have to change, so both its processes and its employees are more innovative. Making HR a leader in innovation is no easy matter because HR has a history of being conservative and risk adverse. That of course raises a controversial question, which is "Can you convert the current HR staff and make them innovative or do you need to recruit new HR professionals who are already innovative?" As an HR professional, it only makes sense that you examine yourself, your capabilities and your approaches to HR in order to determine how you can learn to better drive innovation within the HR func-tion and throughout the business.

Closely related to the concept of innovation is the need for rapid change and continuous improvement. It's well-known that the speed of change in business has increased dramatically over the past decade. As a result, now products need to be replaced much faster and business processes and solutions now become obsolete in a matter of months rather than years. Fortunately, the Six Sigma process is an excellent continuous process improvement tool, but more is needed. As a result, one of the goals of HR excellence should be to increase the speed of change and improvement in HR so that it matches the speed of change and improvement of the organi-zation's products and services. If your products are improving at the rate of 25% per year, it only makes sense that HR processes and results also need to improve at a comparable rate of change. Obviously, HR can't be a leader and gain respect if it improves at a rate significantly slower than every other business function. And, finally, if you want to lead the push for innovation, the important catchphrase to guide your actions is that everything must be continually getting "faster, better, and cheaper."

Increasing Learning Speed and Sharing Are Critical Factors of HR Excellence

The fourth and last complementary component of HR excellence is increas-ing organizational learning. Fortunately, one of the major benefits of any Six Sigma process is that it identifies errors and inefficiencies. Although errors cost you money and time, they do have a side benefit in that they provide you with more opportunities to learn. If you conduct failure analysis after every major error or problem, you provide your team with the opportunity to find out what went wrong and why. Having a process that identifies the root causes of problems provides leaders with an opportunity to not only prevent the same problem from occurring again but also to identify and prevent related problems with similar causes. A strong learning process is essential if the organization is to come up with new and more effective solutions to the problems that Six Sigma identifies. When an organization is innovating, learning becomes even more critical. This is because when you are a leader, you are going first and that means that you must learn the fastest. Unfortunately, that learning becomes much more difficult because by definition, there is generally very little written in a brand-new field. As a result, HR needs to increase its capabilities in the area of informal and self-directed learning because there is little time to develop formal learning programs. Unfortunately, in traditional HR, most don't measure organizational learning speed, and even fewer have a formal process for increasing it throughout the organization.

Closely related to learning is best practice sharing. Best practice sharing is a process that involves rapidly spreading information throughout the organization about upcoming people management problems and the most effective solutions to them. For example, in a global organization, if you identify a training problem in one country, it's important to realize that the same exact problem is likely to recur in many other countries where your firm operates. And even if all of your leaders are warned about the training problem, each one will have to start from scratch and use a trial-and-error process to come up with an effective solution. The most effective process for stopping problems from repeating throughout the organization and for minimizing the need for trial-and-error learning is a formal problem and best practice-sharing process using an internal website or a wiki. Unfortunately, most traditional HR functions do not have an effective people management practice-sharing program.

Final Thoughts on the New Direction of HR

As you read *Achieving HR Excellence through Six Sigma* you will find dozens of approaches that can help you in your transition to HR excellence. When you are implementing them, I urge you to avoid considering yourself as merely a manager of HR processes. A superior approach is to instead consider yourself to be an internal productivity and innovation improvement consultant. If you take this approach to your role, as a consultant, you will not only respond to problems when managers bring them up, but you will go the next step and proactively seek out problems. Early identification will be much easier because you will have a toolkit full of Six Sigma and metrics approaches.

As a productivity and innovation consultant, you should also take a broader view of what solutions you recommend. You should avoid being "employee or headcount centric" when you are faced with business problems or opportunities. Instead, you should consider a broader range of solutions that should include alternatives to the traditional HR approaches. Instead of always recommending an "employee-based" solution, you should also consider technology substitutes for labor. For example, you could recommend staffing a call center, but you could also recommend purchasing IVR technology that doesn't require the expense of a large staff in order to have calls answered. Rather than being an advocate of full-time employees, you should also consider offering "non-full-time employee solutions," which might include the use of contingent workers or outsourcing work. In summary, as a productivity and innovation consultant you will need to have a complete toolkit of proven approaches and recommendations for both solving and preventing people management problems, and in that role, your success should be measured by the increase in productivity and innovation after you finish consulting with the team.

John Sullivan, PhD
Professor of Management
College of Business
San Francisco State University

Acknowledgments

When I committed to writing this update of our 2013 title with Productivity Press, I was under the impression that a rewrite was a relatively simple task. It ended up being far from it. When I reviewed the original text, I found things I wished I had done another way and those changes are incorporated in this book.

Over a decade ago I began a journey. It was not a journey of self-discovery. It was not a journey to some specific place or time. It was a journey into the reasons why some of our processes were not as smooth running as we would like. It was a journey to explore the inner workings of business organizations and being able to gain a more comprehensive perspective on why we do things the way we do. Many of the processes we utilize on an everyday basis, when carefully screened, are hurting us in the long run.

The more I dove into the HR process, the more I found things we do every day that just did not make sense in the real world. Since 2013 over six different titles I have tried to make sense of these inefficiencies. I hope that I have been able to show you those and also showed you how to eliminate them. However, I would be remiss if I did not acknowledge those who have helped along the way.

First, I have to thank the people at Productivity Press for their patience while I got the task completed. Due to some personal issues it got extended way past the due date. I deeply appreciate the relationship with Michael Sinocchi built over the course of the books we have worked on together.

In addition, I need to thank the contributions to this work from the various fellow consultants in the marketplace, who have provided a sounding board or agreed to give me permission to use some of their intellectual property including Bob Sproull, William Mazurek, Robert Ferguson, and Peter Stark.

The evidence-based argument for the premise of this book is the real-time example of the tools within the methodology. We were very fortunate to have the assistance of a number of individuals who supplied us with the examples you will find throughout the book including Jay Arthur, President of KnowledgeWare, for his assistance in developing human resource uses of his QI Macros software, which is used in the TLS Continuum Toolbox discussion in later chapters of the book; the contributors of the case studies used in Chapter 7, who provided the evidence-based data to demonstrate that the methodology can and does contribute in the HR arena including Joseph A. DeFeo, President of the Juran Institute; Kyle Toppazzini, President of Toppazzini and Lee Consulting; John Higgins, Vice President of Ceridian Corporation, BMGI, and Guidon Performance Solutions.

During my Six Sigma Black Belt training I learned my lessons well and with some effort have found the path to relate them to the HR arena. Despite learning those lessons it was still critical that my efforts be reviewed by independent eyes with the mission to determine whether we got the material across in a manner easily understood by the everyday human resource professional. For their willingness to review the final work we thank Steven Browne, the owner of HRNet, Nicole Ochenduski and Christine Gasparino, both of whom are past clients having attended the two-day class on which this book is based.

We also had the honor of having some HR pros review the manuscript and Dr. John Sullivan of San Francisco State University for writing the Foreword to the first edition of this book and to Dr. Phillip Samuel of the Lean Methods Group who wrote the Foreword to this second edition.

I would also be remiss if I did not acknowledge the contribution of two individuals to the journey I have undertaken. Eliyahu Goldratt, whom I never had the pleasure of meeting and who left us way too early, through his work *The Goal* and subsequent related titles, started me on this journey. His introduction on how to identify the obstacles in our organizational functions was an eye-opener into some illogical efforts on the part of many organizations, and as stated above, William F. Mazurek, a continuous improvement champion for Maz-Tech Consulting who over the past three years has filled the functions as my instructor, my advisor and guide through the Six Sigma arena. He is the instructor of the Six Sigma Black Belt program at St. Petersburg College.

We also acknowledge the contribution of the participants who have attended our "Driving the HR 500: Achieving HR Excellence through Six Sigma" seminar, who through their questions showed me that there was a need within the profession for a book of this kind and nature.

About the Author

Daniel T. Bloom, is a well-respected author, speaker and HR Strategist,who during his career has worked as a contingency executive recruiter, a member of the internal HR staff of a Fortune 1000 corporation, a HR consultant, and as a corporate relocation director for several real estate firms. He is an active participant in the HR social media scene, maintaining Blogs since 2006, and has written over 40 articles which have appeared online and in print, as well as published seven books. He also serves on the St. Petersburg College Six Sigma Black Belt Review Board. He is dual certified as a Senior Professional in HR (SPHR) by the Human Resources Certification Institute and as a Six Sigma Black Belt (SSBB) through the Applied Technology Program at St. Petersburg College. He is the founder and CEO of Daniel Bloom & Associates, Inc., an HR consulting firm dedicated to empowering organizational change in the HR community.

Other Books by Daniel T. Bloom

Just Get Me There: A Journey through Corporate Relocation (2005)
Achieving HR Excellence through Six Sigma (2013)
Field Guide to Achieving HR Excellence through Six Sigma (2016)
The Excellent Education System: Using Six Sigma to Transform Schools (2017)
Reality, Perception, and Your Company's Workplace Culture: Creating a New Normal for Problem Solving and Change Management (2019)
Employee Empowerment: The Prime Component of Sustainable Change Management (2020)

TLS Continuum Acronyms

ASQ   American Society for Quality
BIHR   Business Impact Human Resources
BMGI   BMGI Center for Strategic Problem Solving
BPMS   Business Process Management System
CAP   Change Acceleration Process
CFO   Chief Financial Officer
CEO   Chief Executive Officer
CHRO   Chief Human Resource Officer
COE   Center of Excellence
COPQ   Cost of Poor Quality
COR   Cost of Recruitment Worksheet
CSF   Critical Success Factor
DDC   Dow Design and Construction
DISC   Dominance–Influence–Steadiness–Conscientiousness
DMAIC   Define–Measure–Analyze–Improve–Control
DPMO   Defects Per Million Opportunities
DSS   Design for Six Sigma
EHS   Environmental, Health and Safety
FMEA   Failure Modes and Effects Analysis
FMLA   Family Medical and Leave Act
FT   Honeywell Functional Transformation
FTE   Full-Time Equivalent Employee
GE   General Electric
GPHR   Global Professional in Human Resources
HR   Human Resources
HRM   Human Resource Management
HUE   Honeywell User Experience
ISLSS   International Standard for Lean Six Sigma

ISO	International Organization for Standardization
IT	Information Technology
IVR	Interactive Voice Response
KPI	Key Performance Indicators
LSS	Lean Six Sigma
LTV	Life Time Value
MAIC	Measure–Analyze–Improve–Control
MBTI	Myers–Briggs Trait Indicator
MSD	Musculoskeletal Disorder
NC	Necessary Conditions
NLRB	National Labor Relations Board
NPS	Net Promoter Score
OSHA	Occupational Safety and Health Administration
PC	Desktop Computer
PDA	Personal Digital Assistant
PHR	Professional in Human Resources
QFD	Quality Function Deployment
R&R	Repeatability and Reproducibility
RSD	Recruiting Strategy Discussion
SHRM	Society for Human Resource Management
SIPOC	Supplier–Input–Process–Output–Client
SPHR	Senior Professional in Human Resources
TLS	Theory of Constraints–Lean–Six Sigma
TOC	Theory of Constraints
TPS	Toyota Production System
TQM	Total Quality Management
UJSE	Union of Japanese Scientists and Engineers
VOC	Voice of the Customer
VPD	Velocity Product Development
VUCA	Volatility, Uncertainty, Chaos, Ambiguity
WIFM	What's in It for Me
WIP	Work in Process

Introduction to Second Edition

Ten years ago, following the completion of my studies and training for a Six Sigma Black Belt certification, I began the journey to understand how to implement Six Sigma into the human resources arena.

In 2013, Productivity Press took the chance on a first-time author to publish the book *Achieving HR Excellence through Six Sigma*. It was a little bit backward as I did not write the book and then design a training program around it. Instead, back in 2009 we designed and developed the two-day training class and then wrote the book. In the ensuing seven years the feedback I have received from the participants in our seminars and the readers from the book sales is that I presented an easy-to-follow roadmap to change the focus of HR. The course is clear that as HR professionals we need to move from being *at* our businesses to being *in* our businesses.

The second edition takes these suggestions and changes and incorporates them into a new view of the topics. I have updated some information. I have added new chapters and case studies.

Chapter 1, **Organizational Excellence,** has two centers of focus. The first is establishing a definition of excellence in general and specifically from the HR focus. The second focus will be how to utilize this definition in the establishment of an HR Center of Excellence or COE.

In Chapter 2, **The Road to Change,** I would be remiss in taking you down the path toward continuous process improvement and the TLS Continuum if I did not bring you along the journey since its inception at the end of the last world war. This chapter follows that journey from the creation of the Toyota Production System to the present day and shows how it was developed, how it operates and where it has missed the real intent of continuous process improvement.

In Chapter 3, **What Is the TLS Continuum?,** like Chapter 2, with the history of the continuous process improvement effort clearly outlined, my attention turns to just what continuous process improvement is. It also looks at the benefits of the effort to your organization.

In Chapter 4, **Project Design and Team Dynamics**—new to the second edition, I have broken out the discussion of projects and team dynamics into its own chapter. I will look at how you choose projects and the roles, training and responsibilities of cross-functional teams in the TLS Continuum.

In Chapter 5, **Voice of the Customer**, I have also singled out into its own chapter the discussion of the role of customers in the success of continuous process improvement. I discuss how to identify the needs of the customer and how those demands affect the organizational processes.

In Chapter 6, **Organizational Waste**, I will explore the fact that every process has its hiccups that cause the process to break down, sometimes slightly, sometimes dramatically. When the hiccups are hidden, they have a tendency to come back to bite the organization. These hiccups are hidden because the organization and HR have never looked for them. The continuous process improvement and the TLS Continuum recognize nine different types of non-value-added activities that exist in most organizations. In reviewing the nine types of waste I will begin to relate the process directly to HR, by looking at real-world examples of waste within the HR space.

In Chapter 7, **The TLS Continuum Methodology**, I will begin our deep dive into the TLS Continuum methodology by reviewing the continuum from the creation of a project to its successful completion. At each stage I will look at the precise tools that are available for your consideration. Some of the tools will be accompanied by actual HR-related examples. Another aspect of the chapter will be a discussion of QI Macros, which is an Excel-based add-on created by KnowledgeWare of Denver, Colorado.

In Chapter 8, **HRCI Body of Knowledge,** I discuss HRCI, the premier accreditation organization for more than 40 years certifying HR professionals across the globe and the certifying body behind other certifications such as the SPHR and PHR. I use its body of knowledge to define the areas of HR operations where I can discuss the implementation of the TLS Continuum in real time and with real-time implications through the use of HR-related case studies.

In Chapter 9, **How to Implement the TLS Continuum**, I bring all the various strategies I have discussed to transform your organization into a TLS Continuum principled one. It lays out a hierarchy of the exact steps to achieve the goal.

In Chapter 10, **The Road to HR Excellence**, I will revisit our definition of HR excellence and discuss the introduction of the TLS Continuum

Empowerment Model, along with strategies to assist in developing results-oriented solutions, which will drive organizational change.

As a supplement I have provided you with some **Further Reading** titles to assist you if you want to enhance the knowledge you have gained from this work.

Introduction to First Edition

As I am writing this book and equally as you are reading it the world around us is changing. The seasons change. The weather changes. We get older (forgot I was not supposed to remind the reader of that). These are changes that we have no control over. They just happen whether we are actively involved in the change or a passive onlooker. Every day nature undergoes a change to some degree.

Our business enterprises are very much like the world around us. They undergo changes every working day. Some of the changes are very subtle. Some changes are dramatic. Nevertheless, they are changes. Our response to the changes determines whether we survive the change or we cease to function because of the changes in our work environments. The 21st century has seen the workplace evolve from a local perspective to a global one. There has been a dramatic shift in the value of the human capital to the organization. We have gone from valuing our talent assets for what they produce to valuing what they dream. But these changes have forced us to take another look at how we function within the organization. Human resources are not immune to these changes. In fact, the changes may carry heavier penalties for non-action than the rest of the organizational hierarchy. We can no longer function as a silo onto ourselves. The period of functioning silos has gone the same way as the eight-track cassette. (I think I finally got rid of my remaining ones recently.) These changes have brought HR to a vital crossroads requiring very difficult decisions on the part of both HR and management as a whole.

Stop for a moment and close your eyes. Imagine you are driving down this lonely stretch of road and find yourself facing a fork in the road. Think about the following question before you answer, which fork are you going to take? More importantly, why did you take the path you did? Understand that your decision carries some direct outcomes for your organization and your career. Let's consider your alternatives.

The left fork represents the easy route. Human resources and the organization as a whole are complacent with the way things are now. HR management is content in sending the message that they are the go-to resource for putting out fires. You have a problem with your paycheck, come see us. You need to change your benefit package, come see us. You need policy police for the organization, come see us. The problem is that the real message you send is that at the same time you are telling the organization that you are the go-to resource, you are also telling them that you are content working in a state of mediocrity and rapidly becoming a commodity. Where is the justification for the value of your position to the organization? This feeling comes from a view that you are operating at the maximum effort and that your HR processes have no room for improvement.

The right fork is an uncomfortable path. It is a path in which you are forced to challenge the entire process. As human resource professionals you are embarking on a journey that will get you out of your comfort zone. You have been arguing until you are blue in the face that you want to be part of the strategic decisions within your organization, but you have not to this point demonstrated the supporting evidence to put you there. You have moved from being part of the problem to being part of the solution in responding to the changing market conditions as they affect your organization.

This book is going to take you on a journey that will lay out the path to resolve these feelings of uncertainty. This journey serves a dual purpose.

The first purpose is to provide you with the evidence to present to the management that you belong at the table. Human resources play a substantial role in the success of the organization. It shows you as the HR professional how to develop metrics that are creditable, verifiable and appropriate for the circumstances that you are working in. The second purpose is to vastly improve the entire organization by providing the vehicle to run the organization faster, cheaper and better. How do we change our systems and policies to deliver them to the organization quicker, at less cost and without errors?

In the pages that follow, we have laid out a roadmap to take you through the journey we have described. The ultimate goal is to lay out a method that has been used by organizations of various sizes and industries worldwide. It is difficult to explain where you are headed without a clear picture of where you have been. So we will start at the beginning with a look at the history of the quality movement and complete the journey with a look at the future. As a result, the chapters the follow are laid out in the same logical progression. The ultimate outcome will be the ability to demonstrate to the stakeholders within your organization that you have reached a state of HR excellence.

In Chapter 1, we will define **What Do We Mean by HR Excellence?** Trying to determine a basic definition of excellence is as difficult as trying to determine what is beautiful. We will try and arrive at a definition of the term "excellence" from both an organizational perspective and equally as a part of the strategic objectives of the human resource space. The intent is to develop a clear picture as to what our ultimate goal is.

In Chapter 2, **Six Sigma: Where Did It Come From?** we take a look at where we have been. We review the various evolutionary steps that the total quality movement has undergone as we have reached where we are today. On an equal basis the roadmap reviews both the successes and the failures of the past 50 plus years since the continuous process improvement efforts began.

In Chapter 3 we begin to explore **Six Sigma What Is It?** You will discover the basic tenants of the problem-solving method. We will look at the impact on an elementary level as to the principles that govern how we implement the changes to our organizations. We will also consider the roles within a project management along with the requisite training and when the utilization of Six Sigma is best practice within the organization.

In Chapter 4 **Six Sigma Toolbox** we begin our deep dive into the Six Sigma methodology by reviewing the method from the creation of a project to its successful completion. At each stage we will look at the precise tools that are available for your consideration at each stage. Some of the examples of the tools will be accompanied by actual HR-related examples. Another aspect of the chapter will be a discussion of QI Macros, which is an excel-based add-on created by KnowledgeWare of Denver, Colorado.

In Chapter 5, **In Plain Sight: The Sources of Waste**, we will explore the fact that every process has its hiccups that cause the process to break down. Sometimes slightly. Sometimes dramatically. When the hiccups are hidden, they have a tendency to come back to bite the organization. We are not trying to cause a mysterious environment. These hiccups are hidden because the organization and HR have never looked for them. The continuous process improvement recognizes nine different types of non-value-added activities that are in existence in most organizations. In reviewing the nine types of waste we will begin to relate the process directly to HR by looking at real-time examples of waste within the HR space.

In Chapter 6 **Applied Six Sigma and Human Capital Management** begins our journey through the role of Six Sigma within the HR arena. We tried to determine a common ground to review these concepts. The Human Resource Certification Institute has developed a body of knowledge that HR professionals use in preparing for the industry certification exams. After careful review it seemed to us that using these same areas of expectations would provide the basis that every HR professional should understand. As we look at each component of the Body of Knowledge, we will look at real-life projects that could or have been used in each. This chapter also discusses case histories of organizations that have successfully implemented the Six Sigma process.

In Chapter 7 we utilize the Business Model Canvas to create a brand-new business model for HR, utilizing the concepts we have reviewed to this point. The purpose of the canvas is to provide a view of nine tenants of a business model and how Six Sigma influenced each. The business model canvas comes from the book *Business Model Generation.*

In Chapter 8, we bring all the various strategies we have discussed to transform your organization into a Lean Six Sigma–principled one. It lays out a hierarchy of the exact steps to achieve the goal.

In the final chapter we revisit our definition of HR excellence and suggest some very concrete strategies to achieve HR excellence in this new world we have designed.

As a supplement we have provided you with some **Further Reading** titles to assist you if you want to enhance the knowledge you have gained from this work.

Let's begin the journey.

Chapter 1

Organizational Excellence

The idea of excellence is in the eyes of the beholder. Have you ever watched the jaywalking segments on the *Tonight* show? I am not referring to the act of crossing the street in the middle of the block. I am referring to Jay Leno going out on the streets of Hollywood and asking everyday people a specific question on any number of topics. It is sufficient to say that some of the answers are in the range from correct to bizarre. Try a personal jaywalking type of experience in your personal lives. Ask the people you approach what the term *excellence* means to them. I guarantee that you will receive a wide variety of answers, as I said, excellence is in the eyes of the beholder. The responses will be guided by both internalized bias and cultural upbringing. Our ultimate goal is to reach as close to a state of perfection as possible.

Definition of Excellence

You have lived in this global environment, and as such your environment has generated certain feelings toward what is excellent and what is not. Your environment pressures you to answer the question in a particular way or fashion. These biases influence everything we do and say, from a personal perspective. Each person is going to have a concept in mind that defines excellence.

The business workplace is no different. In business, every organization is trying to reach that optimum performance level for its operations.

Organizations seek the ability to say that they excel at what they do. The difficulty, however, is that the definition of excellence is elusive.

As support of what I am suggesting, open any web browser and google "definition of excellence"; the results will tell you the difficulty in arriving at a concrete definition. When I did a Google search of "definition of excellence" I got 328,000,000 results. When I change the search parameters to "defining excellence" the number of results drops to 110,000,000. The dilemma is that when confronted with this wide assortment, as individuals we have a hard time determining a single definition for excellence that satisfies everyone. One way to make that determination is to recognize that there are certain conditions that must be present for us to even begin to talk of excellence.

The website Vocabulary.com[1] tells us several things about the definition of excellence. First, it tells us that it is not easy to achieve, and, second, it tells us that it is hard to define because it is rare to find it in the workplace. The essence of its definition is that excellence represents being the very best at what you do every day.

Consultant Robert Ferguson and his website Ferguson Values[2] suggest that excellence is defined by doing well at what we do—that your organization believes in the quality of the products and services that you produce. They further state that excellence means trying to improve your processes all the time. It means that you are never complacent in the status of your organization, knowing and understanding that there is always a better way.

Merriam-Webster's Dictionary,[3] one of the oldest and most well-known dictionaries, defines *excellence* as a noun that shows an excellent or valuable quality; it also means setting a high standard. So, if we follow the logic from the dictionary, we begin to see that excellence means that we need to demonstrate that we are operating at a level that is perceived to be the best compared to our peers regarding what our responsibility levels are supposed to be.

Jeffrey Spear, president of Studio Spear, in an article for the American Marketing Association "Defining Excellence,"[4] suggested that trying to reach this point of consensus is totally subjective, which adds to our difficulties in our endeavors. He also suggested that in a real sense excellence is something we have created to attach value to the things we create and validate our choices.

Consider another view of the term *excellence*. Reportedly if you visit the U.S. Military Academy at West Point, you will find engraved on the walls of one of the buildings the following definition of excellence written by an anonymous author.

EXCELLENCE is the result of
CARING more than others think wise
RISKING more than others think safe
DREAMING more than others think practical
EXPECTING more than others find possible

The quotation suggests that to reach the point of excellence we have to invest more of ourselves to reach the best in class to attain the indicated goal. The West Point definition suggests that excellence is a set of behaviors or actions that manifest themselves in the way that is perceived by those who influence us. It suggests that to achieve a state of excellence, we are required to change from the path of least resistance to more involvement in the outcomes. It means that we must move away from being purely transactional in essence to a more strategic mode. The changes are required both on an individual basis and on an organizational level. It further suggests that to achieve a state of excellence you have to be an active participant in the change process.

Peter Stark, President of Peter Barron Stark Consulting, in an article for the American Management Association, suggests that there are ten keys to workplace excellence:[5] provide a compelling, positive vision with clear goals; communicate the right stuff at the right time; select the right people for the right job; create a united, team atmosphere; encourage cool stuff—continuous improvement and innovation; recognize and reward excellent performance; demand accountability; ensure that every employee learns and grows; deal with problems quickly and effectively; make sure each employee understands—it's all about the customer.

Provide a Compelling, Positive Vision with Clear Goals

Neil Kokemuller suggests that

> In an effective business, the role of management is clearly distinguished from that of front-line workers. Managers develop and communicate the overall purpose and structure of the company. Managers also build a collaborative company culture and team atmosphere that makes the line between management and employees closer.[6]

As I described in my book *Employee Empowerment: The Prime Component of Sustainable Change Management (2020)*, the empowered manager provides these ultimate policies but in cooperation with the other parts of the organization. From our perspective an empowered organizational management/manager provides the organization and its human capital assets with a standard set of values, defined corporate goals, defined strategy, a defined mission and an underlying corporate culture. It is critical to our discussion that you have a clear picture as to what each means in your organization and your organizational alignment in support of the change.

Corporate Goals—Based on the corporate culture, mission statement and values the organization establishes a strategy to ensure that it is on the right path to meet customer expectations. Every organization establishes a set of specific targets which determine whether the organization stays on the right track. These targets have a specific time and place, and they are quantifiable, meaning that we have verifiable data to support them. The empowered manager understands these targets and how to disseminate them to the organization. The empowered manager understands that these targets are not just some artificial thought or concept but living embodiment of the organization. They are the life blood of the organization.

The importance of these goals is that in order for them to be viable they must meet certain criteria.

First, they must be aligned with the corporate mission, values strategy and culture. They must be not something that exists as a fad at the whim of some manager who heads the latest and best concept without consideration for the entire organization.

Second, your organizational goals must be compelling. Joe Vitale, the Spiritual Teacher, tells us that "our goals should scare you a little, and excite you a lot."[7] Your goals must tell the organization what is in it for them and why the time is right for the goals to be implemented.

Third, the goals must be clear in both their meaning and intent. They must be easily understood by the entire organization without requiring detailed explanations.

Communicate the Right Stuff at the Right Time

Excellence requires that when we communicate the changes, we need to keep in mind two critical factors. First, are we presenting these new goals in the correct format? Are these new goals presented as some new management fad, or are we truly communicating the reasoning behind the changes? The second aspect is the decision of when to communicate the move to excellence. Do we do it as everyone is leaving for the weekend, or do we do it through scheduled orientations to let everyone understand why we are undertaking the effort?

Select the Right People for the Right Job

As we will see later in this chapter, the end game is the creation of a center of excellence. In doing so we need to carefully ensure that the human capital assets that are assigned to coordinate the drive to excellence are those who can complete the effort. This is not the time to assign responsibilities because the individual is the boss's favorite or the person is in a rut and needs a boost up. It is not the time to choose someone to lead the effort based on a manager's biases or stereotypes about the abilities of certain people or groups to perform the responsibilities that are needed.

Create a United, Team Atmosphere

Excellence is a team sport. As we will see later, in the last chapter, one of the pillars of the road forward is to develop the corporate mantra centered around change and process improvement. Everyone from the ivory tower to the front office to the supply chain must buy into the effort. Of all process improvement efforts, 75 percent fail because not everyone is on board with the new normal. It is an atmosphere of that is my story and I am sticking to it.

The acquisition of excellence means that we all have to be on the same page. We all have to be onboard with the effort, why it is necessary and the direction that the organization as a whole has decided to go in. The excellent organization becomes the new normal.

Encourage Cool Stuff—Continuous Improvement and Innovation

As an organization you want an engaged workforce, if for no other reason than it makes the road to achieving excellence that much easier. Make the road fun. Encourage the use of diverse ideas and thinking beyond the box. Don't fall into the trap of thinking that something is a bad idea until you try the idea out. Ask yourself the question, "What if?" What does the problem look like if we tried to resolve it this way? Little changes are what create a winning change effort. As W. Edwards Deming told us, drive out the fear of trying. Celebrate the ideas generated by your subject matter experts on how to resolve the problems facing the organization.

Recognize and Reward Excellent Performance

Excellence means that we have to identify the organizational examples of excellence. It means that we need to identify those human capital assets or departments that are excelling at improving the organization.

The reward aspect does not have to be monetary. Several organizations have constructed whiteboards in the main lobby or in the break room where the successes of the organization can be portrayed for all to see. This effort can be a tool to enhance the organization's buy-in to the improvement effort.

Demand Accountability

Organizational excellence is an organizational priority. No one regardless of their status in the organization can claim that a task on the road to excellence is not their job. Each and every individual within the organization is responsible for seeing that their part of the effort is carried out. If they are not, then management needs to train them to meet their responsibilities and then coach them on how to get to where they are supposed to be. If they can't get there, then management needs to coach them on an exit strategy.

Ensure that Every Employee Learns and Grows

The ultimate goal of the empowered human capital assets is to work for a valued organization. To achieve this goal, they must understand how to get there. The process begins with explaining to the organization and its human capital assets what is in it for them in order to make the change to excellence. From there the process moves to the education of the organization.

The education part of the excellence equation involves explaining to the organization what the changes are and what the new normal expects on their behalf going forward—defining the performance expectations and outcomes of the introduction of the new process(es). Once everyone has been educated on the changes, the next step is to train them on the parts of the process that may not have caught on. With the education and training completed, there is inevitably going to be some human capital assets who just don't get the message. From there excellence means you take those individuals and in a one-on-one coaching session work with them to identify where the problems exist. The coaching process also involves the establishment of an individual improvement plan to help them obtain the necessary skills.

If this does not work, then at some point a new coaching session takes place in which we show the human capital assets the most efficient way to plan for their exit from the organization and lay out a career path going forward for them.

Deal with Problems Quickly and Effectively

Excellence also means that as an organization we need to learn not to procrastinate. I totally recognize that putting a task off that may be uncomfortable or out of your comfort zone may lead you to put off that decision.

Taiichi Ohno told us that having no problems is the biggest problem of all. If we know that there is a problem, then we need to likewise understand that leaving problems unresolved means that the problem will fester and become worse. The definition of excellence means that we understand that organizational health depends on us handling our problems in two ways. First, we need to confront the problems when we find them, and second, we must plan to resolve those issues with the presence of minimal waste in those efforts. It means we need to remove any obstacles that stand in our way to resolution. It means that you need to limit the introduction of efforts of special interests within the organization to sidetrack the problem resolution efforts. It means that while we need to be open to a diversity of ideas that does not mean that we need to be open to ideas that are not related to the problem at hand.

Make Sure Each Employee Understands— It's All about the Customer

Many business individuals from Jack Welch to Tony Alessandra have told us that the primary purpose of our organization is to gain and maintain our customers. The success of your organization is not rooted in the minds of the management in the corner office. The success of your organization is not rooted in your subject matter experts on the front line. The success of your organization is rooted in the minds of your customers.

Your missions, values and goals must have the customer and their needs as the basis of everything you do. It means that everything we do must ask first whether this policy, process or procedure is in the customer's best interests. It means that we need to have our organization aligned with the voice of the customer, as we will see in Chapter 5.

Obviously, we could go on forever talking about a wide variety of definitions for the term excellence and try to generate a generic definition. In the long run, however, it would not resolve the central question of this text. How do we reach the near-perception level of best in class?

Definition of HR Excellence

The purpose of this book is not to discuss ad infinitum the definition of excellence in general but rather to consider what excellence means from an HR perspective. While what I have presented above plays into this definition, there are some characteristics of our organization which feed only into the area of HR excellence.

HR excellence is achieved by putting in place a set of conditions that encourages the development of that excellence state. They are discussed in the following sections.

The Acquisition and Integration of Passionate and Culturally Aligned Employees Who Are Engaged and Aligned with the Organization's Goals

In the early 1900s National Cash Register created a separate department within the organization called personnel. As the business organization evolved, personnel became the go-to resource for putting out fires. The result was that HR had created this small niche in the corner of the organization for itself. You have a policy question, go to HR. You have a payroll issue, go to HR. You have a benefit question, go to HR. Need a new human capital asset, use HR as the gateway to the masses who want to work for your organization. Trying to develop your long-term career within the organization—then use HR as the rung of the ladder to acquaint you with the total organization.

The result has become that we have this silo functioning within the organization that has no true understanding of the organizational business objectives. We have this silo where the members of the department, in many cases, are there to earn a paycheck and not work to build a sustainable organization. Their feeling is that they are this separate entity, and it is not their job to know about the total organization. It means that they are not engaged and therefore not empowered to bring about change.

If we are going to reach a level of HR excellence, then we need to change that outlook. HR excellence is going to require that every member of the HR function consider themselves to be a vital part of the total organization. The HR staff needs to understand that what they deliver is of vital concern to how the brand is portrayed to the marketplace. This comes from employees who are passionate about what it is they contribute to the strategic initiatives undertaken by the department and the organization as a whole.

Using Tools and Processes to Advance the Business Mission

Whether they are on a formal basis or created ad hoc every function within the organization has its share of tools and the processes that are utilized to reportedly make the silo function more efficiently. The difficulty has been that these tools and processes are not based on a complete understanding of the overall organization.

To reach a state of HR excellence, the tools and processes that are utilized in the HR space need to be completely aligned with the total organization. HR needs to understand what the ultimate goals of the organization are and how their tools and processes assist the organization in reaching the organization's mission, strategy and goals.

The Focus on Elements That Are Strategic, Transactional and Compliance Issues

Human resource has a role within the organization, whether we are talking about the new view or the old one, but the question is what is the focus of that effort? Is that focus centered on just getting by, or is that focus on HR excellence? If it is centered on HR excellence, we need to change the focus on whether every action is undertaken from the perspective that what we do enhances the strategic and transactional processes. We recognize that not everything that HR does is non-value added, but much of it is. To reach HR excellence we need to turn the magnifying glass to what is the impact of our decisions on the ultimate strategy of the business.

The Focus on Gaining and Maintaining a Seat at the Table

Google the role of HR in the organization or read many of the HR-related blogs in the blogosphere, and you are bound to find sometimes heated discussions regarding the desire on the part of HR professionals seeking a seat at the boardroom table. These discussions arise out of the need on the part of HR professionals to get out of the silo. Many of us realize that as long as we present the argument that we belong at the table because we add talent to the table, we have not earned that seat.

In order to gain and maintain the seat at the table, HR excellence requires us to change our focus. Rather than being the firemen of the organization, we as human resource professionals need to truly understand the business enterprise. We need to be able to present creditable, verifiable data, which demonstrates that the human resource professional does in fact add value to the full breadth of the discussions at the strategic management table.

The Securing, Training and Retaining of Talent to Meet the Corporate Business Strategies

We talked earlier about the West Point quote and its demands on excellence. If we are going to reach the state of HR excellence, then we need to change the organization. This change does not come from doing things the same way you have always done them and expect the change to naturally happen. It will require changes in behavior in order for it to occur. One of the ways to bring about this organizational change is to implement training to demonstrate why the change is necessary to the sustainability of the enterprise.

This change will be brought about by a new operating philosophy. To be successful going forward the organization needs to move from functional silos to an empowered cross-functional model. Every one of our decisions needs to be centered on what is good for the entire organization, not for Human Resources alone, for example. We need to train both current and future human capital assets on the purpose and intent of the changes. We need to create and put in place a standardized training process for new talent assets. Jeffrey Liker, in his books *Toyota Culture*[8] and his follow-up, *Toyota Talent*,[9] demonstrates a clear picture of the process used in the Toyota Production System to orient the internal and external human capital assets to the new corporate philosophy.

It has been said that if you search long enough, you can find support for just about any view on the web. With that in mind I thought that it was important to get the input of fellow HR practitioners as to what they thought the concept of HR excellence means. I posted on LinkedIn questions and answers, "What is HR excellence?" Over a five-day time span, I received five responses. I also polled some of my HR colleagues for their thoughts.

Of these responses only one individual reported back that I should turn my efforts back to administration and not worry about the other aspects. The single response suggested we should remain focused on the administrative responsibilities as represented by the left fork in our scenario. It represents the path of least resistance. It is the path that Human Resources have always taken. It is a path from which we placed ourselves in this silo if you will. Here are Human Resources. So, what if there are operational issues, we don't have to worry about them because it is not our job or our position duties. We are an entity unto ourselves and based on what we do. As a result, management considered us to be a necessary evil within the organization. You have hiring managers who feel they can do a better job and so circumvent Human Resources at every opportunity.

The majority of the people I talked to found it really hard to provide a solid response to the question. This was due to the nature of the fact that the definition can be very situationally specific. Their answers are very much centered on the organizational culture and goals. Since these characteristics are organizational specific, the resulting definition may vary to some degree.

Based on this evidential information shown above, I can now establish what I believe is a basic definition of HR excellence, which is central to this book.

To me, HR excellence means that we begin with the acknowledgment that HR will now be judged on the basis of what we deliver to the organization strategically. It is our efforts to demonstrate that we are not just this silo within the organization that puts out fires. More importantly it plans out a series of actions which make us become totally involved in the internal processes of the organization. It means that in order to achieve HR excellence, human resource professionals must be actively involved within the continuous process improvement effort throughout the organization.

HR excellence means that we are able to define what HR is in terms of the financial impact of the organization decisions. As we strive to improve the organizational processes based on the strategic objectives, we need to constantly keep in mind how we can deliver these efforts faster, better and cheaper. We need to be able to show the rate of improvement and how the changes have increased the bottom line of the total organization.

It means that we are able to deliver creditable, verifiable data-based metrics to provide management with a clear picture of what we are providing to the organization. The metrics must be able to describe in understandable terms where we were and where we are going. The data collected must be directly attributable to the problem at hand.

I can carry this basic definition further if we return to the wall at West Point and modify the words of the excellence definition. Consider the impact of these modifications.

CARING More about Your Organization Than Others Think Wise

HR excellence means that we don't relegate the organization to a place that just compensates us for our time spent at work. It means we work every day to create an environment that provides value to all involved from our suppliers to our human capital assets to our customers. It means that we care about the image and brand that the organization delivers to the workplace. It means that we tune out the naysayers who try and tell us that this is not what a business does or this is not what we do in this organization.

RISKING More Than Others Think Safe to Change the Corporate Culture

Innovation and improvement come from being willing to take chances. It means that as an organization we must be willing to risk the chance that if we try something we might fail. It means that we must be willing to escape from the box of narrow thinking. Thomas Alva Edison tells us that "I have not failed; I've just found 10,000 ways that won't work." Trying a potential solution to organizational problems means that we recognize that there is an element of risk to anything we try.

There will always be individuals in and around your organization who will try and convince you that this is the wrong path to be taking and that the path is not worth the risk to you or the organization. The risk can be equally great if you don't try the ideas that you come up with. The risk answers the question "what if" from the design thinking realm.

DREAMING More Than Others Think Practical about the Potential for Your Organization

What do your thoughts about your organization tell you about where the organization can go? Are you caught in some narrow rut that allows no room for new thoughts, methods, solutions or directions?

HR excellence means that you are open to the potential improvements and innovations that are coming down the line. It means that we get out of the cover of that is not how we do it here.

EXPECTING More Than Others Find Possible from Your Human Capital Assets

Probably the most important part of the HR excellence model is that you cease the tendency to stereotype our human capital assets into pigeonholes. The HR excellence model sees the potential for actions that enhance the innovations of the organization in each and every one of our human capital assets. It means that the organization allows for the human capital assets to let their minds run with conceiving potential solutions. It means we remember that the marketplace no longer compensates them for what they make but rather for what they dream. Take your post-it notes in your office. If 3M had not allowed one of its human capital assets to dream about what he could do, it would not exist.

With the definitions of excellence and HR excellence in place, we are left with two remaining questions. First, do we know what to work on next? And second, what does HR excellence bring to the table?

What Do We Do Next?

HR excellence is an optimum goal that every organization should strive for to benefit the organization, its human capital assets and its supply chains including its customers. What is not beneficial to everyone involved is to have taken all the steps I discussed above and then put the efforts on some proverbial shelf somewhere and tell the organization that we achieved HR excellence and move on to the net project or fad of the day.

The continuous process improvement effort and the striving for HR excellence is a never-ending process within not just your organization but every organization. However, that does not mean that we can do everything once and forget about it. HR excellence means that we have the ability to look at the organization and choose the best opportunities for improving the organization. These opportunities allow us to understand not only where we are but also what we will look like when we get there. Our efforts to improve the HR function must have a clear picture of both current and future states and what it means to the organization as a whole.

If our desire is to reach a true state of HR excellence, I believe we do not have a choice to remain in the status quo. If you determine that you want to reach the state of HR excellence, then there are some succinct steps to take. First, HR departments must look at the way they operate and identify the ways that HR impedes the success of the organization. We have to do this through not only a different attitude (at HR or in HR) but also a changed direction (transactional vs. strategic).

HR excellence demands that we look at each and every thing we do through the lens of the total organization, not just HR. HR excellence will require that HR be able to explain in clear terms why we have a larger role to play within the organization.

There must be an avenue where you can put these efforts to work. There must be a place or location or process that the organization can use to demonstrate its continued commitment to the acquisition of HR excellence.

There is such a location as demonstrated by the number of organizations that have created specific centers of excellence within their organizations.

Creating a Center of Excellence (COE)

Before we begin to have a look at the role of centers of excellence and how to create one within your organization, we need to understand what a center of excellence is not.

First, a COE is not a steering committee. Steering committees have a very specific role in our organizations. They are there to provide three services. First, they provide advice to the organization. They are a sounding board for ideas. Second, the steering committee's responsibility is to ensure the delivery of the end results of the project improvement effort, and finally it is also responsible for the achievement of the project outcomes. Notice that nowhere in the above discussion do we talk about creating the solutions.

Second, a COE is not a demand center. A demand center is a central and/or regional hub of shared marketing services, infrastructure and processes. Once again, steering committees do not create solutions for process issues; they deliver existing services to the organization on a regional basis.

If a COE is not a steering committee or a demand center, then what is a COE? The website WhatIs defines a center of excellence as "a team of skilled workers whose mission is to provide the organization with best practices around a particular area of interest (which is why you can find COEs in healthcare, marketing, IT, finance, etc.)." The COE also helps with the remediation of knowledge deficits within the organization. It enables the organization to reach out and obtain resources to answer questions that the organization may not have readily available to resolve issues. The COE is a key to eliminating inefficiency as we can centralize the organizational knowledge base in one location rather than chasing an issue through the breadth of the organization. Finally, the COE disseminates knowledge about its specific area of interest and provides the organization with support for implementing the best practices.[10]

Pega Technology Systems suggests that the introduction of a center of excellence in an organization will need to undergo five interdependent steps in the process of developing a center of excellence.[11]

In the first stage the organization has heard about the COE concept, but it is some nebulous concept. And the organization believes that this idea about creating a center of excellence may have some merit. A customer (internal or external) has told the organization that there is a problem. The question is how does the organization go about finding solutions to resolve the problem? However, here is the stumbling block. You have no plan to resolve the issue in place. You have a problem, but there is no direction as to where to start and where to end the improvement process. I hate to be the bearer of bad news, but if you do resolve an issue, it is by luck rather than by a standardized, concrete method to do so. You and your organization are in essence flying by the seat of your pants.

In the second stage the organization has taken the first steps toward an organized problem-solving process. You have created a cross-functional team with the roles and responsibilities of each member clearly defined. The team members have a clear picture of what is expected of them in the problem-solving process. The team has reviewed the problem and determined which resources are going to be required to complete the improvement process. The team has identified those steps in the process where the cross-functional team and the organization intersect. With the preliminary structure of the COE in place, the team looks at where the work of the COE incorporates governance of the processes. The active projects are loosely coordinated through the team and the COE.

In stage three, we find a more coherent center of excellence. The resources of the COE are shared with the various cross-functional teams across the organization. It is critical that the teams and the COE identify those touch points where the team efforts and the COE are utilizing shared services. In these cases, the COE coordinates the information flow so that the organization creates skill benches and expertise can be brought to a project and then returned to a centralized location for use the next time those services are needed. This process also enables the COE to monitor the process of projects that are underway and their progress. In this way the

COE is able to identify and evaluate the potential opportunities that may be created to manage the business process of the organization.

Stage four brings us closer to a formal COE. The successes that have occurred so far have laid the groundwork for the development of COEs in other functions within the organization. In stage four we change the nomenclature, and instead of calling them centers of excellence we call them competency centers. An important function of these centers is to define the standards for application development and the various business requirements.

The fifth and final stage has a full COE in place and operating. The center of excellence(s) is going forward driving the sharing of processes across every aspect of the organization. The same operating model is seen in all the business lines. The corporate mantra is in place portraying that the organization is advocating continuous process improvement with the understanding that it believes that there is always a better way of delivering to the customer, therefore listening to the voice of the customer.

We can graphically show the final stage by looking at Figure 1.1 below using HR as an example. The model begins with the HR function establishing what its mission is within the overall organization. Is the HR function in the organization or at the organization? With the written mission statement in place and ingrained in the organization, the focus of the model moves to

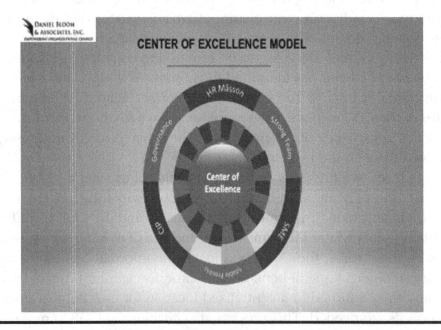

Figure 1.1   Center of excellence model.

the establishment of the COE and the cross-functional teams. For the two entities to operate completely the model identifies who are the subject matter experts within the COE. Who within the COE has the resources, skills and abilities to add value to the project resolution efforts? The SMEs are the guiding forces for the creation of stable processes across the organization. Once the processes are stabilized the focus shifts to constantly improving them going forward.

It is critical at this point that the COE exercises governance over the organization to ensure that the organization is following all the requirements that are imposed on it.

Now is the time for major decision making. If your HR function is still operating from the personnel management view, then moving to the COE model is a waste of your time and energies. You are stuck in a transactional view of HR. You are there to be the organizational fireman and operate from a reactive view of the world.

To have a successful COE you need to begin by auditing your HR function to ensure that several things are in place. First, are your core functions in place where they are supposed to be? Second, are your core HR human capital assets involved in the management efforts? You are the talent gatekeeper. You are the ones who know where the skeletons are buried. You know who is the right one for that project. You need to act your role. Third, does management understand that the HR function can be the differentiator and the competitive advantage on obtaining the human capital assets that will be needed in the future? Finally, the most difficult parts of this exercise. HR has a role to play, but they do not perform the role in isolation. For a successful COE to exist HR must become the go-to resource when issues in their expertise arise. They provide action plans and solutions to these HR issues that are confronting the organization.

Some of you may have already been down the road to COE creation. Others may be just starting the journey. Regardless you are still left with several concerns that need to be addressed as we bring this first chapter to a close.

These issues are, how do I know I am doing it correctly? How do I measure the COE performance? We can answer these issues by looking at the traits and characteristics of COEs and the answer to five guiding principles of successful COEs. First, I believe that if you are going down this path you have improved your own organization's own expertise. We do not create COEs with the belief that since we created one everything will be fine. In that line you should at this point have developed all the necessary resources to respond to the organizational needs. Further, you should have management buy-in at this point since you need to change the corporate culture to encompass process improvement. The skill bench that comprises the COE staffing must be willing to share that expertise. This is not the time or place "this is not my job" mentality.

The final issue is, how do we measure the performance of the COE to see if you have achieved your goals and intentions in constructing your HR center of excellence? The easiest way is to ask yourself pointed questions suggested by the Perficient Consulting firm in a blog post titled *Five Guiding Principles of a Successful Center of Excellence.*[12]

Metric#1: Have you standardized your processes?
At this point all your processes should be established based on creditable, verifiable data. With this process data in hand the goal is to make every process repeatable, meaning that if you do it once in a particular way then you should be able to do it the same way the next time. It also means that if another department requests information regarding one of their process issues the approach to resolution is the same as if another department asked the same question. Consider an HR-related issue. If we hire a candidate in this fashion today, we should be able to do the exact same process on the next hire.

Another aspect of the standardization question pertains to whether you have aligned the COE with the organizational goals, mission, values and strategies. If you can't answer that question in the affirmative, then before you proceed you must ensure that alignment takes place.

Metric#2: Have you leveraged all of your organizational assets?
The services of the HR center of excellence mean that you are the knowledge resource for the organization. You must leverage that knowledge by identifying all your subject matter experts along with both offline and online resources. It means that you must be the facilitator for organizational collaboration efforts. In their book *New Power*, Jeremy Heimans and Henry Timms describe the nature of this new age of collaboration—an era where the information to resolve the organizational problems comes from anywhere and everywhere, both internal to the organization and outside the organization. We need to capitalize on these resources for finding potential solutions to the process issues that confront the organization.

Metric #3: Are we measuring the performance data of the COE?
It is imperative for the documentation of the COE successes that we measure everything we do. These measurements must be backed by

creditable, verifiable and evidence-based data. Dr. Mikel Harry told us that we don't know until we measure, we don't measure what we don't value. Your performance metrics must show that if we, as an organization, do this, this is the expected return on the changes you introduce to the organizational new normal.

Metric#4: Are we meeting our obligations from a governance view? Governance has two components. The first is what I discussed earlier in this chapter. But there are some additional factors that also need to be included. First, governance needs to look at what is expected from the organization based on the regulations that are influencing how you operate: rules that govern the workplace environment, environmental issues, state and local regulations and so on. The other aspect of the governance aspect is how do your organizational policies affect the process improvement efforts. Are those policies a hindrance or some help? Finally, governance must look at the focus of the improvement efforts and how in the long run the organization deals with the changes.

Metric #5: How do we balance the needs of the organization, and how do we select the SMEs?

To begin with, you want subject matter experts with broad experience in the organizational processes. The SMEs must have a clear basis of knowledge on how the process is and should be working. This means that the majority of your SMEs should be front-line workers. The selection of SMEs must be centered on those individuals who are willing to share what they have learned with the entire organization. This includes conclusions, data analysis, data collection results and methods. Your chosen SMEs must also be continuous learners. They must be looking for ways every day to improve their knowledge base of the various organizational processes and issues. Finally, in this volatility, uncertainty, chaos, ambiguity (VUCA) age we are in, your SMEs must have a clear online presence, participating in groups that affect their areas of expertise. They should become actively involved, for instance, in appropriate LinkedIn groups.

The seeking of HR excellence is the key to successful process improvement. The definition alone does not guarantee this success. In the chapters that follow, we will create the road map that will allow us to reach this point of organizational and HR excellence. We will be able to show what we need to work on, what is not adding value to all the stakeholders (internal and external) and how to improve the processes so that stakeholders are getting their money's worth from HR, and finally to be able to describe in concrete terms what the ultimate organization looks like and why we have a critical part in that perspective. The final chapter of this book provides a road map with specific steps to reach HR excellence.

Notes

1. Vocabulary.com Definition of Excellence. https://www.vocabulary.com/dictionary/excellence
2. Ferguson, Robert. *10 Best Definitions of Business Excellence.* June 29, 2018. https://www.fergusonvalues.com/2018/06/10-best-definitions-of-excellence-in-business/
3. Merriam-Webster Dictionary. *Definition of Excellence.* http://merriam-webster.com/dictionary/excellence.html. 2011
4. Spear, Jeffrey. *Definition of Excellence.* n.d. http://studiospear.com/downloads//DefiningExcellence.pdf
5. Stark, Peter. *10 Keys to Workplace Excellence.* January 2019. https://www.amanet.org/articles/10-keys-to-workplace-excellence/
6. Kahneman, Daniel. *Thinking Fast and Slow.* New York: Farrar, Strauss, and Giroux, 2011. Pages 83–88.
7. Kokemuller, Neil. *Brief Description of the Role of Management in an Organization.* AZCentral.com. https://yourbusiness.azcentral.com/brief-description-role-management-organization-22173.html
8. Vitale, Joe. https://www.thelawofattraction.com/joe-vitale-quotes/
9. Liker, Jeffrey. *Toyota Culture.* New York: McGraw Hill, 2008.
10. Liker, Jeffrey. *Toyota Talent.* New York: McGraw Hill, 2007.
11. Definition of Center of Excellence. https://whatis.com
12. https://blogs.perficient.com/2013/02/11/5-guiding-principles-of-a-successful-center-of-excellence-coe/

Chapter 2

The Road to Change

> If you can't describe what you are doing as a process, you don't know what you're doing.
>
> **W. Edwards Deming**

Introduction

Marshall Goldsmith back in 2007 told us in his book *What Got You Here, Won't Get You There* that we can't rely on the past to get us to the future. It is also critical as we explore continuous process improvement and HR excellence that we understand the background of the movement that has gotten us to this point.

Dr. Deming clearly tells us that everything we do within our organization is based on some type of process. When we review these processes, we find that the continuous improvement process is the baby of the world. Our finance processes can be traced back to ancient Egypt and Luca Paioli who created the double-entry accounting system in 1880. Our human capital management process can be traced back to the days of personnel and the National Cash Register in the 1800s. Our sales management process likewise can be traced back to the 1800s.

The remainder of this chapter will take you on a journey through the decades on the development of what we today call continuous process improvement and the TLS Continuum.

1940–1950

Following the end of the war there was a concerted effort to reconstruct Japan following the devastation of the two nuclear bomb drops.[1] Under the supervision of Gen. Douglas MacArthur, the United States and its allies formed the Supreme Command of Allied Powers, which began the work of reviving the Japanese economy.

In collaboration with the Union of Japanese Scientists and Engineers (UJSE), they brought in experts such as Dr. W. Edwards Deming and Joseph Juran to facilitate the efforts.

In viewing the devastation, the UJSE and the Allied Forces came to the conclusion that the best path forward was to select a few organizations to begin the reconstruction process. That concept still persists today. One of the industries that was selected was the Japanese textile industry. It was here that the Toyota Production System has its roots.

Sakichi Toyoda was the owner of one of those companies. He created an automatic loom, which automatically shut down when an error occurred.

The Toyota Production System was created in 1948, and the Toyota Website[2] tells us that it was based on two principles: "jidoka" (which can be loosely translated as "automation with a human touch"), as when a problem occurs, the equipment stops immediately, preventing defective products from being produced; and the "Just-in-Time" concept, in which each process produces only what is needed for the next process in a continuous flow. These principles were centered on the removal of overburdening work and the elimination of inconsistencies or variations along with non-value-added activities. It is important that you understand that the TPS-based organizations do not operate the way most American companies operate.

There are several points that the TPS put in place that have a bearing on the discussion in Chapter 9. Regarding how we achieve HR excellence. First, TPS organization does not view the manager as a "drill sergeant" but rather as a leader and a teacher. The manager's role is to educate, train and coach his/her department in order to achieve the goals and problem solutions of the organization. The resulting system is as much a continuous process improvement effort as a way to create a new culture model without solving the problem. The road to HR excellence is never about the people involved.

The second point is that of a consideration of the standard of work. HR excellence is not about removing creativity and innovation. It is about identifying a process and maintaining a definitive step-by-step system for performing the process. The key to the effort is to identify a standard method of solving workplace problems. We could go on for some time about the system, but as mentioned previously the Liker book provides a thorough review of the TPS. His treatment is far more to the point of the inner workings of the system. The role here is to present the various perspectives that led to the introduction of Six Sigma as it is used today.

1950–1960

The evolutionary track of the process improvement efforts remained on track with the further development of the Toyota Production System (TPS). More and more Japanese industries joined the efforts as the TPS began to manifest its success and triumphs. More companies began to feel that if it could work for them it could work for us.

1960–1970

As we began the third decade in the continuous process improvement evolution, we began to see the effort to try to add additional tools to the efforts. One such tool was quality circles, which were introduced in 1962.

Created by Kaoru Ishikawa, the idea was introduced at Nippon Wireless and Telegraph. Quality circles functioned essentially the same regardless of the organizational structure. The concept behind the quality circles was that they were comprised of small groups of managers and employees who voluntarily got together to solve intercompany problems. The members were trained in the tenants of statistical process control, giving them the basis for identifying and analyzing processes within the organization. The meetings were held around the normal work schedule, occurring either during lunch or before or after work. It should be noted that the solutions were designed to handle issues ranging from safety and health to product design and manufacturing process improvements, so we are not talking about large-scale problems. Further, despite the principles set forth by Deming, the circles were more than likely within the same department or silo. Once a solution was developed, it was presented to management for permission to implement the steps to change the process. After gaining management approval, the solution was implemented. In some cases, the members of the quality circle were awarded bonuses based on the amount of savings generated by their solutions.

In order for quality circles to be successful, the organization needed to complete some preliminary steps within the organization. First, it is absolutely a requirement that all levels of management understand what the organization's purpose is. In conjunction with the understanding of the purpose, management also needed to have in place an effective organizational process for dealing with the issues that may arise out of the quality circles. Second, we all know that any organization is a breeding ground for office politics and chains of command. The quality circle does not function in that environment. The attention must be focused on the process at hand. Third, as we stated earlier, the quality circle members must be trained on how to work together as a team and trained on how to solve a problem.

HUMAN RESOURCE EXCELLENCE 101: QUALITY CIRCLES

Mary Johnson has been a member of the human resource function at Excellence Manufacturing for nearly 15 years. One day she is reviewing an e-mail from a department manager, in which they are lamenting about the length of time it takes to obtain approval for a new hire to take place. Mary talks with both the manager and some of her fellow department members to determine where the process is breaking down.

Based on the conversations, the people directly decide they will try and improve the process. The team consists of Mary, two of her fellow HR team members and the department manager. They begin to meet once a week after hours looking at the current process. From their review they identify what the problems are, select the final issue that needs to be resolved and analyze the impact of the problem on overall operations.

Following the completion of their studies they compile a report on the problem that was identified and the recommended solution and present their report to the organizational management team. Management, after the review of the completed project, gives the team the go-ahead to implement the solution.

Their solution decreased the new hire process, saving the organization approximately $100,000 in cost reductions. In turn the quality circle members received a 2 percent bonus in their pay due to their efforts.

I discussed earlier in our look at quality circles that part of the development was training in statistical quality control. Kaoru Ishikawa wanted to find a way to democratize quality. He wanted to make the idea of quality control understood by all workers. From this idea he created the seven tools of quality, which was based on his concept of quality circles.

1970–1980

In 1972, based on the success of quality circles in Japan, the improvement staff at Lockheed Martin Space Missile Factory in California brought these circles to the United States. Japanese organizations demonstrated that the circles brought about major changes in their organizations. The interest came about after representatives visited an assortment of Japanese manufacturing facilities and saw the quality circles in operation.[3]

Despite the efforts of Deming, Ishikawa and others, not everyone was enthralled with this thing called the quality movement. Not every organization was excited about the potential for quality circles and their potential for legal obstacles. In 1974, these organizations turned to a new movement called total quality management (TQM).

Unlike quality circles, TQM returned to the ideas of Deming and others and structured its principles around the work of W. Edwards Deming. To achieve this, TQM looked at both the quality of the products that were produced and the reduction in variations in the internal processes.

TQM does not have a universal introduction process; however, it provided to be more effective than quality circles. Contrary to quality circles, the efforts to improve the organization were introduced to the entire organization. We no longer consider the silos but rather how each of the identified problems impacted the organization as a whole. Total quality engineering on its website[4] introduces a simple model to understand the impact of the efforts to remove non-valued-added activities from within an organization.

The process begins with gaining a clear understanding of the wants and needs of the customer. What is it that the customer really needs? What are the customers willing and able to pay to make their lives easier? The view of the customer needs relies on the customer obtaining the products or services they need, when they need them, at a value that meets their needs. As discussed further in the review of the Six Sigma methodology, the perspective of our organization from the way the customer sees it is critical to our meeting the continuous process improvement efforts. There are a wide range of vehicles to obtain the information.

Once the organization had gained a clear picture of the customer needs, these needs were integrated into the planning process. It is important to stress here that we will make much to do about standardized work later on in this book. Suffice it to say at this point that whenever an internal process deviates from the expectations of a customer regarding our delivery process we have deviated from the standardized work. It is also critical that as we introduce the customer needs into the various internal processes, we also need to manage the processes to ensure that the customer expectations are the basis for any and all process improvement.

As we again will see later in this book, the next step after introducing the customer needs into the planning process is to analyze the points where we are creating non-value-added waste to the process and see where and what we have to do to bring them back within the standard of work model. The ultimate goal is to remove the non-value-added efforts so that we get as close to that point of perfection we discussed earlier.

The final stage in the total quality engineering model is that of total participation. As was demonstrated by such organizations as General Electric and others, the mission or value statement was that the sense of improving the organization to meet the customer needs had to be organizational wide. It also led to a review as to whether these customer wants and needs were in alignment with the organizational strategic objectives. This meant that every function within the organization from the C-suite to the maintenance staff had to be included in the effort to satisfy the customer wants. The beginning of the creation of cross-functional teams was intended to assist the organization in making continuous process improvement a part of the corporate culture.

When we look at the TQM world, we find that it is guided by a series of operating premises, which take the efforts and begin the process of creating Six Sigma methodologies. Like quality circles Lockheed Martin was the first U.S. organization to introduce TQM to their organization.

The Japanese model of TQM consisted of four separate steps. The first step was a Kaizen Event (**Kai-zen**), which focused the organization on the implementation of continuous process improvement throughout the organization. The second step was Atarimae Hunshitsu **(Atar-i-mae Hun-shit-su)**, which exemplified the Japanese attitudes toward continuous process improvement, which believed that if we did what we were supposed to do, in the long run everything would be as it was supposed to be. As I discussed above, our point of view must be customer oriented. The third step, AtKansei **(Kan-sei),** tells us that TQM is dependent on looking at how the customer uses our products or services. The final and fourth step, Miryokuteki Hinshitsu- (**Miryo–ku-teki Hin-shit-su**), may be the most important of the four steps in TQM, since it extends the concerns of management regarding quality to the entire organization.

1980–1990

This decade was clearly the most active in the development of the continuous process improvement effort. The decade began with Bill Smith and Motorola. In 1986, a scientist at Motorola had been studying the Toyota Production System and was intrigued by the outcomes. He was in need of a method for describing the number of defects found in a particular process. So, with the help of Bill Smith, the company moved from measuring these defects from the number per thousand opportunities to one of defects per million opportunities, providing the organization with a smaller sample of the available defects. A Motorola publication described the work of Bill Smith as "developing this new methodology was the first step on our journey and gave us the tools to begin measuring and comparing the quality improvement rates of our business groups. Six Sigma became our performance metric and was reflective of a product or process that has just 3.4 defects per million units or opportunities. Over the years, we built on this methodology to include the use of statistical tools and a step-by-step process to drive improvement, innovation and optimization." Through the direction of former CEO Bob Galvin, we made the Six Sigma methodology available to the world. We implemented large-scale training efforts and applied the methodology beyond manufacturing to transactional, support, service and engineering functions. Six Sigma became a collaborative effort between our customers, suppliers and stakeholders and an important tool to engage our employees in a culture of continuous improvement.[5] Bill Smith created what we now know as Six Sigma. If any organization holds the rights to the concept it is Motorola. The term *Six Sigma* is a registered trademark with the U.S. government.

   In 1982, W. Edwards Deming authored the book *Out of the Crisis*, in which he introduced his 14 Points of Quality, which today still provide a framework for our continuous process improvement efforts. The 14 points comprise Deming's System of Profound Knowledge. Before we continue our journey of discovery regarding the evolution of the movement, it is worth our time to spend some time looking at the 14 Points of Quality individually.

Point #1: Create consistency of purpose for improvement of products and services—One of Deming's Points of Quality is that we have approached the concept of quality with a single goal in mind. It makes no difference whether we are dealing with a process that makes something or a process which ends in the provision of a service—the basis is the same. What is our intended destination once we reach our goal? Our purpose must be to identify the non-value-added waste within your organizational operations and remove them. The basis of this purpose is that while the results are important, there is a more important aspect of the methodology. Deming's book on *Toyota Culture* stresses that what is important to Toyota is not the end result but rather the problem-solving steps we take to get there. This consistency of purpose that Deming speaks of is based on this view. Consistency of purpose means that we have to be willing to challenge the status quo every day. We need to understand that every process has its hiccups. It is a natural condition of reality in any organization. Within the HR arena these hiccups may mean errors in the way we do things.

Point #2: Adapt the new philosophy—How many times have you tried to implement some changes within the HR department, only to be told "that is not the way we do things around here." Do not feel bad; it happens in virtually every organization globally no matter what the size of operation it has. If we are going to reach that point of HR excellence, we discussed in Chapter 1, we need to change our outlook as to the way we operate as an organization. We have to recognize that we are either part of the problem or we are part of the solution. If we want to be part of the solution, it means we need to change the way we do things for the sake of the very survival of the organization.

Point #3: Cease dependence on mass inspections—We must not, and more importantly, cannot, determine how we are performing by looking at the operations as a whole and saying they are fine. We can't say, "Hey we are hiring the people we need to, so what is the problem?" We need to look at each process in detail and follow the money if you were to process success. Toyota trains its managers in part by putting them through the circle exercise. The process asked team members to stand in a circle and really observe what is going on.

Point #4: End the practice of awarding business on the base of price tag—Look, I totally get it. I understand that every management team in the world is looking to maximize the dollars within the organization. I understand that the tendency is to buy as inexpensively as possible. But what if the problem here is that the lowest cost provider does not have the capability of meeting the needs of the customer? Are you still going to use them? I would think not. Instead of working off price point competitiveness, we need to change focuses on who can do the best job in delivering the needs of our customers. The key to reaching HR excellence is not to figure what is best for the organization based on how cheap we can find it. In the context of our ultimate goal, this means that we can present our efforts over time as costing less to the organization in terms of non-value-added steps being removed. We will consider this point in more detail in later chapters.

Point #5: Improve constantly and forever the system of production and service—There is not a single process within any organization worldwide that is perfect. This new world we are proposing requires us to consistently and constantly look for a better way to perform as an organization. The voice of the customer changes as the work environment changes. We in turn need to change our processes to comply with the customer's requests. Deming stated that in order to reach the quality level we seek we must improve the system.

Point #6: Institute training—I would not expect that if you were to find out that you were in need of a heart transplant then you would ask your general practitioner to perform the operation. Business is no different.

Our ultimate goal is to reach the point where our human resource operation is considered the best in class; we need to obtain buy-in from both the management and our fellow employees. The best way to reach this is through providing explicit training for the entire organization. The training needs to look at what we are doing, why we are doing it and where the organization will be following the training. The training also needs to demonstrate what the organization will look like when we are finished with this segment of the process. The outcome that is sought is that the human capital assets doing the work (a) know how to complete the process and (b) know how to complete the process without any intentional errors.

Point #7: Institute leadership—If you want your organization to reach HR excellence, you are confronted with two paths, somewhat different than what we described earlier. One path is that the HR management of the organization can tell the FTEs within your organization that we are making the change and live with it. The other path is that the manager expecting the organization to reach HR excellence can walk the walk and talk the talk. You can demonstrate that you are willing to dive into the change process along with everyone else within the organization. You as the lead toward excellence must show that you are willing to share in the sacrifices that might be required. The message that needs to be delivered is that the management of the organization is able to identify those aspects of the organization that need help, using the creditable, verifiable metrics to demonstrate that we are meeting the strategic objectives of the organization.

Point #8: Drive out fear—Take a page out of Taiichi Ohno and look at his "Stand in the Circle" exercise. In doing that you will find that many organizations operate from an authoritarian view of the organization. If someone makes a mistake it is the employee's fault. The result is that the employee becomes afraid to make a suggestion for FEAR that it will have negative effects on their job and career path.

Change is frightful. Change is scary. Change is about developing a problem-solving method that works for your organization. Change is about taking the risk that your suggestions may be in error. What Deming was suggesting in his Points of Quality is that the organization's view of risk needs to reinvent itself to the point that no one in the organization is afraid to make a mistake. In the Danbury Hospital Model in the end of the book, we will look at this topic more in depth. Our goal is to identify how we can deliver HR resources to the organization faster, better and cheaper. Our goal is not to drive fear into the organization by challenging any attempts to change the organization.

Point #9: Breakdown barriers between staff areas—Decide now whether you want to bring HR excellence to your organization. If you do not, then I suggest you put this book away because that is not my intended outcome for the reader of this work. I firmly believe that the only path to success is to have everyone within the organization on the same page. I firmly believe that the only way to achieve this is to foster the belief within the organization that we are all part of one universe. There is no room for grandstanding and the image that one group is above another. Patrick's room for grandstanding and the image that one group is above another. Patrick Lencioni clearly points out the dangers of this philosophy in his book *Silos, Politics and Turf Wars.*[6]

Point #10: Eliminate slogans, exhortations and targets for the workforce—Management has always for the most part operated from the belief that the way to motivate employees was to put cash in their pockets. They believed the way to motivate the employee base is with fancy slogans which actually mean very little to the workforce. In most cases that I have observed as part of my work career, the fancy slogans and mandatory targets do not work. The goal of HR excellence is to meet the voice of the customer, not to meet some superficial concept developed by management and then placed on the heads of the human capital assets.

Point #11: Eliminate numerical quotas—I am sure we have all operated with the framework of an organization that told its operations that you needed to reach a certain level of output. I am equally convinced that there have been times that you have wondered where they found these numbers, as they made no sense when you looked at the operations as a whole. To reach our intended level of HR excellence we need to avoid setting arbitrary expected outcomes. We need to let the methodology identify what the process is telling us and what the anticipated future state of the organization is. Our eventual outcomes must be based on creditable, verifiable results, not on some number pulled out of the thin air by management edict.

Point #12: Remove barriers to pride of workmanship—Every organization believes that there are ways to better meet the needs of the customer. The improvements are usually handed down from the top. Organizations need to come to terms with the idea that the part of the organization that knows best how to improve organizational processes are those who are on the front line of the organization. In reaching for HR excellence, we need to recognize this premise and fully engage the entire organization within the effort of identifying the non-value-added wastes within the organization. We need to demonstrate that we value their input. We need to instill within the corporate culture the belief that rank and file is critical to the improvement of the relationships with the customers. Take the time to listen to their observations and their suggestions to improve the processes.

Point #13: Institute a vigorous program of education and retraining—Once you start down the path of continuous process improvement understand that it is never-ending. This means that your organization will be in a constant state of change. Each and every time you complete a process change, it will call for further training within the organization on why the change and how the change will be implemented. We can't expect automatic acceptance and utilization of the new process without showing the process before and after. This comes from extensive training to introduce the changes to the organization.

Point #14: Take action to accomplish the transformation—If we look at the business landscape and at our personal lives, we can find countless examples of where we talked the right game, but we never walked the walk. Just by management stating that we will change will not make it happen. The Six Sigma methodology, we will discuss beginning in Chapter 7, requires us to take specific steps to bring about the efforts to remove the non-value-added steps to our processes.

A couple of years later, a colleague of Deming, Philip Crosby, along with Joseph Juran, added to the knowledge base with the release of his four absolutes of quality. Like Ishikawa, Crosby was the first to put quality in terms that the non-engineering members of the organization could comprehend. This led to the creation of the idea of the cost of quality. The concepts were presented in his book *Quality without Tears*.[7]

In Chapter 1, I spent a fair amount of time discussing the idea of excellence. Part of our continuing effort of improving your organizations is to ensure that the products or services coming from the organization are of better quality than the prior version of those offerings. Crosby argued that the ultimate quality of your products and services can be defined as conformity to certain specifications that are set forth by management. Quality is not this vague concept that something is good. He further stated that these specifications are not something pulled out of the air but rather are set according to the needs and wants of your end users both internal and external to the organization.

Based on the above definition, Crosby created the four absolutes of quality, which he introduced in his book *Quality without Tears* referenced above. It is worth taking a moment to consider the four absolutes further.

Crosby's First Absolute: The definition of quality is conformance to requirements

As stated in Crosby's definition of quality everything is based on customer-based specifications. Crosby stated that improvement based on the definition of quality is based on the concept of doing everything right the first time around. This requires management to set the requirements and supply the method or process and the tools to meet those requirements. Having done that management's role shifts to coaching the team on how to meet the requirements.

Crosby's Second Absolute: The system of quality is prevention

Crosby believed that if you had to do reviews of the process after you completed it, you failed. The goal of the organization is to ensure that the mistakes or defects did not happen in the first place. You, as an organization, did not want to base your success on these post-process appraisals. Repeat the goal is to not make the errors in the first place.

Crosby's Third Absolute: Performance standard is zero defects

As I have stated, Crosby believed that management set the specifications for the process. In order to determine whether those specifications are meeting the goals, you need to set a level of performance standards which create your organizational metrics. The basis of these performance standards is that there is no willingness to accept any deviations from the established standards.

Crosby's Fourth Absolute: The measurement of quality is the price of nonconformance.

The fourth and final absolute of quality in the mind of Crosby was an additional metric by which to judge your organization. That metric is manifested in the answer to the question, "If you make a mistake what is the financial effect on your organization?" What is the cost behind rework when you have to run the process again in order to meet the needs of the customer? What is the value of lost revenue from a dissatisfied customer to take their business elsewhere?

At the same time as Crosby was introducing his four attributes of quality, an Israeli business guru was suggesting a new way to look at continuous process improvement in an organization. Goldratt believed that the reasons behind organizational problems could be resolved through the use of critical thinking tools. He introduced these tools in his book *The Goal*. Written as a business novel, *The Goal* discussed business processes and how they affect the end product.

The basis of *The Goal* was the introduction of the theory of constraints (TOC). It works primarily at the level of the chain, driving the organizational focus to the weakest links and then to the linkages between that constraint or weakest link and other aspects of the system. TOC, with its logic-based tools, provides strength to the process through the use of qualitative analysis, helpful for dealing with those rock-and-hard place dilemmas that we all face.

Joining his peers, Deming and Crosby, Joseph Juran entered the discussion in 1986 with the introduction of what has become known as the Juran Trilogy. Juran is widely credited for adding the human dimension to quality management.

The critical concept behind Juran's definition of quality management was that it extended outside of the walls of the brick and mortar building to encompass that were the non-manufacturing processes including those that were thought of as service related such as HR.

Juran's Trilogy was divided into three parts: planning, control and improvement methodology. It began with utilizing the resources of the organization to identify your organizational stakeholders, laying out the problem-solving steps and plan on how to implement the findings. Further it established the principle that quality planning is a concurrent exercise, which involves all the affected parties that touch the products or services, so they can provide inputs and give early warnings of problems arising.

Once the plans are in place, Crosby moved to the control of the processes. You begin by defining what quality means along with the expected targets of the processes and the methods for evaluating how the process is performing in real time. The final step is to compare, through the use of tools such as gap analysis, the performance gaps between real time and the goals and plan on how to remove the gap.

At this point you should be ready for the breakthrough improvements to the organizational processes. The breakthrough is created by improving the process with fresh new ideas on how to resolve the performance issues.

In the same decade another major corporation made its impression on the process improvement effort in American business. In 1989, General Electric (GE) introduced the GE Workout.[8] In 1960, a University of Massachusetts trained chemical engineer named Jack Welch joined a company called General Electric. In 1971 he was chosen to be the eighth president and chairman of the board of the organization. Our research found that he understood that our organizations were overburdened by bureaucracy and non-value-added parts of the process that had nothing to do with the customer needs. As a result, Jack Welch pushed the operating companies to find ways to improve how they did things. Based on some of the strategic efforts he put in place, the value of the organization increased to 4,000%.[9]

From the very beginning of his tenure, within the C-suite, he took every opportunity to find ways to clean up if you will the organizational structure of the organization through careful analysis of the individual processes from the perspective of effectiveness and efficiency.

One tool that came out of this new focus of the organization was the implementation of the GE Workout around 1989. The GE Workout consisted of a very structured system to resolve problems within the organization. The continuous process improvement developed along the paths is shown in Figure 2.1.

Welch firmly was against the overbearing bureaucracy found within the GE organization. What he did believe in was the ability of every employee, no matter what his or her role within the organization, to have a say in its future. The basic premise of the GE Workout was that cross-functional teams would identify a problem and create solutions to solve that problem. This process of cross-functional teams being the conduit for change within the organization was the impetus for the Workout program.

The GE Workout consisted of a five-step process as we describe below:

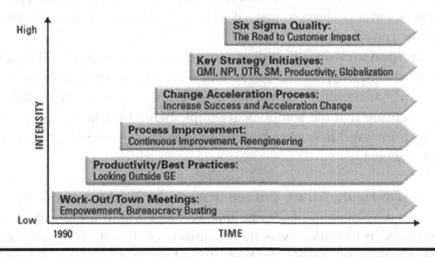

Figure 2.1   Change culture within General Electric. QMI—quick market intelligence, NPI—new product introduction. OTR—order to remittance, SM—supplier management.[10]

Step 1: Problem identification—In the process of delivering the services needed to meet the customer needs, employees determine that there is a problem with the process which prohibits the organization from meeting the customer's deadline. As a result, a collaborative effort is made to identify exactly what the process roadblock is and its impact on the organization.

Step 2: Team development—Following the identification of the problem, a team was put in place, which consisted of both rank and file and management, and they need to apply a review process to the indicated problem. The team's make-up consisted of both internal and external stakeholders. The key to their inclusion was, what was the impact on them from the solution to the problem?

Step 3: Town meeting—Once the solutions to the identified problems were designed the team brought the discussion of the problem to a town meeting where both the teams and the members of the upper management were present. These town meetings could, according to David Ulrich's book on the workout process, could last from one to three days. Each team presented its findings and recommendations to the management team. The report presentations also included the justification behind the solutions.

Step 4: Upper management decision—At the conclusion of each team presentation, upper management was provided with two alternatives. The first is that they could completely reject the suggestions from the team, but they would have to explain their reasoning for saying no. They were not in a position to just say no, or they wanted to take it under further consideration.

Step 5: Sponsorship—If upper management gave its approval to go forward with the problem resolution, one of the team members steps forward[11] as the problem resolution sponsor. It is their responsibility to ensure that the solutions are implemented within 90 days typically. It involved frequent progress reports back to the organizational management.

If we return to Figure 2.1, we can see that within GE, the workout was the base for the development of change management within the organization. The next step up the ladder was the beginning of the efforts among business organizations to identify the best of the best. In that vein, GE began the process of looking at how similar organizations were handling the same issues. It was the beginning of the Best Practices efforts in American corporations.

Based on the work of Michael Hammer and James Champy, GE began the efforts to reinvent the organization through re-engineering. This effort brought to the forefront the concept of continuous process improvement. The idea was supported to say that in everything we do, there is always a better way to do what we are doing. All levels of the organization were pushed constantly and consistently review every operation and look for areas where they could produce better results by running more efficiently.

We have already mentioned several opportunities and will continue to do so throughout the book, that one of the characteristics of the new cultural model is that it is a never-ending road. As the years passed a group of GE management began to look at how we could improve the workout process. Understand it was not that anyone disapproved of the workout process; it was just this inbred part of the GE culture that you constantly looked at on how to improve the process to make it more robust. The result was what GE called the Change Acceleration Process or CAP[12].

The CAP pilot was run out of the GE training center at Crotonville, New York, as was originally termed the Leadership Development Series. At the same time Larry Bossidy, who later went on to write the book *Execution*, developed another program with similar elements and goals. The two were combined to form the CAP. It consisted of a model, which contained six steps that were reviewed on the basis of where we are today, where we are going to end up and how to make the transition. The process began with the requirement of management to lead the change effort. Management had to buy into the change in order for it to function successfully.

Following management leading the change process, the CAP established the reason that the organization had to share the need across the entire organization. They demonstrated why the change that was introduced needed to cross the entire organization, not departmental silos alone. They demonstrated to the rank and file how this change was going to make their job easier and better. Keep in mind that our ultimate goal is to produce our services or projects cheaper, better and faster. The rank and file needed to understand what it was that was in the process for them.

Having proven the need for solving the problem, management turned to create a vision for the organization. This vision provided a roadmap much as we are doing with establishing our road to HR excellence. To this point the organization had established the buy-in by management and con-vinced the organization at all levels why we needed the change and where we expected to be after the change process. Now it was necessary to get employees away from the feeling that this was nothing more than the fad of the day to a feeling of being in an exciting place and time. This was the time when management got the entire organization behind the efforts to introduce change to the organization.

The final two steps of the model could be considered the most important. First, we needed to ensure that the changes made by the model would last. It does the organization no good to introduce this viable system for change only to have someone say, down the road, this is great, but I am more com-fortable doing things the way we have always done them. One of the meth-ods to ensure the longevity of the change process is to measure the progress we have achieved toward our end goal.

We can't have the change take place within an organization without one final step. Change means sacrifice. Change means rethinking the way we do things. Each of these means that in order to achieve our vision of HR excel-lence we must change both the way the organization is structured and the systems that govern our operations.

Both the GE Workout Process and the Change Acceleration Process bring about the required changes in both areas. They teach us how to become better stewards of the organization by locating areas that might be hinder-ing the organization and taking dynamic steps to change the system and the structure. While we improve the systems, we also change the format of the organization through the removal of silo mentality within the organization.

As we have seen, the 1980s was a busy tie in the development of con-tinuous process improvement. While it was an active period, there were still new evolutions to follow, as shown below.

1990–2000

The decade began with discussions in some circles that we were not making the improvements fast enough. In 1990, Leap Technologies introduced the Rapid Workout,[13] which was based on benchmark studies completed on the GE Workout Process. One of their key findings, which were substantiated by industry studies, was that continuous process improvement efforts typically failed for several reasons.

The first factor was a lack of commitment from senior management. We have already discussed and will later in the book that we can reach a state of HR excellence only if management of the organization buys into the concept we are presenting to them. Some managers get it; others feel that it works for others but not in their organization. We need to remember that upper management drives the culture of the organization and if they are not ready to support your efforts to improve the HR process, it will be difficult.

The second reason for improvement process failure is the reluctance on the part of middle-level managers to release personnel for either belt positions or team members. Many organizations today still operate from a point of view that the primary concern is that a department meets set goals on productivity. Letting even one person move to another area of the organization may have dire outcomes to meeting those goals. What is missing is the ability of middle managers to see the benefits of running a leaner organization.

The final reason is that the rank and file fear change. They fear the outcomes usually based on misinformation as to what this change process all means to the organization. They are mired in the belief that there is only one way to do things, the way they have always done it. The natural outcome is that where there is fear there is an obstruction to anything that might change their world.

The Rapid Workout is based on a different working model for Six Sigma–related projects. It sets up different goals for the process. First it is based on an increased speed of delivery. Rapid workout is based on the assumption that the entire improvement process will take 60 days to complete, compared to 120–350 days in a true Six Sigma–based process. One of the initial points of a Six Sigma project is the requirement that you need to provide training for the team members to understand what they are trying to achieve. This new method is based on what the organization already knows and can bring to the table. In essence Leap Technologies has removed the requirement for initial training of team members. Like the GE Workout it is based on making decisions and taking action based on the use of built-in tools. The tools are presented in the design of four interconnected steps:

Step 1: Engage people to build the case for change

The case for change is presented from the emotional connection to the problems, not just the numbers. The stakeholders being involved define for themselves what is in it for them to change.

Step 2: Design for 60- to 90-day "sprint" campaigns

The team agrees on what the important goals or solutions to resolve the issues at hand, with the upfront agreement that the improvement process will be completed in 60–90 days. The team then matches the best people and the right tools for each critical improvement that is needed by the organization.

Step 3: Recruit and launch fast-change teams

As I will discuss more in depth in Chapter 4, the core to reaching HR Excellence is the involvement of cross-functional teams. In order for the team to function in a fast-change environment the organization needs to engage the team members in order to open pathways to a wide variety of views on how to resolve issues before you. The organization needs to ensure that the TLS Continuum toolbox is readily available to the team at all times.

Step 4: Manage the clock and score completions

The final step in the Rapid Workout is that we need to clock the progress of the workout. Remember we are on a 60- to 90-day spend time, so we need to keep track of where you are on that time frame. You want to track how you spread the workload so that no single person or segment of the team is overburdened.

At the same time, on a weekly basis, you want to track the completion of the project milestones for completion levels.

Step 5: Recognize the contributions and sustain the gains

The final stage calls for you to recognize those contributions that have pushed forward the schedule. It can be informal, but you need to ensure that the team members know that their involvement is valued by the organization. It is also necessary that you sustain the improvements through formal recognition of the team both as a whole and individually.

Quality circles continued to be utilized in this country until 1991, when a complaint was brought to the National Labor Relations Board. In the case *NLRB v Electromation*, the NLRB determined that certain quality circles called labor management committees were in violation of the Wagner Act. Signed by Franklin Delano Roosevelt in 1935, the purpose of the legislation was to guarantee the right of employees to join a union or labor organization through an organization of their own choosing.

In the Electromation case, the NLRB determined that the quality circles were established by the firm, and the agenda was determined by the firm.

Further, the action management teams (as they were called) addressed the conditions of employment. Several years later, the NLRB issued a similar decision in *NLRB v. DuPont Corporation.* The NLRB accused DuPont of using quality circles to circumvent the union management negotiations.

In 1993, Allied Signal entered the continuous process improvement field. Larry Bossidy was a friend of Jack Welsh and is the one who pushed Welsh to bring six sigma to GE, was hired as the CEO of Allied Signal. Larry Bossidy, the author of the book *Execution,* and his work at Allied Signal convinced GE to make the jump. The results were quick and a huge benefit to Allied Signal's bottom line.

Based on part on the Motorola Six Sigma process, Allied Signal changed the focus of its efforts away from pure reduction of waste and began the process of looking at the use of business metrics. One of these new business metrics was whether the organization was operating within the operating margins. The Allied Signal system was based on two programs to study process improvement. The first was called Total Quality Leadership, and the second was referred to as Total Quality Speed. Combined, the two programs created a new way of thinking about work within the company. As can be observed in Figure 2.2, the Allied Signal model for resolving problems

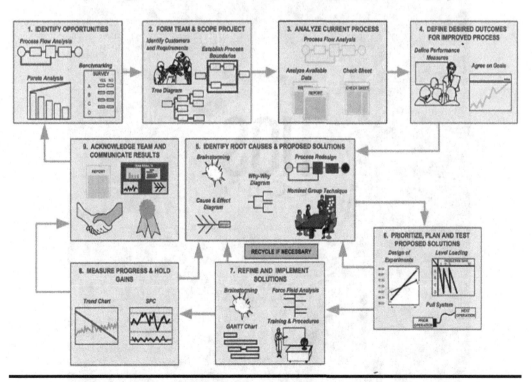

Figure 2.2   Allied Signal's problem-solving method.[14]

involved nine steps. It begins with identifying the opportunities for improvement. With the opportunities identified Allied Signal constructed the team that will work on the opportunity or project.

Once the team is in place its first task is to analyze the current process to find where the problems/opportunities are found. It is important to understand that unlike other continuous process improvement efforts previously explored above, Allied Signal was looking at the total organization. With the current state identified the next step is to define the outcomes you are trying to obtain and at the same time identify what the causes for the problem are.

With those two factors in place, it is time to prioritize the plan and rear the solutions. It represents the third step of the Design Thinking process when you answer the question of what works. Once you identify what works you refine and implement the solutions. Once the solutions are implemented you want to measure the process and maintain the gains. The final step is to recognize the team for its work in bringing solutions to the table.

Five years later, Honeywell introduced its Gold plan to match Allied Signal's efforts (Figure 2.3).

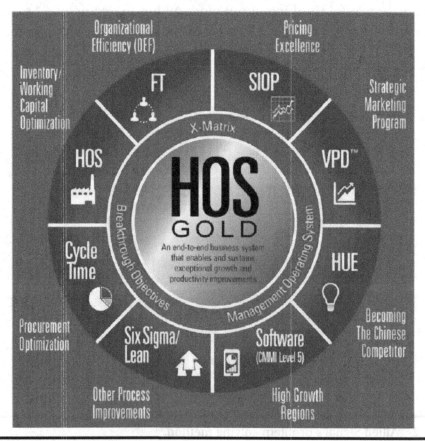

Figure 2.3   Honeywell Gold Process.[15]

The Honeywell Total Quality journey began in the early 1990s, and some of its businesses started using Six Sigma "language" in 1995. Although the businesses that make up Honeywell today are very different, they now have a single, common way to describe their work toward becoming premier—by applying Six Sigma to all of their work processes.

Honeywell had two (2) programs which ran simultaneously. The first was the Honeywell Operating System (HOS), which comprised much of the Six Sigma methodology. It was comprised of kaizen projects, visual management, the 5S, rapid problem solving and standard of work. The other component was the Honeywell Quality Value, which was based on the criteria of the Malcolm Baldrige National Quality Award.

The model foundation was found in eight high-level initiatives. The first was functional transformation (FT). The second was Honeywell Operating System. The third was cycle time. The fourth was Six Sigma/lean. The fifth was software, and the sixth was the Honeywell User Experience (HUE). The seventh was Velocity Product Development (VPD). The final was the Sales Inventory operating Plan (SIOP). This is not an extensive discussion of the Honeywell system but rather just an overview so you can get an understanding of how the model was an integral part of the evolution of continuous process improvement.

In 1998, after ongoing discussions Allied Signal and Honeywell decided that the best track forward was to merge the two operations into one under the Honeywell name, which continues today. As a result, the Honeywell Gold and the Honeywell Quality Value programs were merged with Allied Signal's Total Quality Leadership, and the second was Total Quality Speed; this culture combination resulted in the new Six Sigma Plus. Six Sigma Plus combined the robust change management tools of the Honeywell systems with the activity-based management tools of the Allied Signal programs.[16]

2000–2010

In 2009, Bob Sproull wrote his seminal book, the Ultimate Improvement Cycle. In his book, Bob contended that everything in the world evolves or changes in some way. With that understanding Bob applied that to the change management field. He was witnessing a drawn-out battle between those who felt that the way to improve our organizations was found in the lean manufacturing philosophy that was originally found in the Toyota Production System and those who believed what Bill Smith did at Motorola.

The Ultimate Improvement Cycle stated the belief that the two are not mutually exclusive. It becomes the idea of why you would bake only a third of the pie in trying to improve your organization.

Bob suggested for the first time that we combine the three methods for improving our business processes – the theory of constraints, lean and Six Sigma into a single methodology.

The Ultimate Improvement Cycle begins with utilizing the critical thinking tools to identify what is holding up the processes. What is creating the problems that the customer is bringing to the attention of your organization? Once we have identified those obstacles, the lean methodology uses its tools to remove the obstacles and non-value-added activities. Finally, the Six Sigma methodology creates the standard of work, removes the root cause variations and ensures that all your processes are repeatable.

2010–2020

As we reach the last decade in the journey, the components of the Ultimate Improvement Cycle begin to be introduced to the HR arena. In a 2001 article for *Mobility Magazine* titled "Driving the Relocation 500," I applied the

Figure 2.4   Six Sigma cycle.

tenants of the theory of constraints to the Corporate Mobility process, reducing the process from 500 to 250 days.

This time period also gave me time to reflect on the impact of the methodology to HR as a whole. One concern that I had was that the common method of portraying the improvement efforts was in the form of a circle with the basis of thought that once you made it around the circle you started the process all over again (Figure 2.4).

We talk about the idea of continuous process improvement almost every day so the idea that you could make it around the circle and then just stop your efforts did not sit well with me. Therefore, I created the concept of the TLS Continuum. You may be asking what is the difference. The *Dictionary of Oxford Languages*[17] cites a cycle as being a series of events that are regularly repeated in the same order. It further defines a continuum as a continuous sequence in which adjacent elements are not perceptibly different from each other, although the extremes are quite distinct.

In 2013, I authored the first edition of this book that is in your hands, which combined the three methodologies for the first time to the area of human capital management.

Notes

1. US State Department. Occupation and Reconstruction of Japan, 1945–52. https://history.state.gov/milestones.1945-1952/japan-reconstruction
2. Toyota Production System. https://global.toyota/en/company/vision-and-philosophy/production-system/
3. Kucera, David. *Quality Circles*. n.d. http://enotes.com/quality-circles--reference/quality-circles
4. Total Quality Engineering. n.d. http://www.tqe.com/TQM.html
5. Pierce, Freddie. *Motorola's Six Sigma Journey: In Pursuit of Excellence*. Digital Supply Chain. September 25, 2011. https://www.supplychaindigital.com/procurement/motorolas-six-sigma-journey-pursuit-perfection
6. Lencioni, Patrick. *Silos, Politics and Turf Wars*. San Francisco, CA: Jossey-Bass, 2006.
7. Crosby, Philip B. *Quality without Tears*. New York: McGraw-Hill, 1984.
8. For a more in-depth understanding of the GE Workout process, we suggest that readers take a look at David Ulrich's book on the topic. *GE Workout*. New York: McGraw-Hill, 2002.
9. http://en.wikipedia.org/wiki/ack_Welch. March 3, 2009.
10. General Electric Corporation. *What Is Six Sigma? The Roadmap to Customer Impact*. GE Document #19991438-1. Unknown Year.

11. According to discussions with Kent Linder, who was part of the team at GE Motors, various units of GE operated differently. At GE Motors, the team sponsor was chosen by senior management and always included a team member as a co-leader.
12. The notes on the Change Acceleration Process are based on conversations with Kent Linder, who was part of the original team that developed the CAP and review of internal GE documents that can be found on the web.
13. The information on the Rapid Workout is based on the material sent to me and the conversations I had with Rick Tucci, who is the president of Leap Technologies, creator of the Rapid Workout. http://www.improvefaster.com
14. Allied Signal Process Solving. https://goalqpc.com/cms/docs/journals/Spring2 000.pdf
15. Honeywell HOS Gold. https://twitter.com/honeywell/status/5731453469494 47682
16. Honeywell Six Sigma Plus. https://www.qualitydigest.com/dec00/html/hone ywell.html
17. Definitions for Cycle and Continuum from the *Dictionary of Oxford Languages*. https://languages.oup.com/google-dictionary-en/

Chapter 3

What Is the TLS Continuum?

Introduction

In Chapter 2, I laid out a clear picture of the journey that the industry has taken toward developing the continuous improvement process we work with today. However, I minimized discussions of two areas in that material. Before we go forward, we need to take some time to address those two issues.

Transactional HR vs. Strategic HR

The first issue is the challenge that our fellow HR professionals face every day. The challenge confronts you whether you work for a Fortune 100 corporation or a small- to medium-sized enterprise. I discussed this challenge in the introduction to the first edition (see page 24) of this work. As HR professionals we need to identify what our role is in today's business world. This is regardless of whether you function as a generalist or a specialist within your organization. Is it that of the organizational fireman? Do you view your function within the organization as an HR transactional person? Is your function to provide services that are issue focused? I would contend that if you are stuck in this focus, you are literally working yourself out of a job. If this is your focus go get yourself a calendar and start marking off the days until you are out of a job.

Whether you are a generalist or a specialist the other option is for you to begin to function as a strategic HR professional. You do so by viewing HR as in the organizational processes. You do so by not being some department that we go to when we need to put out fires. We do this by learning that HR is a system with its own set of sources, inputs, processes, outputs and end users. We understand that everything we do must be aligned with the overall organizational goals, values, strategies and goals and the corporate culture. It means that as HR professionals we must not only understand the language of Human Capital Management but speak the language of business as a whole.

The Nature of the TLS Continuum

The second issue is that we did not clearly define what the TLS Continuum is and how it contributes to the discussion of achieving HR excellence. While the previous chapter looked at the evolution of the total quality movement from post–World War II to the modern formats, we still did not delineate just what the journey entails. This chapter begins our in-depth path through the methodology and how to apply it in your HR function.

We would guess that if you asked a random selection of individuals both within and outside the business community what Six Sigma is, you would receive a wide variety of responses. I can tell you from my personal experience when I say I have a Six Sigma Black Belt a fair number think I am talking about some martial arts discipline. From the business perspective their responses can be narrowed down into three responses. Before we delve into just what the Six Sigma methodology is, we need to consider these responses more in depth.

It Is a Manufacturing Thing

In the beginning of the total quality movement, as we discussed in Chapter 2, the world was firmly entrenched within the industrial age following World War II. An organization's brand and reputation in the marketplace were based on the quality of the products it produced. Deming and those who followed him were reviewing problems that arose out of the resulting process. The constant goal was to produce end-user products that were readily available to the marketplace and that provided products that the end users would pay for. The end user is seeking products which are delivered and which perform the usage for which they were intended. They are seeking products which are free from defects, making them less valuable to their organization.

Deming, Ishikawa and Smith saw processes that were basically flawed from the very nature of their existence. These processes were not meeting the needs of their customers due to reworks arising from the defects in the production process.

As a continuous process improvement student, I will concede that the vast majority of the Six Sigma training programs in existence are the result of manufacturing issues. Organizations are looking at the widgets we produce and trying to determine why we are not meeting the customer needs. Some of the solutions are very simple; some are more complex in nature.

In the manufacturing space, we are able to see, identify and find solutions to these problems. We have a physical object which either met the voice of the customer or did not. The rank-and-file employee could, by the very nature of their job responsibilities, know if the process was not working. In many cases these problems arose out of a backlog of material coming down the assembly line and no place to put it. Every member of the organization could somewhat easily comprehend this scenario.

But what happens when the organizational structure has similar problems? What happens when we are in a position where we can't see, identify and feel the end widget? We, on the transactional side of the equation, are in that position.

Like the production side of the coin, the transactional side also produces widgets. The difference is that our widgets are less tangible in nature. Our widgets, as Ken Miller argues in his book *We Don't Make Widgets*,[1] are the process outputs that are generated as human resources deliver their services in order to serve the stakeholders of the organization. Just as in the production realm, our processes have critical outputs that can affect the entire organization. These critical outputs are what we use to align HR with the organizational strategic initiatives. Our widgets are items like applications for candidates, policy descriptions when we create handbooks and manuals, the end results of harassment investigations and other final reports. However, these widgets are still a vital part of the organization. Because they are not tangible in nature our widgets are not something that a staff person can necessarily turn to and say, wait a minute, something is wrong. While the widgets are not measurable like on the factory floor, the HR function is a factory of sorts. This means that the output from the HR Factory is measurable just like if we were on that factory floor. Our HR widgets are still able to produce credible, verifiable data measure points to solve the process defects.

We Tried That and It Didn't Work in Our Organization

As human beings we have a tendency to want the newest and greatest tool that becomes available to make our lives "easier." Business annuals are filled with examples of management decisions to get that latest great tool. What is also prevalent are incidents where management tried to take shortcuts to implement these tools, only to be met with disaster.

The implementation of Six Sigma in an organization requires some fundamental changes to the organization. When we try and implement the latest tool without thinking it through, the premise going in is flawed. Six Sigma–related improvement efforts fail because the organization has not made the required changes to the basis for making decisions. The perspective on the business marketplace needs to shift from the organization to focus on what the customer wants and needs. In many cases, as we will show later in this book, when we introduce Six Sigma to an organization, the first requirement is a culture change. Management touts the changes but wants to do it on the terms of the organization at that moment or in the past. It is these kinds of circumstances that bring about the response that the system does not work. These are the kinds of circumstances that bring out the response that it is not right for our organization. While management wants the successes that have been reported, it is not interested in making the changes we will discuss in future chapters. The Six Sigma process is a structured response to a problem, but one of the critical factors here is that to fully realize the benefits to the organization and the customers, we need to create a new way of doing business. Failure to achieve this organizational change is what leads to the failure of Six Sigma improvement efforts.

It Is Too Highly Complex to Be Used in Most Organizations

As we discussed in Chapter 2, the whole basis of the total quality movement was the work of Dr. Deming, who was by trade a statistician. His fellow champions of the quality movement mostly were engineers. By their very nature they are steeped in a detailed analysis of data. We totally understand that high math is not everyone's cup of tea. Further, this high demand for high-level math has lost followers on the way along our journey. Motorola today no longer offers the high-level training it used to due to the complexity of the data and the training requirements. I will in Chapter 7 present a solution to this dilemma.

The remainder of this chapter will first present an overview of the TLS continuum, followed by an in-depth view of each of the critical parts of the TLS Continuum.

What Is the TLS Continuum?

I got into a discussion in the past days over the use of acronyms. The comment was passed that nobody understands acronyms so why use them. The letters TLS stand for the three components of the continuum. The letter T stands for the Theory of Constraints (TOC), created by Dr. Eliyahu (Figure 3.1).

Goldratt, in his book *The Goal*, defines the Theory of Constraints as a critical thinking–based system for determining where the obstacles lie within an organization. Through the use of various tools, the system asks you to determine where the obstacles are in the process. The purpose of the TOC involvement in the continuum is to determine what needs to be changed, how to change it and how do we accomplish the change. TOC operates at the level of the chain, looking for the weakest link. It is in essence the hypothesis of the problem-solving method, overall. The letter L stands for *lean*. Most organizations are familiar with the concept of lean. It is centered on removing waste from the organizational processes so that the customer receives their orders faster. Understand that faster may not mean cheaper or better quality; it means only that we expedite the process. The final letter is S, and it represents the concepts of Six Sigma. The primary goal here is to remove variation from the processes. If we combine the three letters of the acronym, we find that the TLS Continuum is organized around a process in itself. We use the Theory of Constraints to locate and identify the obstacles within the system. What is holding up the process? Where is the weakest link in the process?

Bob Sproull has provided the perfect view of this action in his piping diagram, as shown above. From the diagram you can clearly see that the weakest link is the point where the flow is narrowed at Point[2] E. With the introduction of TOC, the system asks you to elevate the obstacles and determine how to remove them.

We use lean to do what it is meant to do, that is, to remove the obstacles. We have identified the obstacle and determined through the critical thinking tools how to remove that obstacle and then use the lean tools to actually remove the waste. Finally, the system utilizes the Six Sigma tools to create

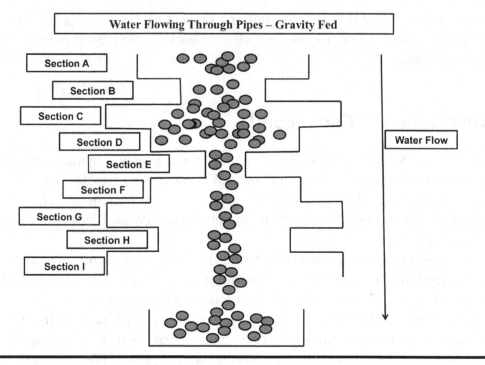

Figure 3.1 Bob Sproull's piping diagram.[2]

the standard of work and remove any variation from the process. When we do this, we have completed the improvement process by creating a progressive system for resolving the problems that occur within many organizations. It is an evidence-based effort to identify, remove and improve the system so the problem does not reoccur.

How does this apply to HR? The TLS Continuum provides a roadmap to guide you through the improvement process. The graphic for that roadmap appears at the top of each segment of the series of posts related to the topic at hand. It helps you explain why one organization discovered that the job requisition was reviewed and approved three times in the course of hire, *by the same person*. It helps explain how one organization was able to reduce the time to hire by 61 percent in six months. When we recognize that the improvement process is tackling a world system as proposed by Dr. Lawrence Miller in his article "Whole-System Architecture: A Model for Building the Lean Organization,"[3] then we understand that the TLS Continuum is a vital tool in resolving those world system problems and system obstacles. It is a dynamic system designed to provide you with new insight into how your organization operates and processes flow. The base is not concerned with whether you are talking about a process that produces something, or a process that is service oriented. The end result of either process is the requirement for a widget of some kind to initialize that process whether we are talking about the need for a candidate for an open position or the introduction of a new mindset to the organization.

As presented above the remainder of this chapter will look at the basic principles behind each of the three components, beginning with the Theory of Constraints.

Principles of the Theory of Constraints

Frank Patrick of Focused Performance probably most succinctly provided us with the basic principles of the Theory of Constraints when he compared the TOC to Six Sigma.[4]

Principle #1: TOC works primarily at the level of the chain, driving focus to the weakest link and then to the linkages between that constraint and other aspects of the system.

As I stated in Chapter 2, the TLS Continuum is a series of actions that continue in a chain of events. The Theory of Constraints works primarily at the level of that chain of events in search of the weakest link or that obstacle in the chain that is holding up the rest of the chain.

Principle #2: TOC, with its logic-based tools, provides strength in dealing with what might be considered "qualitative" analysis, helpful for dealing with "rock and hard place" dilemmas.

The Theory of Constraints utilizes a series of logic-based tools to guide the search for system obstacles. The tools follow a natural progression in completing an analysis of the dilemma before your organization.

Tool #1: Current Reality Tree

You can't even begin to analyze where the system constraints are until you understand the current processes. The current reality tree logically looks at where you are at the moment. It provides a view of the things that are disrupting the system and traces them back to where they intersect the system. It becomes the first indicator of what needs to be corrected.

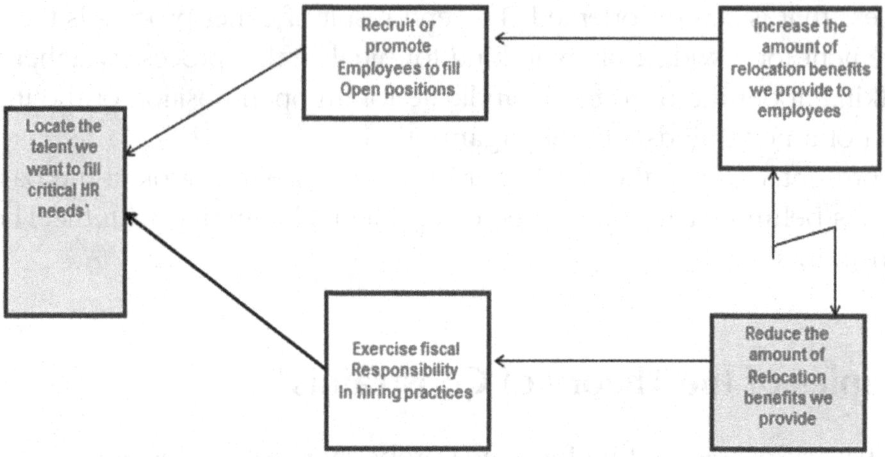

Figure 3.2 TOC evaporating cloud.[6]

Tool #2: Evaporating Cloud

The Evaporating Cloud is designed to uncover the conflict within your processes (Figure 3.2). Consider for a moment the example in Figure 9.2.[5] It states that one of HR's responsibilities is to locate the talent the organization needs to fill critical human capital needs of the organization. The question posed by the Evaporating Cloud is, how do we achieve that goal? The cloud offers two different alternatives. One says the goal is fiscal responsibility, which requires the organization to stay within budgetary guidelines. The other option states that the goal is to recruit or promote employees to fill these critical openings.

The weakest link appears after this segment of the discussion because it directly compares the two approaches. On the fiscal side, the resulting action is to reduce the amount of relocation benefits provided to the human capital assets while still being able to the fill the available positions which is the paramount issue you need to increase the level of benefits. The conflict arises because you may not be able to reduce benefits and still get the level of talent that the organization is seeking.

Tool #3: Future Reality Tree

In design thinking one of the first questions we ask is, "what if?" The future reality tree is the TOC response to that question. It asks you to envision what the system will look like after we remove the obstacles.

Tool #4: Prerequisite and Transition Tree

The prerequisite and transition trees provide a vehicle for determining what is needed to make changes and what objections could be made to the change process.

Tool #5: Goal Tree Map

The goal tree begins with your goal. What is it you are trying to achieve? It then poses the question to you that in order to reach this goal your organization MUST have what? What is the critical success factor which tells you that you have reached the goal? In the problem posed in this book, those critical success factors might be the removal of the barriers to the process flow. It might be a better control system for the flow of parts to the factory floor.

With the critical success factors in place, the next level down in the tree is to ask, in order to obtain the critical success factors what must be in place to get there? What changes in your process will be required to get the new factors in place? In the example in the chart that follows, that organization determined that it wants to maximize throughput. In order to secure that maximized throughput it needs to maximize the incoming sales dollars while controlling costs. As we did with this level the next level down asks you to determine what you need to, for example, maximize revenue. The example tree shows that the way you do that is to have satisfied customers like Morrison.

Finally, at the bottom of the tree you ask again what is needed for you to have satisfied customers. In the example on the next page, it suggests that you need to have a high-quality product. This would bring us back to the Acme Gyroscope side of the equation and causes us to question whether there is something with your product which is not meeting the needs of your customers (Figure 3.3).

Principle #3: TOC's approach to root cause analysis, centered in the Thinking Process known as the Current Reality Tree, starts with a range of diverse problems with which the system suffers and then builds rigorous cause-and-effect logic to identify one or very deep causes at the root of them all.

The most important aspect of continuous process improvement and TOC in particular is to identify what may be the cause for the obstacles to be

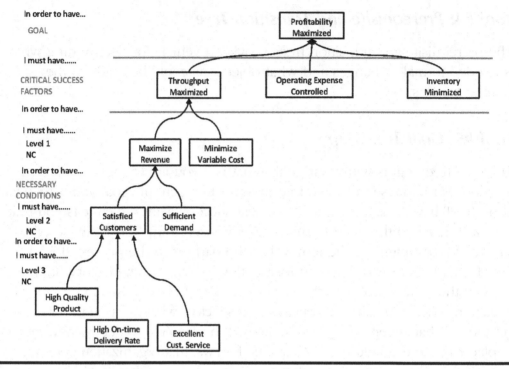

Figure 3.3 Goal tree.

part of the system. What are we doing that is causing the system to present problems that are interfering with our ability to deliver the services that the customer is demanding of our organizations? The current reality tree and its underlying assumptions cause us to look at diverse causes (problems) and identify what the true source of the obstacle is.

Principle #4: TOC first strives to build "logistical" processes that are robust enough to deal with current variation, and through concepts like the Five Focusing steps and "buffer management" identify where attacks on variation will give us the biggest bang for the buck.

With the previous principle implemented the next step is to use the five focusing steps to identify the path forward.

Step 1: Identify the constraint
Step 2: Decide how to exploit the constraints
Step 3: Subordinate everything else

Step 4: Elevate the constraint
Step 5: Go back to step 1

Principle #5: TOC extends its use of the constraints to define maximum value for a market segment or customer in terms of the constraint or core problem of their system. Having identified that, positioning one's product and offering in terms of assisting with that critical issue is the main route to increased value.

By removing the obstacles in the chain, you remove those activities that are non-value-added in nature. It means the organization can concentrate more on the needs of the customer. It means that the process flow, even if it is temporary, delivers products and services in a faster, cheaper and defect-free manner. This change of focus brings about an increased value to the organization.

Principles of Lean Management

Developed out of the Toyota Production System, lean management is concentrated primarily on the speed of the process. How can we shorten the delivery time of products and services? The lean way suggests that there are five principles behind the concept of lean management.[7]

Principle #1: Define Value

Every business day on several social media sites I post a Chane Maestro's Daily Tip. One recent daily tip stated that you should change your process map to a journey map and start with the client's process before yours. Why may you ask? The client of the customer defines what is of value. I will discuss this further in Chapter 5 when we dig deeper into the concept of the voice of the customer. For the moment understand that through the client's demands on what they need, when they need it, how they need it, etc., they establish what they are willing to purchase from that. That is the proof as to what is of value to your organization. Google tells us that there are 148,000,000 results on defining value. So it is no wonder that it is a daunting task.

The critical principle in the lean management area is to find a way to define this value. Find that common ground of what the customer demands and how it fits into your organizational culture and values. Where there are some discrepancies, work together to resolve the issues.

Principle #2: Mapping the Value Stream

Dr. Mikel Harry told us that we don't know what we don't know. The only way to really know and understand our processes is to prepare a process map that plots out the journey from your suppliers to your organization to your clients and then to their end users. As we will see in Chapter 7, with the process map in hand you can convert it to a value stream map and include time intervals to the map.

Principle #3: Create Flow

One of the goals of the TLS Continuum and the lean segment is to remove the obstacles that inhibit the flow of products and services through the chain. We achieve this by seeking out the obstacles that the TOC logical tools uncover.

The created flow provides the organization and its stakeholders with a guide on how each operates within the business operation.

Principle #4: Establish Pull

Another principle of lean management is that we need to alter operational views. Many of our organizations have believed and some still believe that you just push materials along the process as they enter the building. Lean management believes that there is a better way which is found in the philosophy that no piece of material enters the process until it is needed. Toyota referred to this as just-in-time operations.

Principle #5: Pursue Perfection

The proverbs tell us that if you don't have time to do it right you must have time to do it over. That is what lean management tells us. The goal is to ensure that everything that flows out of our organizations is as defect free as is humanely possible. Ford tells us that quality is job one. Toyota believes that it is in their DNA to do it right the first time. This final principle suggests that it is your job as a human capital asset of the organization to do everything you can to ensure that the outgoing product or service meets the values established in the first principle for the client. The client fulfills their needs when they want it, where they want it, how they want it and at the right price.

Principles of Six Sigma

What is this term *Six Sigma*? What does *sigma* mean? These are all questions that must be understood before we look at the guiding principles of the Six Sigma segment of the TLS Continuum.

Remember your school days when we pushed instructors to grade on a curve. The intent was to identify where the average score landed and to grade the exceptions on a curve. This curve was manifested in a tool called the bell curve, as shown in the figure (Figure 3.4).

Our argument to the professor was that based on the fact the scores on the examination fell outside of the expected grade ranges, we wanted them to grade the exam based on the results of the curve, which hopefully would result in higher grades for all after the scores were reviewed. As human beings we, as we have discussed earlier, push for that nirvana we call perfection. Our ultimate goal in life and within the workplace is to reach a point where our output is considered to be as free from defects or as close to perfection as possible. The bell curve provides us with the ability to view our data and determine how close we have come to reaching that goal.

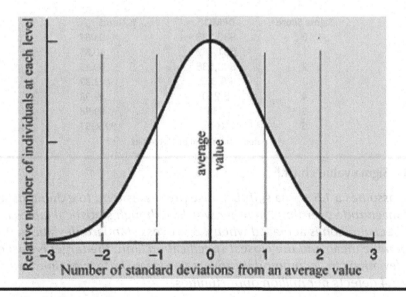

Figure 3.4 The bell curve.[8]

If you remember our discussion of the history of the total quality movement and the role of Motorola, we discussed that one of the goals of Bill Smith was to seek a way to count defects within its processes.

Coming from the Greek, *sigma* refers to the summation of the numbers or quantities indicated.[9] In statistical terms, the term *sigma* allows us to measure the data in the bell curve and the rate of variation within our processes. It represents the amount of variation that occurs relative to the specific customer's specifications. The bell curve tells us that in most cases, we allow for one standard deviation above or below the mean score. Each deviation from the mean is equivalent to 34 percent, above and below the average point or the point of error-free processes. The bell curve provides us with a clear perspective on how close we are coming to meet the voice of the customer. We can take the bell curve and apply it to a DPMO chart.

If we review the table below, we find that as our defects per million opportunities decrease, the level of the yield or those items which meet the required customer specifications increases. The smaller the variation from the requirement, the closer we get to the goal of perfection. As a result, when we reach a level of Six Sigma, the defect rate or the variation from the voice of the customer is so small that the resulting product or service is 99.99966 percent on target to the customer specifications. It is hard to get much closer to our goal of perfection than that. We usually display these results in what is referred to as a Six Sigma Defects per Million Opportunities Chart, as shown in the figure (Figure 3.5).

Sigma Score	DPMO *	% Good
0	933,193	0.067
1	691,462	30.85
2	308,538	69.15
3	66,807	93.32
4	6,210	99.38
5	233	99.98
6	3.4	99.9997

* - Defects per million opportunities

Figure 3.5   Sigma value chart.[8]

*The table assumes a 1.5 sigma shift because processes tend to exhibit instability of that magnitude over time. In other words, although statistical tables indicate that 3.4 defects/million is achieved when 4.5 process standard deviations (Sigma) are between the mean and the closest specification limit, the target is raised to 6.0 standard deviations to accommodate adverse process shifts over time and still produce only 3.4 defects per million opportunities.

Toyota, through its Toyota Production System, has shown that at its very essence, the Six Sigma methodology is a unique, structured system to resolve critical workplace issues. Some organizations have tried to approach the process from the point of view of an established quality department. Six Sigma can't operate as a silo and expects to achieve the goals we anticipate from our continuous process improvement efforts. Its goal is to take the culture of process improvement and imbed it in cross-functional personnel, determining where the problems are and potential solutions to the issues that arise. These potential solutions are not a finance problem, nor an HR problem; they are an organizational problem. It is not necessarily squarely centered on the ultimate results but rather on how we got there.

The process.st[10] website presents us with seven principles regarding the Six Sigma methodology – customer focus, workflow, process flow, waste removal, removing variation, organizational buy-in and making efforts evidence-based. As I have done with the other segments above, it is worth our time to review these individually.

Principle #1: Always Focus on the Customer

As I stated earlier the customer is the essence of an organization. You can't live without them. That said, every organization needs to make sure that it understands its customer. Who are they? What is their corporate culture? What are their values? What are their current needs? What are their future needs? Allow me to flip the coin for a moment. What is the life tie value (total sales divided by years as a customer) of the customer to your organization? As we will see in the chapter on the voice of the customer, they are the basis or need to be the basis for every action you undertake in the process improvement efforts.

Principle #2: Understand How Work Really Happens

As an organization you and your human capital assets must obtain knowledge on how your processes work in the workplace. Just because you think a process works in a particular fashion does not mean that is the way it does operate. Dr. Mikel Harry has told us we don't know what we don't know. The goal is to know. You should be able to walk the entire process of every process within the building and externally to the building—at your suppliers, at your customers.

Principle #3: Make Your Process Flow Smart

As I discussed in the discussion of what the TLS Continuum is, the initial goal is to remove those activities which are not providing value and are hindering the process flow. The Six Sigma principle tells us that one of our tasks is to diligently seek out those obstacles and continuously improve the processes each and every day.

Principle #4: Reduce Waste and Concentrate on Value

If you see something, say something. If you see a process not working, correct it. Toyota allows the human capital assets to push the anon button or pull the anon cord if it sees something go wrong within a process. Our focus must be centered back on principle 1 and what the customer needs. I will discuss in Chapter 6 about the various types of efforts we involve ourselves in every day that create no value to either the organization or the customer.

Principle #5: Stop Defects through Removing Variation

In order to maintain continuous process improvement, our processes must be based on creditable, verifiable and repeatable processes. This means that if the process to develop product A is done today, it must be done the same way the next time you do it. This must be the same for every process within your organization.

The primary way we achieve this goal is to ensure that as much variation in the process is removed so that we have a standard of work for that process. Variations are a waste for the organization. Variations are a waste for the customer.

Principle #6: Get Buy-in from the Team through Collaboration

As we will see in the next chapter, the critical component of the achievement of sustainable change management is based on empowerment and engagement within the organization. This occurs when everyone is on the same page, when everyone believes that their ideas and suggestions are valued by the organization, when management accepts that its subject matter experts are the front-line workers.

Principle #7: Make Efforts Systematic and Scientific

We need to review our decision trees carefully to ensure that they are grounded in evidence-based data. That the potential solutions we arrive at are based on clear evidence that there is logical reasoning behind why we think a particular solution is valid for that moment and circumstance.

As I have tried to present in this chapter, the TLS Continuum is a strong tool in the continuous process improvement effort. I could have spent a vast amount of print space talking about the tools more in depth, perhaps. But there are those who came before me who could do a better job— Continuous Process Improvement professionals such as Bob Sproull in his book *Epiphanized* or H. William Dettmer in his book *The Logical Thinking Process*. My intention to this point has been to provide the theory behind the TLS Continuum by establishing the definition of HR excellence and the history of the process improvement movement. It was then necessary to present you, the reader, with the tenants of the TLS Continuum. The succeeding chapters will begin to look at the TLS Continuum from an application focus, beginning with the look at teas and projects.

Notes

1. Miller, Ken. *We Don't Make Widgets.* Washington, DC: Governing Books, 2010.
2. Sproull, Bob, Bruce Nelson. *Epiphanized*, 2nd Edition. New York: CRC Press, 2015. Pages 13–15.
3. Miller, Lawrence. *Whole-System Architecture: A Model for Building the Lean Organization.* https://www.lmmiller.com/wp-content/uploads/2011/06/Whole-System-Architecture-Article1.pdf
4. http://focusedperformance.com/articles/tocsigma.html provides us with a clear picture of the tools.
5. Taken from the article "Driving the Relocation 500." http://www.dbaiconsultig.com/Articles/Articale9.pdf
6. The Lean Way. *Principles of Lean.* https://theleanway.net/The-Five-Principles-of-Lean
7. The bell curve is from the course materials in the Six Sigma Black Belt training at St. Petersburg College.
8. The DPMO chart is from the course materials in the Six Sigma Black Belt training at St. Petersburg College.
9. Dictionary.com. *Definition of Sigma.* http://dictionary.reference.com/browse/sigma?s=t. Based on Random House Dictionary. 2013.
10. Process.st. *Principles of Six Sigma.* https://process.st/six-sigma-principles

Chapter 4

Project Design and Team Dynamics

All improvement happens project by project and in no other way.

Joseph M. Juran

Introduction

Before continuing with the road to HR excellence it is necessary to establish some guiding idioms. First every process is a system. A system includes sources, inputs which feed processes, outputs to the customer and the end user. HR is no different.

Dan Heath, in his new book *Upstream*, suggests that "each system is designed to get the results it gets."[1] Think about that for a moment. Dan Heath is suggesting that our processes run the gamut as they are supposed to. Every system (process) takes the products or services from our sources and receives some kind of input which feeds our processes, which in turn produces outputs in the form of products or services, which we deliver to the end user in the exact way as the process or system was designed to do. However, every process and every system along the way have its hiccups. Every process and every system have situations where they do not perform exactly the way they are designed to perform. Some of these hiccups may be human error, or they may be a defect in the parts we utilize. When they do not, then we need to turn to projects and cross-functional teams to find the new path to get to the desired solutions.

The opening chapters of this book tried to set the foundation for you to understand the culture change process or system we are embarking on. They were presented from both a theoretical view and a historical view. The theoretical view was from the perception of the definition of excellence, which we will carry forward through subsequent chapters. The historical view came from tracing the development of the continuous process improvement efforts over the past half-century of efforts upon people who cared about getting the systems working in a proper fashion.

These efforts are carried out through the well-defined process solution projects and well-constructed cross-functional teams.

Therefore, it is necessary to understand both of these areas before we move on to actually solving the problem at hand. This chapter will begin with the exploration of how to operate and construct the teams and then will walk you through project selection and construction.

The continuous process improvement effort will not be successful without the presence of two components. You need a functioning cross-functional team and a project structure.

Without a carefully chosen project and then a truly functional team your process improvement efforts are doomed for failure.

Team Essentials

If you look at the business world the subject of business teams is a major area of concern. How do we construct them? Who should be part of them? What do we do with the result of the work of the team? Google the term *business teams*, and it results in 1,210,000,000 items. If we change the search criteria to ask for business team books, the result is 223,000,000 titles. If we turn to Amazon and Barnes and Noble websites and ask them to search for business teams, we get 30,000 and 360 titles, respectively.

Obviously, the concept of workplace teams is a point of critical discussion. The real question becomes how they operate within our workplaces. In one of our webinar programs titled "Who Am I? The Role of Human Capital Assets in the Global Workplace," we present the fact that teams either formally or informally have been around since the 1700s, the first teams being the family farm and the way in which the family worked as a team to complete the necessary steps.

In 1909, with the publication of his *Principles of Scientific Management*, Frederick Winslow Taylor first introduced the idea that workers and managers needed to cooperate with each other. From this idea Taylor began a series of Time and Motion studies to discover how to more effectively run the workplace.

These studies resulted in Taylor's Four Principles of Scientific Management.[2] In his first principle Taylor advocated that organizations should replace working by "rule of thumb" and instead use the scientific method to study work and determine how most efficiently to perform specific tasks. In other words, Taylor suggested that we actually have a process to complete a task. The second principle suggested a different way of assigning tasks. Rather than simply assigning workers to any job, we should assign workers based on capability and motivation. One of the tenants of my *The Road to HR Excellence through Six Sigma Master Seminar Series* is that team members should be selected based on their skills and attitudes. From this point Taylor, in his third principle, suggested that the worker's performance should be monitored and provide instructions and supervision to ensure that they are using the most efficient ways of working. This principle reinforces the Toyota premise of the manager as a coach. The final principle advocated that the work between managers and workers be allocated so that the workers were allowed to perform their tasks efficiently. The drawback to these principles is that they are based on the idea that there is only one way to do something and that does not allow for innovation or expanded views of the problem.

The modern-day cross-functional teams are not the teams of the earlier examples of business teams. Today's teams take advantage of the best resources to resolve organizational issues based on the voice of the customer, which expands the focus of the organization into areas outside of the norm. It adds new resources that are often overlooked by the classical teams.

Unlike the quality circles discussed in Chapter 2, the modern teams view their function with the inclusion of the diversity of ideas, new decision tools and team methods of operation.

As can be seen in Figure 6.1 the empowered team must view its purpose from the view of diversity, full-spectrum thinking, new decision tools and the method in which we construct teams.

Diversity of the Team

What got the quality circle concept in trouble, and what characterizes the "classical" team in trouble, is that the final decisions are made by management—the classic command and control environment. The views of the team do not matter if they are in conflict with the manager's view.

The modern view of the cross-functional team is vastly different. The new cross-functional team thrives on the divergence of input into the problem-solving effort. Diversity in the empowered team arena looks at who is included in the deliberations. There exists in any organization a spectrum of thought if you will. To completely resolve the issues confronting the organization it is necessary that you include everyone who touches the problem in any way or manner. So who I am talking about? Consider as you construct your teams the entire supply chain from start to finish. Consider what is beyond the customer. Take into consideration the function of your customer's internal teams. The initial question for the team is, who do you call first? You want to reach out to everyone involved in the production of that product or service at both ends of the spectrum.

This is the concept behind the consideration of stakeholders versus shareholders. Let's review for a moment the difference between the two. Any corporations contend that their purpose is to meet the needs of their shareholders. First let me make it abundantly clear that all shareholders are in themselves stakeholders. The difference is that their involvement in the organization is purely financial in nature.

R. Edward Freeman suggests that there exists an interconnected relationship between a business and its customers, suppliers, employees, investors, communities and others who have a stake in the organization. The theory argues that a firm should create value for all stakeholders, not just shareholders.[3] The stakeholder theory talks about the community. The empowered team will ensure that the solution that is arrived at includes the widest spectrum of thought regarding the issue at hand. It needs to identify and include the openness to diverse thoughts on the solution, not the confined view of most organizations.

New Decision Tools

This reliance on diversity of ideas means that the team can bring to the table new tools that the typical team would not have: tools like the Theory of Constraints logic–based tools; tools like the process maps to be discussed later in this chapter; tools like the utilization of design and full-spectrum thinking, which expand our search for information and data; tools that not only explore the current state of the problems but what the process could look like. Then explore what could possibly work to resolve the issues.

New Team Processes

In their book *New Power* Jeremy Hines and Henry Timms suggest that one characteristic of the new business world is the need for collaboration. The millennials have no hesitation in order to resolve a problem jumping on their computer and asking for assistance from whoever is resolving the issue. The key to the success of the cross-functional team effort is the act of collaboration using the power of a site called InnoCentive[4] resolved problems that the in-house experts could not.

The team will look at broadening its reach into the problem by looking at all aspects of the problem at hand, considering not just what is thought to be wrong but what is wrong. They will consider not just anecdotal views of the problem but the data-driven view of the issue. They will undertake full-spectrum thinking. The next question becomes, how large of a team do you need?

Team Size

Earlier in this chapter, I stated that the cross-functional team should include EVERYONE who touches the process. That could potentially lead to a huge team. At a bare minimum the team should consist of a representative from human resources, management, finance, sales and marketing, front-line workers and customer service. Safi Bahcall, in his book *Loonshots*, suggests that the magical number for team size is 150 members.[5] I totally understand that having 150 individuals in one room at the same time and expecting to get anything done is a bit unreal. What I am suggesting is the stakeholders can be rotated in and out of the problem-solving process as they are needed. As we progress through the project not everyone's expertise will be needed 24/7 on the project. John Ricketts of IBM suggests the creation of a skill bench.

When you are developing your project, resources consider creating the skill bench to represent all the skills that will be needed to resolve the issue. The skill bench allows you to form a skill depository. As a particular skill is needed the project team can reach into the skill bench for that skill.

The skill expert joins the active team to utilize their skills. When that part of the project is complete the resource is returned to the skill bench until the next time it is needed. This becomes part of the HR Center of Excellence. The remaining question then becomes, what roles and responsibilities are required by the cross-functional team?

Team Role and Responsibilities

With the suggestion that an ideal team size is around 150, I am not suggesting that the team operations are nothing but a free-for-all. Every team has a hierarchy of roles and responsibilities that the team utilizes in the search for the right solution. Notice I did not say *result*, but rather *solution*. I will repeat over the following chapters that the real key to success is how you resolve the problem, not how you solved the problem. We can get a better handle on these roles if we look at them in depth. While we have stressed several times that the key to making Six Sigma work is the functioning of cross-functional teams, the process has its own team responsibilities. This is not to say that we are talking about command and control here but rather about who has the responsibilities to guide the ship and make sure that the team is staying on task. This section will look at each of the roles, the training required and what their contribution is to the finished product.

Senior Executive

The senior executive's role in the process is to make management buy into the change process. The senior executive is the gatekeeper between the team and upper management. They are the ones who make the pitch to senior management on what the problem is, why we need to solve the problem and why the proposed project is the correct route to take. They are also responsible for conducting reviews of project progress and reporting the results of the review to the cross-functional teams, the rank-and-file human capital assets and the senior management of the organization.

Executive Committee

Comprised of the members of senior management, the executive committee pushes the methodology out into the organization. While there is some degree of discussion about the role of senior management in the process, if the executive committee and thus senior management do not buy into the process it will not result in successful conclusions. They also have the responsibility to ensure that the required resources needed by the project team are made available.

While it would be helpful, there is no published requirement that either the senior executive or the members of the executive team must have any training in depth into the methodology and how it works.

Champion (Project)

The role of the champion is to be the rudder of the project. They are the ones who make sure the teams stay on target and are working to delivering the milestones when they say they will be delivered. They are responsible for reviewing the project's long-term impact on the organization. If the team runs into an obstacle, it is the champion who helps them get around a solution. The champion in addition holds the purse strings for the project, authorizing the release of the fund for various aspects of the project. Because of the nature of the duties of the project champion, the person in this role should have earned at least a Yellow Belt so they have some understanding of the process the team is working through.

Level	Years of Experience	Training Requirements	Responsibilities	Reporting Path
Champion	None	Should ideally have Six Sigma Yellow Belt	Translates company vision to develop a plan	

Process Owner

Since the first word in this book, we have made mention of the critical factor in the success of the TLS Continuum Methodology is the voice of the customer. The project owner is that voice. They are the ones who have a direct impact on the project. In today's business climate many managers and employees ask the question of what is in it for me. The process owner is no different. They know they have a problem and have asked the cross-functional team to assist in the finding of a solution. The expectation is that the process owner is going to be able to find a positive solution to the problem because of the process we have undertaken and thus we will have met the voice of the customer. It is also important that you understand that the process owner may be inside your organization but just as likely may be external to the organization.

From this point on, the roles begin to require more in-depth training in how the process works. There are many sources out there to obtain the training both live and online, and we will not suggest to the reader which is the best direction in which to obtain the training. We did however need a standard source to describe the basic training requirements going forward, so we turned to the Certification section of the American Society for Quality[6] as a basis for the resources in this area.

I need to divert our attention for a moment to an issue within the quality industry at the present time. There is much discussion underway about whether we have since its inception at Motorola trained too many "belts" within our organizations. If you poll professionals within the quality field, you will receive a mix of responses. Motorola had the formula that you needed: one Master Black Belt for each ten Black Belts and 1 Black Belt for each ten Green Belts. GE went so far as to require anyone seeking leadership positions within the organization to have at least their Green Belt. The real question is, have we concentrated too much on the certification process and not enough on the system for resolving the organizational problems?

Level	Years of Experience	Training Requirements	Responsibilities	Reporting Path
Process owner	None	None	Stakeholder with the eventual benefit from the project	

Master Black Belt

A Master Black Belt is expected to have a minimum of five years of experience or successfully completed ten Six Sigma Black Belt projects showing expertise in three areas: teaching, coaching and mentoring; occupational experience and responsibility; and technical knowledge and innovation of the field. It is inherent that they have a clear knowledge of strategic plan development and deployment, cross-functional competencies and mentoring responsibilities.

The Master Black Belt is the leader of the Six Sigma improvement process and in some cases also will take on the responsibilities of the project champion in smaller organizations. They are also responsible for the implementation of programs that will aid the continuous improvement effort along with training the Black Belts and Green Belts in the Six Sigma methodology. In the cases where you have constructed the HR COE, the Master Belt can be the lead of the Center of Excellence.

Level	Years of Experience	Training Requirements	Responsibilities	Reporting Path
Master Black Belt	5+ years in the role of Black Belt or Master Black Belt	Completion of ten projects	Trains and coaches' Black Belts and Green Belts. Internal Six Sigma consultant	Reports to champion or sponsor

Black Belt

The next level down in the pyramid is that of the Black Belts. Black belts are expected to have completed two projects with a signed affidavit on each plus three years of work experience. In order to be successful, they must be able to explain the philosophy and principles to others within the organization. It is also preferred that they have at least a four-year college degree. They become the first-line supervisor of the process. The immediate supervisor is the Master Black Belt. It is the expectation of the organization that a Black Belt will complete projects, which will lead to $250,000 to $500,000 in savings to their organization per year spread over between four and six projects per year. Both the Master Black Belt and the Black Belts are full time in their responsibilities, so their primary vision is on how to improve the organization from the perspective of removing waste and variation from the processes.

Level	Years of Experience	Training Requirements	Responsibilities	Reporting Path
Black Belt	3+ years of experience	BA degree and two completed projects with signed affidavits	Leads problem-solving projects. Trains and coaches project teams	Master Black Belt

Green Belt

The Green Belt, like the Black Belt, should have at least three years of experience in quality efforts so that they can be familiar with the tools. Under guidelines from ASQ, the candidate for a Green Belt will have completed 64 hours of instruction in a classroom situation learning the methodology. In the course of their duties, they will analyze and solve elementary quality problems. They may also lead smaller teams. In most organizations the role of a Green Belt is a part-time one. The potential savings for the organization from the projects they work on are in the range of $25,000 and $50,000. Their improvement efforts pay for the program training.

Level	Years of Experience	Training Requirements	Responsibilities	Reporting Path
Green Belt	3+ years of experience	64 hours of training	Assists with data collection and analysis. Leads smaller projects	Black Belt

Yellow Belt

The Yellow Belt certification is reserved for those individuals who will be assigned as team members on the improvement efforts. It typically requires between 16 and 20 hours of training in the tools of the Six Sigma methodology. While they will not be leading specific projects, it is necessary that they understand when and how they should use the individual tools at each stage of the process. They also learn how to relate these concepts to the business's overall strategy. Remember that the ultimate results of the project process are the creation of creditable, verifiable data so they need to understand how to read the data points so they can be interpreted correctly.

Level	Years of Experience	Training Requirements	Responsibilities	Reporting Path
Yellow Belt	None	16–20 hours	Participates as a team member	Black Belt

White Belt

The bottom layer of the roles within our cross-functional teams is the White Belts. This could be opened to anyone within the organization who wants a general knowledge of the process. Typically, a White Belt candidate undergoes only about eight hours of training, which is centered on an overview of the process and the tools.

Level	Years of Experience	Training Requirements	Responsibilities	Reporting Path
White Belt	None	8 hours	Works on local problem-solving teams	Black Belt

Project Essentials

At the beginning of this chapter, I quoted Joseph Juran, who said, *All improvement happens project by project and in no other way.* If Juran is correct and we believe he is, then we need to gain an understanding of just what a project is.

The *Project Management Professional Study Guide*, 2nd edition,[7] clearly tells us what a project is and what it is not. Phillips defines a project as an endeavor that creates something and is temporary in nature. An endeavor does not exist in a vacuum and requires some structure. Part of that structure is the cross-functional team. The other part of the structure is the project effort itself. Having looked at the nature of the cross-functional team, I will now turn to the project side of the equation.

Once the problem has been identified, the team creates a roadmap for the project in the form of the project charter.

The Project Charter

The project charter (a copy of the charter can be found on the following pages) is a concise form which lays out the project scope and work. It begins with identifying the project that you are planning on working on. It answers the question regarding what you expect to achieve. It also identifies which organization or department is sponsoring the project. This is typically the one that will gain the most contribution from the process improvement efforts. If you remember we also discussed earlier the role of the various human capital assets involved in Six Sigma projects. One of those roles was that of the project sponsor. The sponsor is the key to the success of the project as they are putting their name on the project as being one of utmost importance. They are the gatekeepers to keep the project active through upper management levels.

There is no chance of success in an improvement project if you remain enclosed within your functional cocoon. The key is a look at the problem from all angles within the organization. The team of individuals who are responsible for implementation must come from a cross-section of the entire organization and includes a representative from every segment that is touched by the problem in question. The next part of the charter form shows the names of the cross-functional team members and what their specific roles are within the project. Some, like the finance representative, may be obvious, but other team members will have vital roles to play, but their role might be less obvious. Still, you want to designate their exact role within the project team for each member.

The ultimate goal of the project is to meet the needs expressed by the customer. In order to complete the project in detail we need to identify who are the stakeholders who are most likely to gain the most from a successful outcome and further to identify what the benefit is. The next block on the charter requires the project sponsor to sign off and date the form. It is from here we begin to develop the inner factors in the project.

One of the outcomes of the project schedule is to develop a set of milestones which are recorded on the project charter. A milestone becomes an indicator of how the project is advancing.

When I underwent my training for the Black Belt, my project was dealing with the effectiveness of training an organization's human capital assets. In the project charter we listed seven milestones. My indicated milestones were scope of the project, submission of the charter, determining the evaluation methods, analyzing the data, construct the dashboards and the balance scorecards and finally delivering the final project report. Each milestone indicated a target date for delivery, the actual date for delivery and sponsor approvals.

Following the milestones, the next task is to develop a detailed description of the problem that you believe is present within your organization. It may also be an opportunity statement if you are introducing a new process.

Project Charter Statement

Project Name/Title:	
Sponsoring Organization:	
Project Sponsor:	
Team Members (Name)	**Role**

Principal Stakeholder		Proposed Benefit		
Sponsor Approval Signature/Date:				

Preliminary Plan (Milestones)		Target Date	Actual Date	Approvals

Project Name/Title:

Problem/Opportunity Statement

Project Goal: Solution/Recommendation

Resources Requested (What you need, $, personnel, time, etc.)

Project Impact Statement

Having established the problem statement, the cross-functional team now develops for management review of the goal of the project. This includes your proposed solution and recommendations for changes within the organization. It is at this point you may begin to see some pushback from within the organization from those aspects that are reluctant or afraid of changing what they have done for time eternal.

You not only want but need buy-in from upper management for the process to work successfully, so one of the data points that must be presented is what is the process going to cost the organization. This section of the charter asks the team to delineate the resources needed. For each resource requested we need to tell management precisely what you need in terms of funds, time away from traditional work expectations and added equipment. The list could go on forever, but it needs to be detailed to provide a clear picture of what it will take to achieve your goal.

Regardless of whether you are a floor person or the CEO of the organization, your immediate question is, WIFM or what's in it for me? The final section of the project charter is space for the team to delineate what the impact on the organization will be if you are successful in completing the project. The project impact should also provide a view of the dollar savings that could be expected if the changes you are suggesting come to be within the organization.

Completing the preliminary project charter, the team is confronted with the dilemma of how to select the right project to work on. The next section will look at that process.

Project Selection

Your organization believes that there is a problem with the organization, so the tendency is to try and repair everything at once. While on the surface that may seem like the right direction for the organization, this approach seldom meets the end goal.

We can find a series of factors in the process of determining which project to choose when beginning the continuous improvement process. In presenting our Master Series course on the topic of this book, I developed the ten commandments of project selection to aid you in making that decision.

Commandment #1: Thou shalt become one with the customer

Start with the understanding that the customer rules. They determine what your organization does. They determine the process flow through your organization. The end user of our products and services is our customers. They determine what they need, when they need it, where they need it and how much they will pay for the products and services. It makes no difference whether the customer is internal in the organization or outside the organization into the global marketplace.

The first goal in project selection is to become one with the customer. You can't just say here is our products or services. You need to get into the head of the customers. You need to understand how they think and feel. You need to understand their organizational goals, missions and values. You need to understand why they feel they need our products and services. In the end, you should behave as if you are the customer. Everything you do must be performed from the view of the customer.

Commandment #2: Thou shalt align all projects with corporate values, missions and goals

In order to run error free your organizational processes do not exist as an island. Each of the processes must rest in the values, missions and goals of the organization as a whole. We still will be changing the overall corporate culture and the end of the improvement effort, but they must still reside within the critical bases of your organization. In the end, the three pillars will guide the implementation process. Each process improvement needs to be aligned with the values that have maintained the organization through its history. Each process improvement needs to be aligned with the missions of the organization. Finally, the improvement process must be aligned with the corporate goals for the future.

Commandment #3: Thou shalt seek total organizational alignment with project outcomes

You have selected your project and identified the potential outcomes. The next step is to preset the proposed process changes to two different groups within your organization. First, you need to present the business case to upper management as to why this course of action is good for the organization as a whole and second to the organizational bottom line. Simultaneously, you need to present the business case for the changes to the rank and file within the organization. You must show them what is in it for them when we make the changes. You need to present the business case for why you are making the changes. You need to show them what happens if you don't make the changes including the possibilities of job losses.

The bottom line is that from the front door to the corner office everyone must be in alignment with the path forward to continuous process improvement.

Commandment #4: Thou shalt seek a positive return on investment on all projects

As you progress through the methodology toolbox you will uncover a wide variety of possible projects that need attention. Just because you have a project potential does not mean that you should work on it. The goal is to implement those projects that have the greatest potential for a return on investment. You want to concentrate on those projects that will have a positive benefit on the organization's bottom line. Only when you can show how the process improvement effort will make things better can you properly select the project.

Commandment #5: Thou shalt ensure that all resources are in place

In our discussion of the project charter above, I talked about identifying the required resources to complete the project. You should absolutely ensure that all required resources are identified and secured. Do not begin a project unless you have in place the resources to complete the effort. You need to have the commitment from management levels of the organization to release the necessary human capital assets to complete the effort. It does not assist the effort when as the project rolls out, managers turn around and say you can't use this person because I need him to complete a particular project of his or her own. This defeats the whole journey toward continuous process improvement.

Commandment #6: Thou shalt ensure that all projects are concentrated on true process causes

Perception is reality. We look at everything either by looking in a mirror or by looking outside a window. They are two different views. This is a proven nature of being a human being. You need to ensure that any improvement efforts that you enter into are based on real causes, not one-time occurrences. You will find from time to time that one of your processes performs in a non-normal fashion. You will find that circumstances may just cause a rapid solution that is perceived to be the perfect solution but may in fact not be the best solution. As you begin this journey, be sure that when you determine what the causes of your problems are, they are the real causes, not a perceived cause.

Commandment #7: Thou shalt ensure that all projects will be implemented

It is human nature to tend toward procrastination. However, The TLS Continuum is not lip service to improving the organization. If you or your management is not intent on caring through the effort, it is a disservice to the efforts to become one with the customer by just going through the efforts without the commitment to actually meet their needs by improving your processes. Delaying the implementation of the process changes is not fair to your customers or to your human capital assets that strive to put together the project outcomes. As we will see in Commandment #8 time is of the essence.

Commandment #8: Thou shalt ensure that all projects are based on urgency

There is a tendency for humans to put off until later those things that are uncomfortable. I totally get that change is hard. However, in order to meet the voice of the customer, you need to dedicate yourself to reaching the end of the process improvement effort as soon as you can reasonably reach that point. Typically, the project needs to be completed within a 90-day time frame.

Commandment #9: Thou shalt strive to have all projects are based on evidence-based metrics

The solutions to your organizational problems are not grounded in "I think this is the problem" or "I think this is the right solution." These are anecdotal thoughts about the problems confronting you. True continuous process improvement and the TLS Continuum are not based on static information. They are based on creditable, evidence-based data. In order for your solutions to be viable for both your customers and your organization the solutions must be based on these creditable, verifiable evidence-based data. Data that clearly demonstrates the solution chosen meets all the conditions of what the customer demands to have in place. Failure to do so leads to a worsening of the problems.

Commandment #10: Thou shalt strive to have all projects deliver the end result cheaper, faster and better

Every time you embark on the TLS Continuum journey you should have one goal in mind. You must make it your mission statement to deliver your product or service post-process improvement effort cheaper, faster and better. We mean that the customer's demands are less costly in terms of production costs. We mean that the customer's demands are delivered faster than the customer expects. By this we mean that the sooner you can deliver the end result the more money your customer makes. Incidentally the more money your customer makes the more money your organization makes. Finally, you need to strive to deliver the end result better than the customer demands. It means that after the improvement efforts the product or service needs to be delivered with as little chance for errors in the product or service as possible.

These ten commandments lay out a checklist to determine your potential project trajectory. A positive response to the commandments will take your organization closer toward success in improving your organization. The checklist is a critical factor going forward.

Project Maps

The first of these process maps is the Gantt Chart. Lynne Hambleton in her book *Treasure Chest of Six Sigma Growth Methods, Tools, and Best Practices* tells us that the goal of the Gannt Chart is to organize the project activities and to display and communicate the project's planned activities as well as the progress toward completion.[8]

The Gannt Chart begins with a list of the milestones we identified in the project charter. The milestones are inserted in the far-left vertical column. Across the columns going from left to right are the dates that you have established for the project. As you enter the data into the chart as you complete a task, it appears on the Gannt Chart in the form of a bar across the page showing the progress. The subsequent bars represent each task and the path toward its completion. You can find templates for a Gannt Chart in Office 365 templates as well as in software programs such as QI Macros.

In the presentation of the project charter, many Black Belts will look for the presence of the Gannt Chart as a way to track the project and report back to management (Figure 4.1).

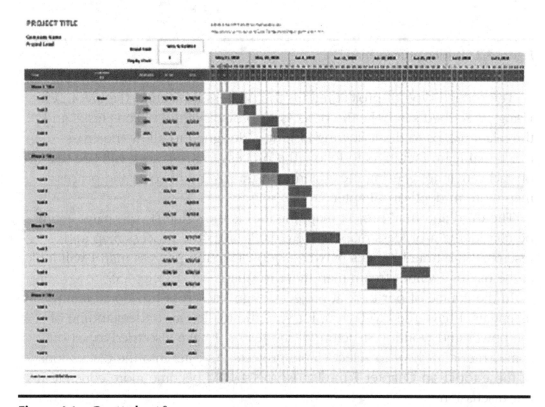

Figure 4.1   Gantt chart.[9]

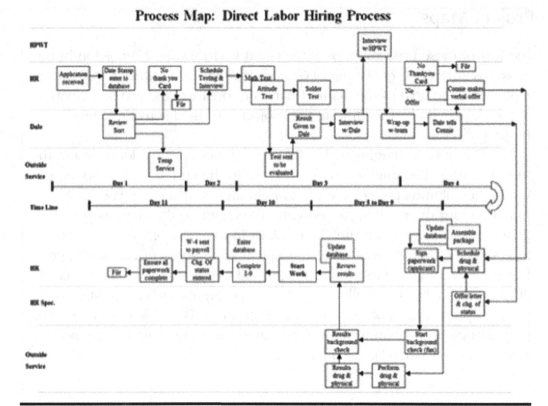

Figure 4.2   Hiring process map.[10]

The second type of project map is the process flow chart (Figure 4.2). Using prescribed symbols, the process map displays the various tasks and the relationships to the following task. It is designed to allow the cross-functional team members to follow the process to see if they can see the obstacles that are causing the system constraints. I will cover the process map more in depth in Chapter 7.

The third and final project mapping tool is the value stream map. It can be considered a process map on steroids. It takes the process map and inserts all the time intervals between steps. Like the process map I will look at the use of a value stream map more in Chapter 7 (Figure 4.3).

In the course of our look at project design and cross-functional team essentials, I have tried to lay out for you, the reader, an understanding of the power and working structure of the teams. I have also tried to set out some criteria for how to select viable projects. As I get into the discussions of these topics in Chapter 7 the landscape should become more concrete in our discussions.

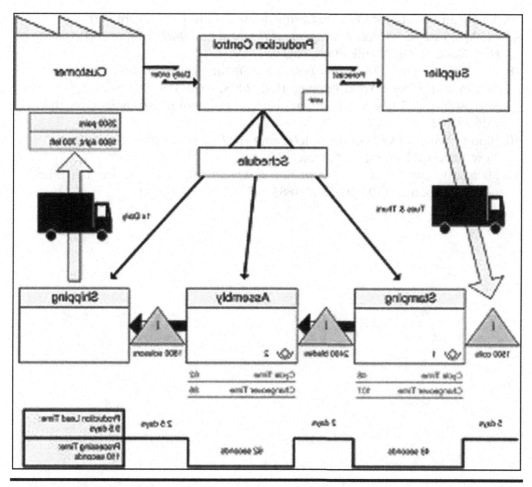

Figure 4.3   Value stream map.[11]

Notes

1. Heath, Dan. *Upstream*. New York: Avid Reader Press, 2020, Page 26.
2. Mindtools.com. *Frederick Taylor and Scientific Management*. https://mindtools.com/pages/article/new/TMM_Taylor.htm
3. Dr. Edward Freeman created the stakeholder theory, which is a view of capitalism that stresses the interconnected relationships between a business and its customers, suppliers, employees, investors, communities and others who have a stake in the organization. The theory suggests that a firm should create value for all stakeholders, not just shareholders. http://stakeholdertheory.org/about
4. Epstein, David. *Range: Why Generalists Triumph in a Specialized World*. New York: Riverhead Books, 2019, Pages 177–178.
5. Bahcall, Sadi. *Loonshots*. New York: St. Martin's Press, 2019, Pages 199–202.

6. American Society for Quality. *Certification Tool.* https://asq.org/cert
7. Phillips, Joseph. *Project Management Professional Study Guide*, 2nd edition. New York: McGraw-Hill, 2006, Page 9.
8. Hambleton, Lynne. *Treasure Chest of Six Sigma Growth Methods, Tools, and Best Practices.* New York: Prentice-Hall, 2008, Page 315.
9. Microsoft. *Gantt Chart.* https://templates.office.com/en-us/simple-gantt-chart-t m16400962
10. Bloom, Daniel. *Field Guide to Achieving HR Excellence through Six Sigma.* New York: CRC Press, 2016, Page 124.
11. Microsoft Support. *Value Stream Map Template.* https://support.content.office. net/en-us/media/8f704492-5800-4885-aa5c-7176d7a7539f.gif

Chapter 5

Voice of the Customer

Introduction

Dr. Tony Alessandra, in his book *The Platinum Rule*, tells us that the reason organizations exist is to acquire and maintain customers. Joseph Juran tells us that quality planning consists of developing the products and processes required to meet the customer's needs. Jack Welch, in a presentation to GE stockholders, said,

> The best Six Sigma projects begin not inside the business but outside it, focused on answering the question—how can we make the customer more competitive? What is critical to the customer's success? … One thing we have discovered with certainty is that anything we do that makes the customer more successful inevitably results in financial return to us.

Kathy Schissler, of Destination Breakthrough LLC, tells us that in order to play in the game you need to choose to play, stop and think; seek to appreciate your customers; and learn to execute by hearing the voices of the customer.

The impact of these views can be found in the voice of the customer paradigm, which was inspired by Kathy Shissler's "In the Game" presentation, as shown in Figure 5.1.

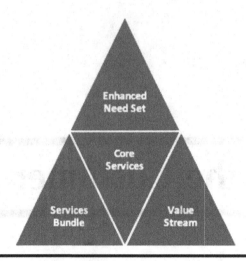

Figure 5.1 Voice of the customer paradigm.

Core Services

To begin our discussion of the voice of the customer we need to establish a theorem about why our organizations exist. Understand that a theorem is a general set of principles that we believe to be true. In the case of the voice of the customer, that theorem is that my company and your organization each exist to contribute something to the global marketplace. Your organization does not exist in a bubble. Your clients do not exist in a bubble. In order for us to acquire customers we need to have something to contribute to the marketplace. Typically, this is the form of products and services. Thus, the first part of the voice of the customer paradigm is our core services.

The core services are those products and services that your organization makes available to the global marketplace. The voice of the customer tells us what products and services they need. It makes no difference whether these clients are internal to the organization or out in the marketplace. They will not be the same with every customer, so as an organization we need to strive to have a wide variety of core services. It is also a necessity that you understand that these core services may be offered on an interim basis. As the client needs change so must your core service package. That voice tells us what it is about those products or services that brought them to us rather than one of our competitors. Our message tells the customers that we are able to meet their basic demands—can they get our products when they need them? Can they get our products where they need them? Can they get our products how they want them? Can they get our products at the price they want them? Failure to meet these voices means that we will not acquire and maintain customers. It means that they can look at the marketplace and see who else may also fit their needs. There is no such thing as customer loyalty in today's marketplace. The way we maintain customers is to genuinely listen to the voice of the customer.

Services Bundle

The second component of the paradigm is that of the services bundle. Based on the customer needs what other services can you offer that complement their needs? Consider the following example. While the example does not have a bearing on our pursuit of HR excellence, it does however provide an example of what I am implying.

You are an avid bowler. You go into a sports shop to purchase a new ball, and the store associate shows you the ball you wanted but also the bag to go with it.

The service bundle allows you to more completely answer the voice of the customer as to what they need at that moment. This allows the voice of the customer to make you further understand the value of their needs.

Enhanced Need Set

The third component of the voice of the customer paradigm is that of enhanced need set. You know how you get a handle on the needs of the customer—you do it by becoming one with the customer. You do it by knowing your customer so well that you can anticipate their needs before they know they need them. Once you do that you need to be ready with the product and services that answer those needs with the customer making contact with your organization.

Value Stream

The *Merriam Webster Dictionary* tells us that value is defined as the monetary worth of something, the fair return or equivalent in goods, services or money for something exchanged or the relative worth, utility or importance.[1] Everything we do must be value-added in nature. This means that the value flows throughout the supply chain. This is true regardless of whether we are talking about the lifetime value of a client (LTV = total sales/tenure as a client) to your organization or the benefit the client receives from the product or services they obtain.

It is imperative in our listening to the voice of the customer that we ascertain the value stream of our products and services. It is imperative in our listening to the voice of the customer that we ascertain just what the customer is seeking to gain from our services. The easiest way to determine the value stream is to follow the supply chain and seek to remove the non-value-added parts of the process. In Chapter 6, we will delve deeper into what constitutes these non-value-added parts of our processes.

This chapter is an exploration of that voice. It is an explanation of how we learn what they need and how they need it. Before we get deep into that discussion, there is one other facet that we must explore and, that is, who do we serve?

Stakeholder vs. Shareholder

That may seem like a crazy question, but it is mandatory that we understand the answer to that question. Pick up any organizational annual report. Open any corporate website. I am not a betting man, but I am willing to bet that almost all of them will make reference to in some fashion serving their shareholders. They will make some reference about returning the shareholder's financial investment in the organization through a larger bottom line.

But is that really who you really need to be servicing? Is that the only people you need to be listening to? This brings us to that other facer that needs to be explored. What is the difference between a shareholder and a stakeholder? The place to begin is to look at the definition of the terms.

Many corporations contend that their purpose is to meet the needs of their shareholders. First, let me make it abundantly clear that all shareholders are in themselves stakeholders. The difference is that their involvement in the organization is purely financial in nature. Your shareholders are those individuals and entities who own shares of stock in your organization. They come and go based on how well your organization is making money. The opposite side of the coin is the stakeholders.

The Pearse Trust tells us that shareholders are the owners of the company and provide financial backing in return for potential dividends over the lifetime of the company.[2] A person or corporation can become a shareholder of a company in three ways: by subscribing to the memorandum of the company during incorporation; by investing in return for new shares in the company; and by obtaining shares from an existing shareholder by purchase, by gift or by will.

Their involvement is not the same as stakeholders, as we will see below.

The stakeholders play an active role in your organizational processes. It considers the active role that the various stakeholders play in the organizational processes. It is both the external and internal stakeholders. It is worth our time to stop for a moment and define what we mean by stakeholders.

In 1984, Dr. Edward Freeman suggested that stakeholders are any entity that is either affected or can affect the business processes.[3] Dr. Freeman's concept suggests that we take a broader view of the organization to take into consideration how our actions and processes affect the entire global perspective of the outputs of our organizations.

Dr. Edward Freeman created the stakeholder theory, which is a view of capitalism that stresses the interconnected relationships between a business and its customers, suppliers, employees, investors, communities and others who have a stake in the organization. The theory argues that a firm should create value for all stakeholders, not just shareholders.

With the definition of stakeholders in plain view, the next task is to determine who they are in our organization. One of the easiest ways to do that is through the use of a tool out of the TLS Continuum Toolbox in the form of a SIPOC.

SIPOC

In order to better understand the voice of the customer it is imperative that we understand the roles each of the stakeholders plays in the process improvement efforts. The easiest way to achieve this is through the usage of a tool called the SIPOC diagram. Created during the push for Total Quality Management, the SIPOC is a tool that can be used to identify the stakeholders and their roles. Remember in Chapter 2 I said the TLS Continuum is just that. It is a chain of a series of actions resulting in process improvement. In order to begin the implementation of process improvement within your organization, we need to gain an eagle's eye view of the processes and the performance gaps from the customer's point of view. The first step is to conduct a stakeholder analysis of the organizational processes.

The first step in the journey is to look at the organization from above and identify the players in the mix. The SIPOC can be used as a stakeholder analysis process.

SIPOC Diagram Template				
Suppliers	Input	Process	Output	Customers

Template Provided by Bright Hub Project Management.

Figure 5.2 SIPOC diagram.[4]

Using the form, as seen in Figure 5.2, the process begins with the construction of a SIPOC analysis of your operation. It provides an eagle's eye view of the various components of the process.

In order to achieve this analysis, the SIPOC is divided into five segments or columns which lay out the steps in the process chain. While we eventually will be concerned with the critical few, at this macro viewpoint, we want to include all that are applicable to the process in each column.

The S in SIPOC refers to the suppliers to the system. They are represented in the first column of the diagram. They represent those entities that contribute the materials that are used to produce our products and services.

These materials are delivered to the organization in the form of an input of some kind.

The I in the SIPOC refers to the inputs. As an organization you seek out suppliers to provide you something. Whether it is materials or software, you still seek out their inputs. Those are your process. Inputs come from sources within and outside our organizations. They are designed to furnish or provide (a person, establishment, place, etc.) with what is lacking or requisite to make up, compensate for or satisfy something missing from a process. These inputs ultimately feed into one or more of your organizational processes.

The P in SIPOC and the third column represents the processes that flow through your organization. The system is designed as such where the suppliers and their inputs feed the processes by which your organization functions. You need to have a precise path of how the supplier's inputs are utilized in making the product or delivering the service to meet client needs. Your definition of the process involved must be clearly noted.

We do not conduct a process without expecting the process to result in some sort of product or service. The O in SIPOC refers to those outputs. When we complete a process, it needs to present something tangible. The process is undertaken because it is creating something. This thing is the output. It is the product or service that you deliver to the end user.

The C in SIPOC refers to the last stage of the stakeholder analysis. It stands for the customer or end user. Understand both the supplier and the end user are able to complete SIPOCs at their individual ends of the chain, going back in time or forward in time, respectively.

How Do We Measure the Voice of the Customer?

Remember that we can't take steps to implement the TLS Continuum and Continuous Process Improvement without some creditable data. So, where do we get those data points? The easiest way is to ask them directly. The difficulty here is that their immediate answers may not be the full story here.

The TLS Continuum toolbox contains a tool called the Quality Function Deployment (QFD) tool, as shown in Figure 5.3. The QFD is actually a process within a bigger process and is designed to more effectively define that all-important voice of the customer. The end goal is that with the customer telling us what is critical to them, your organization is better able to establish those products and services that meet those voices. It is the completion of the voice of the customer matrix that completes that goal.

To get a better understanding of how the matrix works, turn back to Figure 5.3, and I will take you through the various components of the matrix and their interactions with the rest of the form.

Running horizontally across the top of the matrix is the delineation of the phases of the process in question. In this case the phases are laid out as plan, develop, market, deliver and support. Under each of these are three options that might be undertaken for each phase. For instance in the

Voice of the Customer

Legend: ● 4 Strong ○ 2 Medium △ 1 Weak

Customer Requirements	Importance (1-5)	Internal Consultant	Customer Surveys	X functional Team	Internal controls	Talent Screening	Dept partnerships	Policies	Procedures	Process	Sourcing vehicles	Talent search	Employmnt offers	Pre-Interview steps	Pre-hire steps	Onboarding
		Plan			Develop			Market			Deliver			Support		
Better																
Treat me like you want my business	5	1	2	2	4	2	4	4	2	2	2	2	2	1	1	2
Deliver services that meet my needs	5	2	2	2	2	2	2	2	2	2	2	2	2	2	2	2
services that work right	3	2	2	2	1	2	2	2	2	2	2	2	2	2	2	2
Be accurate, right the first time	4	2	2	2	1	2	2	2	2	2	2	2	2	2	2	2
Source us the right candidate	5	2	2	2	1	2	2	2	2	2	2	2	2	2	2	2
Faster																
I want it when I want it	3	2	2	2	1	2	2	2	2	2	1	2	2	4	2	2
Make commitments that meet my needs	4	2	2	2	1	2	2	2	2	2	2	2	2	4	2	2
Meet your commitments	4	2	2	2	1	2	2	2	2	2	2	2	2	4	2	2
I want fast, easy access to help	4	2	2	2	1	2	2	2	2	2	2	2	2	2	2	2
Don't waste my time	5	2	2	2	1	2	2	2	2	2	2	2	2	2	2	2
if it breaks, fix it fast	4	2	2	2	1	2	2	2	2	2	2	2	2	2	2	2
Cheaper																
Deliver irresistable value	4	2	2	2	1	4	2	2	2	2	2	2	1	2	2	2
Help me save money	5	4	2	2	1	4	2	2	2	2	2	2	1	2	2	2
Help me save time	5	4	2	2	1	4	2	2	2	2	2	2	1	2	2	1
Total Weight		135	120	120	80	148	130	130	120	120	117	120	106	137	115	115

Figure 5.3 Voice of the customer matrix.[5]

planning stage the options shown are internal consultant, customer surveys and the cross-functional team.

On the far left is a vertical column denoted by the three goals of the TLS Continuum. We want to strive to get your product or service to the end user better (less defects), faster and cheaper (not in the total cost but in the outlay of funds to produce the end product).

By entering this data into an excel type spreadsheet you construct a grid between the components. The next step is to ask the customer, what would characterize a "perfect product for them"? Your task then is to assign a number to each response on a scale of 1–4, with 4 being considered a strong want by the customer.

Your final task is then to identify the customer priorities in their response on a scale of 1–5, with 5 being the strongest want. When you enter the priority ranking into the column, the matrix is preloaded with weighting formulas for each square. The last horizontal row is the calculation of the totals of each column, giving you the ability to identify what is most important, thus giving you the critical few items that must be worked on immediately.

As we have seen the voice of the customer is a critical part of the continuous process improvement effort and the TLS Continuum. As we will see in Chapter 7, it is a necessary task in defining the process obstacle that is confronting the organization.

Before we look at the methodology in action, there is one other aspect that we need to consider and that is the identification of the non-value-added wastes in your organization.

Notes

1. Merriam-Webster Dictionary. *Definition of Value.* https://www.merriam-webster.com/dictionary/value
2. Pearse Trust Blog. *The Role of a Shareholder.* https://www.pearse-trust.ie/bl og/roles-responsibilities-of-company-shareholder#:~:text=The%20shareholders %20are%20the%20owners,the%20lifetime%20of%20the%20company.&text=By %20investing%20in%20return%20for,by%20gift%20or%20by%20will
3. Freeman, R. Edward. *The Stakeholder Theory.* http://stakeholdertheory.org/ about
4. SIPOC Diagram https://drive.google.com/file/d/17gj65PNuqIuZ5EeWVn3EAw RNSV5Ao8Xr/view
5. Taken from the Black Belt Training Program at St. Petersburg College.

Chapter 6

Organizational Waste

Introduction

Shigeo Shingo told us that "the most dangerous kind of waste is the waste we do not recognize." The business literature tells us someone stated that "removal of waste in our processes makes the organization more sustainable."

Every process in the workplace is destined to have hiccups. Those hiccups are typically due to waste or non-value-added activities of some kind. As Shigeo Shingo stated, the most dangerous kinds of wastes are those we don't recognize. In many cases the reason why we don't recognize the wastes in our processes is because we don't look for them even though they are in plain sight. The easiest rule of thumb is that the examples of waste we will see in this chapter are those activities that add nothing to the task of meeting the demands of the customer.

In this chapter we are going to look at wastes that are found within the HR processes.

Consider as an example your talent acquisition process to bring new talent into your organization. Our organizations have been really good at adding steps to the process, whether it is from the suggestion of upper management or someone in the human resource management space who felt that the new step would assist the process. Many of the steps have been added without consultation with their customers, internal or external. I would assert that if we were able to look at any organization in existence throughout the global workplace, there would not be a single

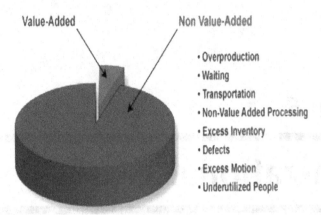

Value-Added   Non Value-Added

- Overproduction
- Waiting
- Transportation
- Non-Value Added Processing
- Excess Inventory
- Defects
- Excess Motion
- Underutilized People

Figure 6.1   Types of MUDA or organizational waste.[1]

organization that did not contain waste of some sort. In fact, Jay Arthur of KnowledgeWare suggests that for every $100 of corporate spent in a 3-sigma corporation, $25–$40 of it is wasteful spending.[2]

Depending on what source you reference, there may be seven, eight or nine individual types of waste in existence. Toyota's original list of waste sources consisted of seven wastes. Over time we have added sources to the nine contained in this chapter. Whenever you have any form of movement within your process, you are subjected to the potential for the inclusion of non-value-added steps. Toyota and the Toyota Production System suggested that every organization has actually presented three types of waste. The first is *MUDA*,[3] which refers to those wastes that utilize human activity but do not add value to the customer requirements. The second is *MURI*, which refers to actions by the organization that add unreasonable expectations on the organization, and the final type is *MURA*, which refers to variation and inconsistency within the organization. While it may not meet all our needs, it is simpler to lump all the wastes together under the MUDA umbrella; we need to clarify a concept before continuing. By the term *waste* we are not referring to something that, when it is found within the organization, is taken out to the back of the facility and placed in a container for the waste management company to retrieve. We are not talking about wrapping from food or products purchased for the organization (Figure 6.1).

The remainder of this chapter will look at each of the nine sources of non-value-added wastes with a concentration in human capital management.

Waste from Overproduction

If you are on the manufacturing floor, many organizations operate in a push environment in which the materials needed on the floor are sent through the processes when they come into the building rather than when they are needed. HR does the same things with certain transactional actions each and every day. Part of this is because as human beings we have a tendency to believe that having more is better in the long run even if you have an oversupply on hand. The result is that we get a request for data and we tend to produce way more than the customer asked for or needs.

As I stated above the HR function is just as guilty as the rest of the organization in this regard. As human resource professionals have you ever experienced these situations?

Excess job requisitions

It is normal for your organization at the beginning of each fiscal year to establish a talent management plan in which you determine your manpower needs for the coming year. This plan sets out the number of open jobs, the talent backgrounds needed and the compensation for each open position. Take a moment and think about your organization and its talent management plan and how many open positions you have. Now consider how many open positions you have. Is the number less, equal to or greater than the plan?

If you have more than the plan it is a good bet that the conflict with the numbers is the result of a manager who tells HR that they have a critical need for a particular skill set so they ask you to add to the open positions. In reality, they may be real positions, but many managers ask HR to recruit a particular skill set with no valid opening. The manager gets it into their head that they need to source the marketplace to see what is available just in case someone decides to leave. The collection of talent profiles in case something happens is a waste. This tendency makes the talent management's effort more difficult. The candidates applying get frustrated with the process and with your organization. The managers get upset because they have all this backlog of candidates and when he or she needs them they are not available. This is equivalent to the push environment on the manufacturing side of the business. This is a waste.

If you are like the vast majority of organizations, you are following the compliance requirements and need to enter all the candidates into your applicant tracking system, so you are using the valuable time of your HR staff to input them into the system. You are wasting brand capital because more than likely these candidates are entered and then they never hear from the organization again.

Creation of too much information

If you have ever been at the office water cooler, especially one used by members of management I am sure you have heard the opinion expressed that they could do HR's job better without the hassles.

As human beings many of us operate under the premise more is better. This is equally true when we collect data. There is a simple premise in business, and it states, "Keep it simple, stupid." Here is where the problem is presented. The chief executive officer requests from the head of HR the data on the turnover rate for the past quarter.

HR in turn wants to demonstrate to the organization that there is some value in HR being a critical part of the organization to dispel the water cooler talk. HR gathers the data requested with a twist. They produce the report for the turnover rate for the past quarter and also present the data for each department and compare it to the previous quarters. The added information is a waste. It is not what was requested. Do not get me wrong; the extra data may be valuable, but it is not what the voice of the customer requested (the CEO is the customer).

Creating excess reports

In the same venue, some HR departments constantly plan as part of their procedures to routinely create reports on turnover and time to hire and relay the results to top management of the company. The intention is that HR can justify their existence by demonstrating what it is they do. The problem is that there is no value-added benefit to the extra data reports to the organization as it does not meet the requirements of any of the function's customers.

Not in HR, but a business peer tells the story about where a client of his requested a report and two years later the report sits on his office bookcase because the client changed their mind about what they need. Albert Einstein said that if you can't explain it simply, you don't understand the problem.

Waste of Waiting

Put this book down for a minute and think about how you felt the last time you went to the doctor's office. A while back I was referred to a specialist for an 8:30 am appointment, and when I got there the nurse told me that based on his operating method, I would be lucky if I got in to see him before 3 pm in the afternoon. How would you feel in this situation?

Our second of the nine Muda types is that of waiting. Waiting is non-value added because it is not requested by a customer. It plays no part in fulfilling their demands. We receive many reasons for the delay; however anytime we delay the delivery of a product or service beyond when the customer requests it, it is waste:

Within human capital management it refers to the tendency of both managers and recruiters to put off what they need to do even when there is a deadline in place. We receive many reasons for the delay, however anytime we delay the delivery of a product or service beyond when the customer requests it, it is waste. As we did above consider these examples:

Undefined decision making
The recruitment process in particular requires a very well-defined outline of how the process is supposed to work. What typically happens is that the hiring manager tells HR that they need the new employee hired and ready to report for work in three weeks. HR sends up the ladder all the sourced, qualified candidates, and the hiring manager sits on them for three weeks or three months. In the meantime, the recruiter has gone out of their way to complete a supposed priority only to find that not everyone is on the same timetable. Consider this fact that each hour that the critical decision is not reached costs the organization a minimum of $42 per hour in salary and benefits for the assigned recruiter.

Fill times
In congruence with the undefined decision making, this form of non-value-added waste occurs when the hiring manager tells HR management that they need this position filled in three weeks due to a critical project. It is now three months, and HR has yet to send up any candidates to the hiring manager. The reverse is also true; HR sends up the qualified candidates, and the hiring manager sits on it despite having told HR that it is critical that they find the person immediately. When we experience delays in time to fill, it carries ramifications for the rest of the organization. The holdup of the process creates an obstacle or

constraint, which means that the steps that occur later are also held up. The even flow of the hiring process is dictated by certain events happening at precise intervals in the road to new hires, and anything that interferes with that flow creates new obstacles to the rest of the organization.

Customer unmet needs

Human capital management is unique in the organization's hierarchy because the vast majority of our customers are internal to the organization. This is compounded by the fact that HR has an image problem. That arises out of HR's persona as existing to hinder the flow of the talent through the organization. HR is viewed by many within the organization as a roadblock and that your role is to block the hiring process. Management solution is to work around you and do the hiring themselves.

Consider what the picture would look like if the rest of the organization could not deliver what was needed when it was needed. In many cases the customer would take their business elsewhere. Internal managers have only two choices; they can deal with HR which they believe to be lacking the will to get the job done on time or do it themselves. When this happens, we no longer have a standard of work and thus we have created waste within the organization.

Waste of Overtransportation

Whether we are talking about the Hawthorne Studies or the original work of Frederick Taylor, every organization at one time or another has been concerned with the flow of materials and resources through the organization. I am sure you have all worked in an organization where it seemed that every time you turn around the organization has rearranged the office every time the wind changes. Many times, there is a valid reason for the changes. Other times it is supposed to meet some reported need. The problem is that sometimes the movement creates more problems than believed because the total organization was not reviewed. When this extra movement is present it creates waste.

Unnecessary movement

Look at how our human capital assets work through the organization. Your goal is to get the right person in the right space at the right time to achieve the goals of the organization. The intent is to have your department as productive as possible. Consider that one major organization within the mortgage industry hand-carried a mortgage application from the beginning of the process to the point of acceptance or rejection. When they were finished the application had traveled a total of eight miles. Is this a productive use of the human capital's time and efforts?

Office flow

Consider this scenario: you have a meeting with a hiring manager; how do you get there? I recently sent a fax to a client. After sending it, I called her to see if she got it. The response I got was that she did not know because the fax machine was in the break room on the other side of the floor she was working on. How much time did she lose by walking back and forth to the break room to retrieve a fax? Consider the example of a quality engineer who had her desk moved from the second floor to the first floor, but the organization left all her files on the second floor. Consider how much time came out of her day to walk the entire length of the first floor, get up to the second floor to retrieve the file she needed and then return back the way she came.

Waste of Overprocessing

A member of management attends a conference and hears a new strategy within the HR arena and comes back to the office and implements it without seeing how it will fit into the total organization. Somewhere back in time a minor crisis occurred, and management decided to avoid it happening again so they will implement oversight controls on the HR function. All of these could be great ideas, but if they are not taken in the context of your corporate culture you are asking for added problems. These added steps were implemented to isolate the organization but not meet the needs of the customer. Failure to listen to the customer is waste. Consider these examples where good ideas went bad:

Excess steps in the hiring process

Our organizations make changes to our processes on a routine basis every day of the year. Some of these come about due to a member of management hearing about a competitor and the way they handle the hiring process. Or some organization approaches the company with the latest and best tool for creating a seamless process. Often these changes are implemented without consideration as to the effect of the changes on the corporate culture. In the course of presenting our seminar we have come across many examples in this area. A government agency found that in the course of hiring new talent for their agency the job requisition is reviewed three times—by the same person. Another organization required each and every job requisition be signed off by the HR manager before a recruiter could begin the sourcing process. When we worked in the real estate field handling homes of corporate transfers, if an offer came in outside of a certain price point percentage, the offer was presented to no less than seven additional individuals prior to acceptance. Obviously depending on schedules this would extend the sale of the property.

Let me give you one other blatant example from HR. You have an open job requisition that you have been recruiting for. You had each candidate input their background online; however when you invite them for an interview you have them complete a paper application. Why?

It is crucial that in order to eliminate the non-value-added steps the process be reviewed to see how it fits into the operating culture.

Redundancy

We find in many organizations the tendency to repeat steps in the name of getting them right. The hiring manager informs HR that they need a new IT specialist within three weeks. HR sources and screens the candidates and send to the hiring manager the candidates that best it the job requisition requirements only to have the hiring manager tell HR that they want to see ALL the applications and that he is beginning a search of his own for the right candidate, slowing up the process of selecting and hiring the new talent.

Island mentality

The key to creating high-performing teams is to look at the organization from the outside looking in. Non-value-added activities get created when we look at our role as an ivory tower. In the current business model, there is no room for organizations confined by thought processes that run through a single part of the organization.

Waste of Excess Inventory

Wikipedia defines *excess inventory* as a capital outlay in which there is no return from the customer. We usually consider this from the point of view of a physical item. However, you can also have excess inventory from a service perspective. From the HR perspective we are talking about the accumulation of too much stuff.

Too much work in progress

Later in this book we will talk more in depth about a concept called traffic intensity. The essence of traffic intensity is that in a given workday you have only a set amount of time to get done what you need to get done with the resources available.

Traffic time looks at what happens when you add problem requests with the resources unchanged. There is a point at which it is no longer reasonable to expect that you can resolve all the issues on time. It is at that point where the number of requests exceeds the available resources that waste occurs.

Physical pile of forms

This is a perfect example of the best-laid plans. You develop a new form within the HR function, or any department for that matter, so you order what you think is the reasonable supply of the forms. Lo and behold, two years later you change the form, and you have two year's worth of the old forms remaining. You have created waste as the only real choice you have is to dispose of the old forms.

Waste of Excess Motion

In virtually every corporate facility in the world, if we utilize the spaghetti diagram tool or the Stand in a Circle Tool created by Taiichi Ohno, we can see that we have designed the work floor not entirely in the most efficient way to move human capital within the system. The added steps required to complete the process based on the workflow create waste as we create less productivity. Some real-life examples of this can be found below.

Needless switching of programs

You are working on a word document, and suddenly the hiring manager calls and wants information out of your applicant tracking system. How many steps do you have to take to switch programs on your screen in front of you? Can you view the other program without losing down the first program?

Needless movement of people

I can walk into an office and see examples of this every day. Consider the organization I mentioned earlier in this chapter, which decided to move an employee's desk from the second floor to the first. No problem! That might be totally reasonable. But the organization left all of the employee's files needed to perform the duties and responsibilities of their position on the second floor. To walk the length of the building, go upstairs, retrieve the required files and return to their desk ate up 25 minutes of work time. Consider the business analyst who is trying to review an operating procedure and needs some forms to complete the review. To do so means they have to walk to the other end of the floor to the supply room to obtain the forms instead of printing them on their computer.

Needless movement of information
Your customer asks for a certain report and you generate the report only to find out that the manager did not need the report after all. The movement of information which has no importance to the customer is waste.

Waste from Process Defects

By far this could be the largest segment of the waste types and includes many easily overlooked examples of non-value-added steps in the HR arena. Many of these defects may be simple slips as part of being human, but they do represent waste in the system. They refer to those opportunities where the wrong information is provided, and the result is a disruption to the customer. A disruption requires that the process be reworked in order to correct it so the customer requirements can be met. Consider these examples:

Errors in job postings
These errors can bring huge ramifications to your organization. You are swamped with trying to market your open positions, and in this rush, you type the wrong compensation, the wrong location, etc. The misinformation can lead to the wrong candidates applying for the position, wrong offers being made to the successful new hire or the wrong benefit packages being negotiated based on the presented information. The mistake can be totally innocent, or it could cause a major crisis. No matter why the mistake was made it is still waste to the organization.

Error in job offers
Like the errors in job postings, we are all human and prone to errors. However, this defect example can carry major ramifications for the organization. Consider that you have found the ideal candidate or your

organization, and you issue an offer letter with the wrong salary or the wrong start date. When the candidate reports for work, they are presented with an entirely different set of data regarding the position.

Incomplete metrics

In order for us to "take our seat at the table" we must be able to produce creditable, verifiable data points as we have discussed earlier. In the rush to create this data from the wide variety of data points that are available to us, it is easy to pull the wrong data points. While the data may be correct, they may not be correct for the question at hand. We need to review all of our metrics to determine that we have not only creditable data but valid data for the information requested.

Missed deadlines

The final example refers to those situations when you are given a precise milestone that you need to meet so that the customer's needs can be met. For whatever reason the deadline comes and goes, and you have failed to deliver on your promises. Think out of HR for a moment. If your organization is standardly late on delivering finished products to your customers, how long do you think they will remain a customer? Same scenario, just within the HR space. Missed deadlines mean we are not meeting the voice of the customer, which results in waste in the system.

Waste of Underutilized Human Capital Potential

Can any of you remember the Negro College Fund's slogan that "a mind is a terrible thing to waste"? While this was referring to the opportunities for a young African American trying to get through higher education, the same question can be posed to the internal organization and how you treat your human capital. We can waste the contributions of our human capital asset when we place them in less than an optimal work environment. For example

Idle time

Human potential is compromised when you bring on talent and then have nothing for them to do. Take for example the hiring manager tells HR that it needs a position filled ASAP but leaves the recruiter twiddling his/her thumbs when they have to wait for the official requisition to be signed by all parties involved. Consider when your organization has a less-than-working onboarding system and a new employee reports for work and is shown their desk and telephone and asked to get to work.

Understaffing

Linked to the waiting category, when we understaff a function within our organizations you inevitably make the customer wait for delivery. HR has the responsibility to derive the required staffing levels within the organization, and if we use the wrong metrics, we end up with too few headcounts to complete the work at hand.

Overstaffing

Similar to the previous example, if the metrics are wrong then we could end up hiring too many FTEs, which would leave them sitting at their desks with no work to be delivered.

No time for continuing education

In today's global workplace knowledge becomes obsolete on a regular basis. This is one of the reasons that most certifications require you to earn continuing education credits. Your human capital is in a constant mode of increasing their career portfolios with added knowledge and skills, but unless you plan for it there becomes a scarce amount of time to accomplish this effort. The lack of new skills may hinder the organizational ability to innovate new ideas and products within your industry, leaving your organization less competitive within the marketplace.

Waste of Material Underutilization

The last of the nine types of wastes is that of material underutilization, and it refers to how we use materials within the organization. Every day we do things within the organizational structure, which create waste in the processes and organization such as

E-mails

I am as guilty of this as anyone else. We as humans have a tendency to believe that we might lose something. So an email comes in and we have to rush to make a hard copy of it. I once worked with an individual who posed the question of why after he went out and purchased a desktop PC, a laptop and a PDA he was keeping more paper notes now than he did before. This is an example of the waste that can be created when we underutilize the systems we have in place.

Late arrivals

Finance tells you it is cheaper to schedule teleconferences than it is to send an employee across the country or the globe for a meeting. So you schedule a meeting for 8:30 am in the morning to last an hour. Many of the teleconference companies will charge you based on that 60-minute block of time. John Smith walks into the meeting 30 minutes late, but you get charged as if he was there for the entire time.

Design errors

We are asked to make up a flier, for example, 500 employees, so you make up the fliers two to the page. What happens to the material surrounding the two fliers? It becomes a waste.

If you are still with me at this point, I have provided you with a good background in the continuous process improvement effort I call the TLS Continuum. I discussed what we mean by HR excellence. I have taken you through the growth of continuous process improvement. I have demonstrated the value of the voice of the customer. I have shown you the basics of the process improvement process. Finally, I have shown you the nine types of wastes that occur in every organization, no matter the size of the organization. These wastes occur in the Fortune 100, as well as in the corner mom-and-pop store.

The next part of this book, starting with Chapter 7, will look at how you provide all this information in real time. Chapter 7 looks at the TLS Continuum toolbox and how to use the tools. Chapter 8 looks at the role of HRCI and its body of knowledge. In this chapter I will provide you with some case studies to support our discussions. Finally, in Chapters 9 and 10 I will show you how to implement this process in your own organizations.

Notes

1. Taken from the Six Sigma Black Belt Training materials from St Petersburg College.
2. Arthur, Jay. *Free, Now and Perfect.* Denver, CO: KnowledgeWare, 2012, Page 18.
3. e-coach website. http://www.1000ventures.com/business_guide/lean_waste_types.html

Chapter 7

The TLS Continuum Methodology

Introduction

In this chapter we will begin to see the methodology in action. I will walk you through the entire process one step at a time and explain the how's and why's of everything we do. I will also show you how to use some of the more prevalent tools in the toolbox.

The long-term goal of the TLS Continuum is to create a standard of work. Every time we undertake a problem resolution the solution process should be the same. Further, you should be able to take this process and apply it to issues outside of HR. It is the same method, the same steps and the same process.

Let's be clear, our organizations are operated and governed by processes. The TLS Continuum approach to continuous process improvement is a process and shares all the same characteristics of its sister processes—it has sources, it has inputs which feed processes, it has outputs and it has an end user in the form of problem resolution.

There is one elephant in the china closet if you will that I need to discuss before we get into the meat of the methodology. It is an issue that I discussed earlier. One of the reasons that we hear for not undertaking this process is that it is too difficult. It does not need to be. Granted, I have said that we need to make our decisions based on creditable, evidence-based data, but that does not mean you need to be a PhD or a statistician. In the next section I will show you how to simplify your tasks going forward.

You Don't Need to Be a statistician

My wife tells me that I need to stay away from the check number because I can't add. I will commit to you that math is not my favorite subject. So, when I got into my Black Belt training, I needed a resource that would help me in the way of a crutch to get over the math hurdle. Upon searching the Internet, I found three programs that would provide that crutch—Minitab, QI Macros and Sigma XL.

Minitab—Minitab's website (https://www.minitab.com/en-us/about-us/) tells us that Minitab helps companies and institutions to spot trends, solve problems and discover insights in data by delivering a comprehensive and best-in-class suite of statistical analysis and process improvement tools. Minitab is used by many organizations as their first choice of data analysis tools. However, it has a downside in that it takes 16–20 hours to become at least somewhat proficient. Further, it is not necessarily totally intuitive in nature. It helps users to be somewhat knowledgeable in the use of Excel worksheets.

The remaining two software options are actually built into Excel as add-ons, so it becomes easier for the average person to use the data analysis tools.

SigmaXL—SigmaXL's website (https://www.sigmaxl.com/SigmaXL.shtml) was designed from the ground up to be a cost-effective and powerful but easy-to-use tool that enables users to measure, analyze, improve and control their service, transactional and manufacturing processes.

QI Macros—QI Macros (https://www.qimacros.com/) was built by a businessman, not by a professor. I used the program throughout my Black Belt training. The program consists of a number of tools in the toolbox, along with a wide collection of templates. In all cases you enter your data points, and the program does the analysis for you.

Continuous Process Improvement Matrix

I have referred several times in the course of this work about mapping the processes. The continuous process improvement matrix, as seen in Figure 7.1, is another version of a process map. It begins with the define stage and follows through to the control stage, laying out the milestones under each stage. Along with the toolbox graphic, which will follow later in this chapter, it tells the organization what tasks to begin with and what comes next after you complete them. As stated, one of our goals is to establish a standard of work. The matrix is a graphic of the standard work for the improvement process.

Instructions

TLS Continuum Empowrment Model CPI Index

Organization Status		Importance (1-5)	Manage			Teams			Individual					
			Values	Goals	Strategy	Diversity of Ideas	Full Spectrum Think	Decision Toold	Subj Matter Expert	Engagement	Process Ownership			
Management	**Empowered Managment**													
	Management Controlled	4	3	5	5	1	5	4	5	1	1			
	Values goals and strategy alignment	5	2	3	2	1	1	3	3	1	3			
	Managers serving as coaches	4	1	1	1	3	4	1	2	5	1			
	Voice of Customers intgral part of decisions	5	2	1	1	3	1	3	2	3	1			
X Funct Teams	**Empowered Cross-functional Teams**													
	Management Controlled	2	4	4	4	1	1	1	1	1	1			
	Cross-functional team controlled	5	2	2	2	3	3	3	3	3	3			
	Open sourced ideas for solutions	5	1	1	1	4	4	4	3	2	1			
	Work plan set by team	5	1	1	1	3	3	3	3	3	3			
	Solutions determined by team	5	1	1	1	4	4	4	2	3	3			
	Solutions determined by management	2	4	4	4	1	1	1	1	2	2			
Individual	**Empowered human capital assets**													
	Human capital asset controlled	5	1	1	1	4	4	4	3	3	3			
	Recognized as true subject mtter experts	5	1	1	1	3	2	4	4	3	3			
	Have the ability of change processes	5	1	1	1	4	4	4	3	3	3			
	Smooth proceses work flow	5	1	1	1	4	4	4	2	2	2			
	Total Weight		97	105	100	185	190	204	172	160	139	0	0	0

Legend: ● 4 Strong, ○ 2 Medium, △ 1 Weak — Business Functions

Figure 7.1   Continuous process improvement matrix.[1]

The matrix begins with the understanding of the environment in which you are operating. You want to ascertain management's thoughts and priorities. You want to walk the process and identify where the problems are occurring. The matrix ends with the implementation of the identified solutions. As we make it through the methodology and the toolbox, the matrix will become clearer in nature.

Scientific Method vs. DMAIC Process

The TLS Continuum is based on a concentrated process grounded in a path of discovery. Each and every one of you reading this book has been through a similar process. Take a minute and go back in time to your high school science classes. Each semester the science instructor began the first class with the same lesson for the day. Do you remember what it was? (I know what I am asking because I am a former science teacher, and I did it.) Typically the teacher began with a discussion of the steps of the scientific method.

The scientific method began with constructing a hypothesis, which represented your issue at hand. Once you identified that "what if" stage of the experimental process, you turned to test whether your hypothesis was correct. You did that by taking measurements to prove or disprove your data, and from that you drew a conclusion as to whether your thinking was right or not. When you were done with the first stages you then communicated your results to the indicated audience, your fellow students or the teacher. The scientific method is designed for the natural environment.

The TLS Continuum process is no different. Both the scientific method and the TLS Continuum methodology are designed to solve problems. The TLS Continuum is specifically designed for the business world. I call the TLS Continuum the business scientific method. Similar to the scientific method, the DMAIC method provides a roadmap for cross-functional teams to complete a process centered on improving the quality of your organizational transactional services or the products you produce.

As you can see in Figure 7.2, while the intent is the same, we just have changed the step nomenclature. You begin by defining the problem. What is the system constraint in the system that must be attended to? Once we have identified the constraint, we measure the effects of the constraint on the system to identify the impact of the problem on the organization. As with the scientific method, we take the measurements and analyze the data to find the cause of the problem. Then we use that analysis to improve the system and set up controls to ensure that the constraint does not return once we have removed it.

Scientific Method	DMAIC Process
Construct a hypothesis	Define the Problem
Test your hypothesis	Measure the Problem
Analyze Your Data	Analyze the results
Draw a conclusion	Improve the process
Communicate Results	Control the process

Figure 7.2   Scientific method vs. the DMAIC method.

DMAIC Business Case

Each stage of the TLS Continuum is seeking a specific answer for the reasoning behind each of the steps in the problem resolution.

The define stage, which identifies the problem facing the organization, seeks answers to what is wrong and begins the process of identifying what we are trying to achieve, removing the problem from the specified process.

In the measurement stage we take the problem and again answer a series of questions designed to identify the road forward. We begin by asking what methods or tools we are going to use to measure the problems. While the TLS Continuum has a wide variety of tools and the software programs mentioned above provide us with the toolbox, not every tool is going to be appropriate in every situation. We also need to understand where the data comes from and whether that data source is creditable.

There is an old business adage that tells us that you can make the numbers mean whatever you want them to. It is critical from the very beginning that we ascertain that the numbers we collect represent what we think it does. This means once you collect the first data points you want to verify that the numbers are evidence-based and verifiable. If in fact the data is telling us what we think it does, what is the process, as it currently exists, telling us about the operation. The other aspect of this is, based on the data, how is the current state of the process behaving in the real-time business environment. The final part of the measurement stage is what the voice of the customer is telling you about how the current process is affecting their business.

The subsequent step is to discover what the data is telling us about the process constraint and its effects on the customer. Design thinking methodology tells us to begin by asking "what is?" We do this by determining how the problem works and what are the apparent problem areas? Where are the bottlenecks within the system? Do the existing process and the data tell us the same story?

Returning to the design thinking process, the second step is "what works?" We do the same thing here. We explore the different potential solutions and determine which are more likely to achieve our ultimate goal. It is also essential that we take into consideration the level of risk management that you are willing to take to implement the chosen solutions. Once we have chosen the solution then we have to find out where the organization can get the best return for their investment and how to undertake the changes.

The final stage is to ensure that the improvements withstand the passage of time. Once we make the improvements will they continue to be implemented? It is of no benefit to the organization for you to make the changes to the process and then revert back to the old way of doing things a couple of months down the road.

One of the milestones going forward is the determination of how you will measure success. Your success is going to be based on how well the improved process performs in the future. The other critical key performance indicators of the new process are that we have seen the problem, felt the problem and created a new normal. It means that as we remove the obstacle, we must have a new aligned organizational corporate culture. Equally important, have the changes achieved the goal for the introduced improvements?

The final aspect of the business case is the need to be clear about the timeline to implement the new process. As we will see, the trouble in the room is the tendency to put off what needs to be done until another day. It makes no sense to go through this improvement process and then not implement the solutions. It means that organizational politics must be shelved in favor of the demands of the customer.

Define Stage

The *define* stage is the bedrock of the process to identify the system constraint and resolve the organizational issues. It is where we identify the concerns of the customer and take specific steps to come to a conclusion as to the right path to solve the problem. The define stage is where we begin to identify what it is that we don't know. It is where we create what we think the solution is to the problem based on the direct observation of the process, and what the voice of the customer is telling us is the system constraint.

The TLS Continuum methodology is comprised of more than one tool from which you can choose to assist in your project. We usually define the tools from two perspectives. The first is from the lean side. These tools tend to be less costly and quicker to introduce than the full Six Sigma side. Below is a chart with the tools within the methodology. We will repeat the chart in each of the phases with the precise tools at that stage highlighted in red (Figure 7.3).

DMAIC Step	SIX SIGMA Tools	LEAN Tools
DEFINE	Voice of Customer Project Charter Project Critical to Quality Definition High Level Process Map	Value Definition
MEASURE	Quality Function Deployment Measurement System Analysis	Value Stream Mapping
ANALYZE	Process Capability Analysis FMEA Benchmarking Hypothesis Testing Graphical Tools	Line Balance Takt Time Calculation
IMPROVE	Regression Analysis Design Of Experiments Risk Assessment	5 S Establish Flow / Pull System SCORE Events
CONTROL	Determine New Process Capability Statistical Process Control Control Plans	Poke Yoke Visual Management

Figure 7.3   TLS Continuum methodology toolbox—define stage.

We totally understand that if you were on the factory floor, some of these tools would be of more benefit than those within the human resource space. But there are specific tools that can benefit your processes.

The define stage begins with a review of the process, and what the customer is telling us is not being delivered to them. Frequently the input at this point is from within the organization. It is the true view of the world, not as it is but as we see it. It is the view of the business in the mirror instead of out the window. It is guided by the organizational biases about the process being reviewed. It is the tendency of many organizations to believe that everything is fine as it is. Having determined what we think is wrong we also determine what we would expect the process to look like once the process is completed.

Once we have determined the business case for the problem, we can begin the process of implementing the project. The initial step is to get upper management buy-in for the DMAIC process within the organization. In order to achieve this goal, we must demonstrate to them that there is a long-lasting benefit to the organization. Failure to obtain management buy-in means that our efforts into problem solutions are a waste of our time. One of the ways we do that is through the use of the project charter we discussed in Chapter 4. The charter provides the vehicle for you to explain to management what the problem resolution looks like. It also provides an identification of what is going to be needed in the way of resources, both physical and financial.

With management approval obtained the cross-functional team moves to mapping out the project through the use of the Gannt Chart we discussed also in Chapter 4. It tells us what the milestones or project guides are and when each is due to be completed. Especially if we are working in a Results-Only Work Environment, it establishes that the project end dates that I indicated above were an absolute necessity. The Gannt Chart is in essence a bar chart that provides a visual picture of the project progress. It is critical that you understand that the Gantt Chart is a living document in that as you progress through the process improvement effort, milestones can be extended or shortened. You can add and subtract milestones as we move through the DMAIC process.

In Chapter 4, during our discussion of the project maps, I talked about the use of a tool referred to as a Goal Tree. As I discussed the Goal Tree begins with your goal and then established the critical factors that must be present in order to reach the goal. It then sets out the necessary factors that you need in order to obtain the critical success factors.

I want to turn the Dettmer's Goal Tree on its head if you will. My suggestion is that we change the name of the Goal Tree to the TLS Continuum Problem Resolution Guide. Using the same nomenclature as shown in Figure 7.4, we redefine the components. In place of the term *goal* place the *problem statement*. This problem statement should be in the form of a question. For example, why does the customer say that our product or service is not meeting their demands? The next level down is not the critical success factors but rather answering the question of how the product is not meeting their demands. Be very specific in your answers. These provide your top-level causes. The next level down changes from necessary conditions to the response for the question of if these factors are in place causing the process to not meet demands, why they are not meeting the demands. At

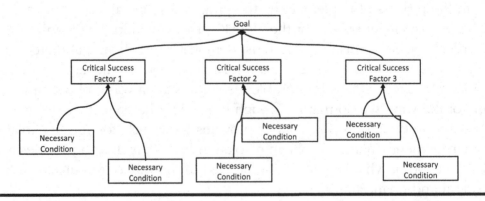

Figure 7.4   Goal Tree.

the conclusion of the DMAIC process, we can revert the TLS Continuum Problem Resolution Guide to the original idea of the Goal Tree.

Having established the problem statement, the cross-functional team now makes management review the goal of the project. This includes your proposed solution and recommendations for changes within the organization. It is at this point you may begin to see some pushback from within the organization from those aspects that are reluctant or afraid of changing what they have done for time eternal.

You not only want but need buy-in from upper management for the process to work successfully, so one of the data points that must be presented is what is the process going to cost the organization. This section of the charter asks the team to delineate the resources needed. For each resource requested we need to tell management precisely what you need in terms of funds, time away from traditional work expectations and added equipment. The list could go on forever, but it needs to be detailed to provide a clear picture of what it will take to achieve your goal.

Regardless of whether you are a floor person or the CEO of the organization, your immediate question is WIFM or What's in It For Me? The final section of the project charter is space for the team to delineate what the impact on the organization will be if you are successful in completing the project. The project impact should also provide a view of the dollar savings that could be expected if the changes you are suggesting come to be within the organization.

The first tool from the lean side is that of value definition. We can't begin to understand what the customer wants and needs until we understand what constitutes "value" to them. As a result, one of the critical tools is for the team to construct a working definition of the term *value*. It needs to be based on what the customer tells you what is important from your organization. Part of the process is to survey the customers to ask them what is important. This definition can't be based on what you think is of value to them. The voice of the customer is based on three specific components. The customer is asked to look at the features of the product or service from the perspective of faster, better and cheaper. By *faster* we mean that the widget is delivered with activities which truly meet the customer's needs. Based on those needs, your organization has removed any steps in the process which add time to the delivery. By *better* we mean that the product or service is free from defects. We do not serve the client's needs when we deliver incomplete or faulty services to them. The final perspective is that of cheaper. In this arena, we look to deliver the service as inexpensively as possible.

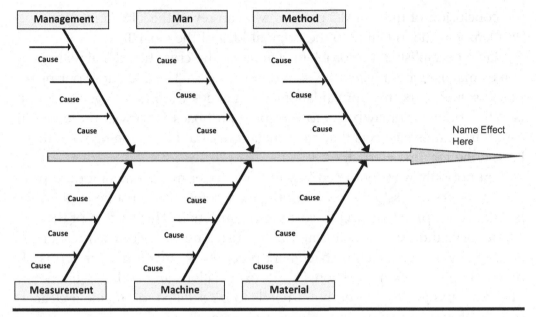

Figure 7.5   Ishikawa Cause-and-Effect Fishbone Diagram.

Another tool that is valuable at this point is a high-level process map. Remember we referred at the beginning of this chapter that one of the utilization indicators is that we don't know what we don't know. The high-level process map becomes the initial look at what we don't know. Following in the exact order, with simple blocks and arrows, the entire process is laid out for the view of how we are delivering the service we have been requested. From our 16-hour course we can tell you that when a process map is created, some really amazing things have come to light.

Once the process map is complete the two remaining tools of advantage to HR professionals are the Ishikawa Fishbone Diagram and the SIPOC analysis (Figure 7.5).

The Fishbone Diagram was created to look at six elements of any process. It looks at management and its role in any decision. Depending on their attitude toward change management can make or break the effort. The second element is the people involved. Have we explained the process we are undertaking to the line employee, but do they understand what's in it for them if we do make the necessary change or we don't? The third element is the method we use to resolve the problems within the organization. We know we have a problem, but how do we resolve those problems? Is there a structured way that you resolve the issues, or is each problem resolved in an ad hoc method? The fourth element is measurement. We have, through the process, accumulated some data, but what do we do with those data points? The fifth element is that of machines. In looking at your process map, have you attempted to automate parts of the process? What equipment is required to complete the project charter milestones?

The sixth and final element is the materials used by the process. This could range from the applications for employment to the forms HR uses to administer the policies and procedures of the organization. For each of the elements, the team asks the organization what are the results if we, for example, have a management philosophy which runs counter to our expressed goals? What does that do to the total integrity of the process we are trying to implement?

The final tool of the define stage is the SIPOC analysis. Taking our process map we begin to look at the total process. From there we identify who the suppliers are. We are administering processes which are involved with the acquisition of talent for the organization. What sources are we using to achieve that point? This would include suppliers both within and outside the organization. The next step is to ask yourself if we use supplier A as an example, what is it they contribute to the process? Having identified what they provide, the next step is to decide to which process the input is assigned. The assumption is that once we identify those steps, then determine what the ultimate output is and who it is delivered to. Let's look at a simple example.

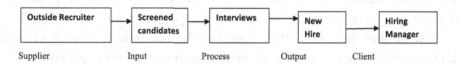

| Outside Recruiter | Screened candidates | Interviews | New Hire | Hiring Manager |

| Supplier | Input | Process | Output | Client |

With the conclusion of the steps in the define stage, we move to the next step within the improvement scientific method—***measure*** stage.

Measure Stage

In the second step of the scientific method, we are taught that once we have established our hypothesis, we then turn our sights on the testing of that hypothesis. This is achieved by conducting a series of experiments to determine whether the results confirm or disprove the hypothesis. It is a standard of work within the scientific community.

The measure stage of the TLS Continuum methodology is no different. During this stage of the DMAIC methodology, we begin to look at what the process tells us. To gain a better handle on the premises of the measure stage, we only have to turn to the work of Dr. Mikel Harry, who in his book *Six Sigma: The Breakthrough Management Strategy Revolutionizing the World's Top Corporations*[2] tells us that most organizations suffer from a lack of data in trying to improve the organization. Dr. Harry says that we don't know what we don't know (the reasoning behind the define stage); we can't do what we don't know (if don't resolve the issues, we can't meet the customer needs); we don't know until we measure (the impetus behind the current stage); we don't measure what we don't value and we don't value what we don't measure.

The intent of the measure stage is to review our processes from the voice of the customer perspective to see if the process is in fact meeting those demands. We discussed in the section above regarding the DMAIC Business Case that the business case for the measure stage asks us to explore six perspectives regarding our current processes. Each of the perspectives asks us to question why we are doing things the way we have been doing them. This is not to say that every time you measure the process you will find something that is out of variance from the needs of the client but if we don't question the process we will not know.

The organization is confronted with operating results which indicate that somewhere within the organization something is directly affecting the end results. Upper management understands there is a problem but is unclear about the cause. The project charter and the project team have identified whether what they believe is the source of the obstacle. The project charter has laid out our hypothesis. We all understand that there is an issue. The real question is how do we determine what the nature of the problem is? How do we reliably arrive at data points that verify the outcomes of the processes? As a result, we need to go back to the project charter and test if what we believe is the problem. Whether you are on the factory floor or in the front office, every day we are confronted with processes which govern how productive the organization is within the marketplace. It is within those processes that certain steps are causing these problems.

In the scientific method step we test the hypothesis. The foremost way we test the hypothesis is to create an experiment that will either prove or disprove our concept developed in testing the hypothesis. It is important to recognize that as we conduct these experiments, we are creating data points which aid us in determining the outcome of the testing process. Recognize that these data points have only two results. On the one hand they tell us that the data proves our hypothesis and we can proceed with the rest of the process, and on the other hand, it tells us that we were wrong in what we expected and then we have returned to the experiment stage and further test the hypothesis or change it.

Every process, whether it is manufacturing a new automobile or completing a transactional process, contains key performance indicators which tell your organization whether you are meeting the needs of your customers. One of the first steps is to identify the indicators and how we are going to measure them. I am not concerned about whether you are following the works of individuals in this field such as Dr. Jac Fitz-Enz or Dr. Wayne Casio; we need to establish the metrics you will use to determine the solutions. These metrics must clearly state exactly what we are measuring and why they are of particular concern to the process in question.

When beginning the measure stage, we need to establish the metrics and key performance indicators for our processes to determine whether we have an obstacle to the workflow or not. Having the KPIs and the metrics is one thing, but the other side of the equation is where does the data come from? Is the data based only on the internal results? Is the data based only on the customer's view of the process? Does the data include the input from the suppliers to the process?

One of the most common metrics used within the HR arena is time to hire. Where do you get your data from to determine the metric? Typically, the time to hire is determined in days and covers the time from the date the position opens to the time the new candidate accepts the position. But the source of the metric data can vary. Do we start from the point of the hiring manager, informing HR that there is a need, or do we start from the point where the job requisition has been approved? The response will differ from organization to organization. The key is knowing where the data is located and what the source of the metric data points is.

In a breakout/meeting presentation we offer, we ask the attendees a simple question. You are sitting at your desk and the financial statements for your department arrive on your desk. What do you do with them? The vast majority of those who have responded answer that they basically check to ensure that there are no errors in calculations. That is fine, but those numbers may also carry another story behind them. Consider that in your process the client requires delivery in three days for an important deadline. Due to your internal processes, you deliver it in seven days. There are costs involved in the missed deadlines. They may be external costs, or they may be in the service level agreement, which says if the client needs the output in three days and you deliver in seven, the organization may incur a penalty for being late. We need to challenge the numbers in order to see if the process is behaving the way we expect it to. When we review the financials as in our above example, we need to do so with an eye toward looking at the process and seeing if the picture we have is in reality what is actually happening.

Part of the measurement process is to gain a picture of what the current process is doing. Consider for example this scenario from a real-life client. They were making a product, and from every indication they were completing the processes on time, but the client was complaining of late delivery. The process metrics showed no real reason for this. When they looked further, they found that the process was completed on schedule, but the finished products sat on the loading dock for seven additional days, causing late delivery. The production process was telling the organization that they were following the service level agreement, but external factors were making the process unreliable.

The flip side of the coin is that the quality review of the product or service shows that there are some defects in the processes. The question then becomes why the process is showing the problems. When you look for example at your recruitment process, why does the process appear to show problems? In a recent seminar we had a team reviewing their recruitment process to see why it tended to drag at times. It appears that in the course of hiring a new team member, the job requisition was reviewed three times—by the same person. The result was that the process got dragged because of the required time for the manager to review a document that they already had reviewed.

The final question is really at the heart of all of our processes. From an internal view, we know what our processes tell the organization. Remember however that the true basis of the success of the organization is how close our processes meet the voice of the customer. With this in mind, does the process output tell you the same thing that it tells your customer? The customer, whether internal or external, is the critical part of the chain, and so the real indicator of the success of the process or failure comes from the perspective of how the customer views it. Part of the measure stage is to measure the process from the perspective of the client as the end user. Is the customer receiving the value that they expect and are willing to pay for? (Figure 7.6).

Each part of the define–measure–analyze–improve–control process has its own set of unique tools and the measure phase is no different. Some of these such as the measurement system analysis can become quite technical;

DMAIC Step	SIX SIGMA Tools	LEAN Tools
DEFINE	Voice of Customer Project Charter Project Critical to Quality Definition High Level Process Map	Value Definition
MEASURE	**Quality Function Deployment** **Measurement System Analysis**	**Value Stream Mapping**
ANALYZE	Process Capability Analysis FMEA Benchmarking Hypothesis Testing Graphical Tools	Line Balance Takt Time Calculation
IMPROVE	Regression Analysis Design Of Experiments Risk Assessment	5 S Establish Flow / Pull System SCORE Events
CONTROL	Determine New Process Capability Statistical Process Control Control Plans	Poke Yoke Visual Management

Figure 7.6   TLS Continuum methodology toolbox—measure stage.

however, there is from a human resources perspective, the one primary tool that will guide us on our journey to HR excellence. In the define stage we discussed the creation of a process map for your recruitment process. At this point we need to return to that discussion.

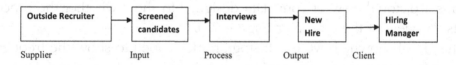

The process map is a review of how you do things from an eagle's point of view. It is performed from a point above the organization to see how a process works its way through the organization. It applies to either a whole organization or a single department on an equal basis. The process map also does not allow for the introduction of the required data points,

In one of the presentations of our seminar, Driving the HR 500: Achieving HR Excellence through Six Sigma, we had in the audience the HR manager, the recruiter and the benefits coordinator. They completed the development of a value stream map of their recruitment process. When it was completed the HR director remarked, "Are we really spending that much time on this process?" The time spent was there; it just was hidden because they had never looked at it in detail.

In the measure stage we bring this eagle's view down to the terra level and expand the pictorial view presented by the process map. The tool that we use in this instance is a value stream map. Look at the process map shown above. From this point we are going to take it to the next level. When you convert your process map to a value stream map, we include every step and process included in the recruitment process. This includes people and materials such as documents, forms and online systems. It also includes the duration of elapsed time between each block and step. Following the completion of the value stream map the organization creates a true picture of what it takes to hire an individual into your organization.

An additional benefit of the measure stage is that it provides support for an area we discussed earlier. We had discussed that every process has its key performance indicators, which tell the organization what is essential for the process to operate effectively. The value stream map is one step in identifying those KPIs. They provide the expected signs of success, which are the basis of this stage. These KPIs are based on the voice of the customer as to what they expect from your organization.

With the KPIs in place and your data assimilated, the last step of the measure stage is to enter the data into a control chart of some sort. We would suggest that one of the easiest tools to use is a histogram. The histogram is a pictorial view of your data designed to show whether the process meets the view of the customer (Figure 7.7).

The visual shown above is a histogram developed to show the frequency of compensation across an organization. It is designed to provide a summary of the data you have collected from the organization. Each bar is

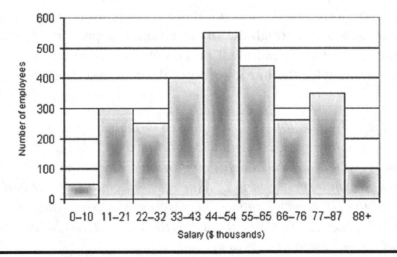

Figure 7.7   Compensation spread.[3]

representative of a data point that was collected during the measure stage. Most of the TLS Continuum–related software programs such as QI Macros contain a user-friendly histogram in which you need to basically fill in the blanks and it will draw the chart for you.

To this point we have defined our problem, aka defined our hypothesis, and we have undertaken efforts to collect data as to the performance of our processes. We have in essence tested whether our experiment proved or disproved what we thought the problem was. The next question becomes, What do we do with the data we have collected?

Analyze Stage

The scientific method tells us that we have to define our problem, arrive at a hypothesis or guesstimate what the solution is, measure our data points and then analyze the results. The DMAIC process is no different. At this point we have determined that we have a problem. We then took steps to collect the data points on the performance of the process in question, and now we come to the next step. We now need to analyze the data to determine what the process is telling us.

The determination of what the data is telling your organization comes in the ***analyze stage***. There is not a day that goes by that your organization does not collect an overload of data that is created by the very nature of the human resources process. The downside to all this data is that as we will saw in Chapter 6 this overproduction of data is a type of non-value-added waste within your organization. In many cases, we collect data for some really good reason at the time, but where does that data end up residing?

It resides in that file drawer on your desk.

It sits on a shelf on the bookcase in your office.

The reports are ordered by a member of management because they think they need the data even if they have no use for the resulting reports.

The DMAIC process sets five areas of concern when we are beginning the analyze stage. Each of the areas of concern is asking us to challenge the status quo and seek to find the real outputs of the process in question.

In the testing hypothesis phase of the scientific method, one of the outcomes of the methodology is to determine whether the results of our experiments prove the hypothesis. In this case we are concerned with whether or not the solution we suggested in the project charter actually solves the elimination of the obstacle within our processes. One of the benefits of the measurement stage and thus the analysis stage is that we get to uncover hidden obstacles that are slowing down the process. The two phases provide us a visual picture of the process that is currently in place. As stated earlier using the tools of the analysis stage makes us view the process in its entirety to determine whether the mission of the process is what we are delivering. For example, a hiring manager tells you that he needs a suitable candidate in 48 hours. Does the process allow the HR function to deliver on those terms?

My favorite statement to clients is if you have a process, then it will eventually experience a hiccup. It is a guarantee that it will happen. The critical question is can we identify those hiccups before they become a problem? Like the example we gave earlier of the organization that had a job requisition reviewed by the same person three times, the analyze phase should seek out, locate and make the necessary adjustments to enable the process to run more effectively. In order to achieve this goal, we need to put the process under a microscope. We want to view each and every step within the process to determine if what we are doing is what the client needs and wants. If not, we have found the problem area, and in the next phase, we will correct the process going forward.

A real-time example can be found in the hiring process. The hiring manager calls your office with an urgent request. His lead IT person just walked out the door, and he desperately needs a replacement within three days. The human resource function does everything you are asked to do, but then the hiring manager sits on the applications for three months. Has the process worked for your organization? Probably not, and more than likely someone will scream that HR is not doing its job.

On the surface when you look at the problem, is it indicating that the problem exists? Does the nature of the problem indicate what is responsible for the problem? Notice we did not ask who was responsible for the problem as the answer is never in the human capital assets but rather the way the process is constructed and unfolded. So our issue becomes that the client is telling us that there is a problem with some aspect of our human resources' way of delivering the services to the client. We then are charged with finding out why the problem exists. The analyze phase concentrates our efforts in looking at what the process is delivering to the system and why it is causing the waste to occur.

Part of the testing process is to confirm that the data collected is both creditable and verifiable. The data collected must be centered on the problem at hand. This is a good point to stress that we are not trying to solve every problem within the organization at one time. We are collecting data on the critical few problems that are affecting the organizational strategic initiatives. It is common for management to disavow that there are any problems. To them the organization is running smoothly. The problems arise when the client tells the organization that your service is not performing at the level they want, and they may have to take their business elsewhere. Then we become forced into reviewing the process for where it is not meeting those needs.

In the define stage we discussed the Ishikawa Fishbone in which we looked at the six elements of the corporate structure that are affected by the elements of the fishbone. Critically we now need to review that diagram to ascertain what happens if we do this rather than doing this. By gaining an understanding of the relationship between the diagram elements and the vice of the customer, we develop a better picture of how our strategic initiatives affect the process in the long run.

As you can observe from Figure 7.8 there are seven distinct tools that come to play within the analyze stage. Of these three can have a distinct role within the human resources processes. The first of these has been used for years by you as HR professionals. You just did not recognize it as part of the continuous process improvement effort. You are considering offering a new policy or benefit component. What is the first thing you do? Most of us would go to the SHRM website or go on to the groups we belong to and ask whether any of the members have implemented a similar program and how did you do it. This tool is called benchmarking. The purpose of the benchmarking process is to identify what went right when others tried to

DMAIC Step	SIX SIGMA Tools	LEAN Tools
DEFINE	Voice of Customer Project Charter Project Critical to Quality Definition High Level Process Map	Value Definition
MEASURE	Quality Function Deployment Measurement System Analysis	Value Stream Mapping
ANALYZE	Process Capability Analysis FMEA Benchmarking Hypothesis Testing Graphical Tools	Line Balance Takt Time Calculation
IMPROVE	Regression Analysis Design Of Experiments Risk Assessment	5 S Establish Flow / Pull System SCORE Events
CONTROL	Determine New Process Capability Statistical Process Control Control Plans	Poke Yoke Visual Management

Figure 7.8 TLS Continuum methodology toolbox—analyze stage.

implement the same process. It also provides you with a roadmap to continuous process improvement steps necessary to successfully introduce the service through molding the process to represent what has worked in the past.

The second tool is the series of control charts, which can again be found in the QI Macros software. The data plots on the control chart indicate whether we are operating within the process limits that we have established. If the data analysis indicates that we are operating within the process limits then we know that we are achieving the results we expected. If, however, the results are outside the process limits, then we know we have a problem. The analyze phase then points out where we have to make changes to the process to bring it within the process limits.

The third and final tool is a concept called TAKT time. TAKT time is a mathematical equation to determine the processing time to complete a process. It is calculated by completing the formula shown below:

(TAKT time) = Net available time to work divided by the customer demand

In other words, the time it takes to complete the process is calculated by the amount of time available to work divided by the number of units per day requested by the customer. See the full example below.

> *If there is a total of 8 hours (or 480 minutes) in a shift (gross time) less 30 minutes lunch, 30 minutes for breaks (2 × 15 minutes), 10 minutes for a team briefing and 10 minutes for basic maintenance checks, then the net available time to work = 480 − 30 − 30 − 10 − 10 = 400 minutes. If customer demand was, say, 400 units a day and one shift was being run, then the line would be required to spend a maximum of one minute to make a part in order to be able to keep up with the customer demand.*

TAKT time can be used in calculating how long it will take to recruit a person depending on the hiring manager's requirements and the available time the recruiter has to source new candidates. There is another version of TAKT time that also comes to play in the analyze stage. That version is called Traffic Intensity (Figure 7.9).

We need to start with some basic assumptions. First every organization, yours included, is presented with a specific amount of both resources and time. We saw that above in our discussion of TAKT Time. Roger Bohn, in

Traffic Intensity Calculation	
Days to Solve	0
# of New problems per day	0
Number of Problem Solvers	1
Traffic Intensity	0.00%
Created by Roger Bohn in the article "Stop Fighting Fires" Harvest Business Review July August 2000	
When traffic intensity nears 100% - Problems sit in queue for a while	
When traffic intensity is greater than 100% - More problems that can be solved	
When traffic intensity is <80% - System works well	

Figure 7.9   Traffic intensity calculator.

his article for *Harvard Business Review* titled "Stop Fighting Fires," suggests that we can use these two assumptions in planning what we are able to achieve when analyzing the problem. The calculator begins with you determining what the deadline is to resolve the issues. In the case of a time to hire scenario, how long do you have to locate, interview and hire a candidate? With that data point in mind, the next step is to determine how many job requisitions management has thrown to HR, both current and anticipated. We said that you only had a set number of resources to resolve the issues. So how many talent acquisition specialists do you have serving in FTEs at this moment? The calculator multiplies the number of days by the number of requests and divides it by the number of staff. This produces a traffic intensity score. If your resulting score is under 80 percent then your system is designed to operate within the confines of both time and resources. On the other hand, if the score is 100 percent or higher, then you need to analyze the number of requests you can take at any one time.

With the identification of the problem, the collection of data on the performance of the system and the analysis of our data points it is time for us to look at how we improve the system in order to remove the system constraint.

Improve Stage

Along with the define stage, the ***improve stage*** may very well be the most critical parts of the continuous improvement process as they set the tone for where we are and where the journey is headed.

In Chapter 2, we made reference to the Ultimate Improvement Cycle, which is designed to identify the roadblocks or obstacles that hinder us from meeting the voice of the customer, identify the causes of those roadblocks and remove them from the process. It is during this stage that we undertake the changes to the process that we are reviewing in the DMAIC process. It is also in this phase that we begin to accomplish the efforts to change the corporate culture in addition to the process.

We need to step back for a moment and consider the impact of the previous statement. Many continuous process improvement efforts fail because the organization looks for fast returns on the efforts or "quick fixes." The real success of the efforts we are discussing comes about due to the organization changing. Changing the way we think about the organization. Changing the way we think about our customers. Changing the way we do things in general. Any successful improvement process involves a change in the cultural view of the organization, not just for the moment but for the long term. It requires the organization to change from an "our perspective" to one of the client's perspective. What we do and how we do it must be centered in that concept of the voice of the customer we have mentioned several times so far in the book. The improve stage is where the focus needs to be established that any changes to the processes within the organization are totally focused on delivering only value-added services to the clients.

In the improve stage, the cross-functional team comes together and looks at the data and questions that have been answered to this point and using that information decides where the organization goes next on this journey. They do this through a review of the organization, the findings and the available solutions. There are four distinct views that the cross-functional team would take to determine the next step.

Via the benchmarking process, the cross-functional team more than likely has come up with a wide range of potential solutions to the problem at hand. While they all are potential solutions, they need to be viewed from the view of which ones would not add non-value-added waste into the existing process. If a certain solution does contribute to the waste within the system, then it is a necessity that it be dropped from the potential changes to the process.

This is the point where the culture of the organization comes into play. The cross-functional team may have come up with some really unique and exciting solutions to remove the process obstacles. However, when we take the culture of the organization into consideration, there are some of them that would blatantly not work in your cultural environment. You may ask how we know in advance that something would not work within our organization. The real response to the question is how the organization feels about change. If there is a natural resilience to change from the functional silos, a dramatic change effort most likely would not work. When we are in these environments it requires a slower pace to make the changes than when both management and rank and file fully support the need for changes in the way the organization functions. At the same time, you have to take into consideration the demands of the customer. If they are in conflict, then changes will have to be made.

Let's face it any time we make changes in the way we perform things within the organization it entails a sense of risk. The TLS Continuum and continuous process improvement are risk issues. We know we have a problem, so what is the impact if we decide that we will leave the status quo in place? What is the impact on the organization if we do this? What is the impact of the rank-and-file employee on the change? We know we have a problem, but is it a life-and-death environment if we choose to ignore the voice of the customer? I would suggest to you that if we recognize that there is a problem the risk factor is greater on the organization if we do nothing. The current process is definitely demonstrating that the customer is not happy with the service they are receiving, and they are left with two alternatives. One is to push to get us to change how we perform, and the other is to move their business elsewhere. Both of these alternatives also carry risk. If they move to another source, they have no guarantee that things will be any better with the new vendor. If they stay put, they are still not guaranteed that things will improve.

Implementation of the chosen solution can have various outcomes. The outcomes are based on how and when we implement the solutions. You have a decision to make. On the one hand you can implement it across the entire organization. This can be a major undertaking depending on the reaction from the employee base. This method has some really good evidence-based knowledge that it can work. This was the way Toyota implemented its process improvement efforts. The other option is to introduce into a single function or department. Let the function become the model for how to do it right and, then using this model, roll it out to the rest of the organization (Figure 7.10).

As we enter the improvement stage, we should have at this point identified the problem, measured the data and analyzed what it all means to the organization. There are several tools out of the toolbox that can help guide the process change along. One of these is to change how we initiate both

DMAIC Step	SIX SIGMA Tools	LEAN Tools
DEFINE	Voice of Customer Project Charter Project Critical to Quality Definition High Level Process Map	Value Definition
MEASURE	Quality Function Deployment Measurement System Analysis	Value Stream Mapping
ANALYZE	Process Capability Analysis FMEA Benchmarking Hypothesis Testing Graphical Tools	Line Balance Takt Time Calculation
IMPROVE	**Regression Analysis** **Design Of Experiments** **Risk Assessment**	**5 S** **Establish Flow / Pull System** **SCORE Events**
CONTROL	Determine New Process Capability Statistical Process Control Control Plans	Poke Yoke Visual Management

Figure 7.10   TLS Continuum methodology toolbox—improve stage.

processes and the steps to completion. In many organizations the natural tendency is to operate from the belief that the best way for any function to make a contribution is to keep the pipeline fully loaded with talent or materials. The reason is the belief that if, say, the IT department needs a particular skill on an ongoing basis, then if HR continually pushes candidates to the IT department, when the time comes the staffing effort is already taken care of. The drawback is that some of the candidates may not be currently available. I discussed the hazards of this approach in Chapter 5 when I looked at the waste from overproduction. The alternative is to set up the process so that the hiring manager receives information on potential candidates only when they request it. We refer to this as a push vs. pull environment. In the push environment the system is consistently filled with potential candidates, while in the pull environment the only candidates in the pipeline are those requested for an actual opening. This allows the organization to control the level of work in the process.

There is one other scenario we need to consider at this point in our review. We have followed all the steps of the DMAIC process to this point. At the conclusion of the analysis stage, we discover that because of the way the process behaves none of the possible solutions will achieve the results we are seeking. The question then becomes what do we do next? The TLS Continuum methodologies contain a different process for resolving this issue. It is called Design for Six Sigma. Like the process, when we are looking at an existing process, DSS has its own process steps. While we will not do a deep dive into the DSS process, as it is outside of the approach this book is taking, we do want you to be knowledgeable of the steps in the process. It is much like designing an experiment in science.

From the book *Design for Six Sigma for Service*[4] we can see that there are some striking similarities in the DSS process. DSS is divided into five phases, resulting in the introduction of the new process within the organization.

In Phase 1 we define the existing problem. It begins with defining the problem through a project charter to lay out the problem as we did in the DMAIC process. Since we are creating a new process, we next need to identify customers who will receive the most benefit from this new process. With the customer in mind, we create a process map of the future state of the new process, laying out the development states. It works exactly the way we did earlier in this chapter.

Based on the charter and the process map we then decide what metrics we need to confirm that the process will achieve our expected outcome.

In Phase 2 we measure the determined metric and how it performs in the new process. This is very much like testing our hypothesis in both the scientific method and the DMAIC process. We are going to handle the metric performance identically to the DMAIC and can use the same tools as we did previously. The results lead us to identify the performance metrics that meet the voice of the customer.

In Phase 3 we analyze the current process by running a process diagnosis on the current process with the assistance of tools such as a value stream map. It is from the first two phases and the resulting analysis that we are able to begin the design of creditable alternative solutions to the existing process.

In Phase 4 the cross-functional team designs the brand-new solution. It takes into consideration all of the data that has been gathered and lays out the steps to reach the ultimate outcome. One useful tool is to run simulations of the process alternatives to determine the best solution to the organizational problem.

In the final phase we are confronted with a lack of information to complete the last step of the DMAIC. We have nothing to improve, nor do we have something to necessarily control. What we do need to finalize the process is to verify that the new solution to the problem is in fact working and resolving the customer problem with the current process.

Control Stage

The final goal of the DMAIC process is to create a standard of work, which governs the way the process is delivered going forward—the ***control stage***. The standard of work is not a guide on how to do something necessarily. It is however a roadmap for the organization as to how a process should be delivered. It is an organization process map to respond to the voice of the customer. Take for example the recruitment process, as we have done throughout this book, and look at not how we recruit new talent but what steps we take to do so. This is the standard of work.

In order to create the standard of work, it is critical that the cross-functional team and the organization have a session devoted to critiquing the DMAIC process. This is very similar to the post-mortem of the military conducts after every mission is complete. We would suggest that this can be accomplished by responding to four questions.

First, just because we have completed the five stages of the continuous process improvement stage does not mean that our review is over. Notice that when we talk about the DMAIC we make reference to *continuous* process improvement. This is not a one-time event, so how is the process going to be measured after the project is completed? Understand the chances that you are going to need to revisit the process in the near future are fairly strong, so what are you going to look for and how are you going to determine if it meets the ongoing needs of all stakeholders.

Second, we discussed earlier that the continuous process improvement and the TLS Continuum are change agents. You will not successfully implement the process improvements without a change in the organizational culture. We can provide an example of this by turning to the training and development space within most organizations. We spend large amounts of money to send employees to a wide variety of training programs. When they return to the office, the manager typically tells the employee the training probably was helpful but to go back to the way they have always done it to get through the work that has amassed while they were gone. This is not a change in corporate culture. It is absolutely essential that the improvements to our organizational processes must become the new business as usual—not just within the functional area where the process resides but throughout the entire organization. The process changes must be understood and implemented from the board room to the factory floor.

Third, in the project charter one of the last sections asks us to describe what we believe the project's impact would be on the total organization. In the control phase we take some time out to compare that impact statement to the reality of the process results. If we stated that we would reduce costs by $100,000, did we actually save the organization that much? The impact statement should also have described other changes within the post-organizational space, and now we have to determine whether we in fact met those goals also.

Fourth, in the project charter we established milestones for this project. These milestones were deliverables that arose out of our efforts. The last of these milestones should have established a date in the future when the final reports were to be delivered to management. At this point we need to look at the project charter and the Gantt Chart and determine whether we will meet that milestone target. Pat of the control stage is for the team to review the process and see if they were able to complete the steps they set out to cover in the time frame they predicted. Process improvement projects are never open-ended; they always have set the beginning date and the ending date (Figure 7.11).

As we stated at the beginning of this chapter, we are trying to establish a standard of work for our human resources processes. The control stage gives us several tools to assist in the development of that standard.

First, we can create control plans. A control plan is a document which describes for the organization the information about the process in play. It informs the user of the name of the process, what machines are used, the name of the process, the allowable tolerance from the standard and how you are going to measure the process going forward. It further discusses what control method is in place to ensure that the standard of work is followed.

The second tool is called visual management. Using a large whiteboard, you can create a visual process map which hangs on the wall. In an article which appeared in *Human Resource Executive* entitled "Lean and Mean,"[5] GE Healthcare described how it created a giant whiteboard, which was divided into sections which corresponded to the steps in their standard of

DMAIC Step	SIX SIGMA Tools	LEAN Tools
DEFINE	Voice of Customer Project Charter Project Critical to Quality Definition High Level Process Map	Value Definition
MEASURE	Quality Function Deployment Measurement System Analysis	Value Stream Mapping
ANALYZE	Process Capability Analysis FMEA Benchmarking Hypothesis Testing Graphical Tools	Line Balance Takt Time Calculation
IMPROVE	Regression Analysis Design Of Experiments Risk Assessment	5 S Establish Flow / Pull System SCORE Events
CONTROL	Determine New Process Capability Statistical Process Control Control Plans	Poke Yoke Visual Management

Figure 7.11   TLS Continuum methodology toolbox—control stage.

work called recruitment. In the chart it posted Post-it notes for each candidate involved in the process. As the candidate progressed through the process, his or her Post-it was moved to the next stage. Any member of the HR staff or management could look at the board and immediately tell whether there was some bottleneck which was holding up the hiring of the required new talent.

The third tool for the control stage is a Japanese term called Poka Yoke. Remember the goal of this phase is the creation of a standard of work, and the ultimate goal is to have that standard be what comes to play every time when you initiate the process. Poka Yoke is intended to make the standard of work mistake proof. It means setting up your workstations so that everything has its place, and it is clearly marked where that location is. For example, if you were needing a 1–9 form to be completed by a new hire, the form could be found in a specific labeled location within the HR workspace.

In the course of the pages of this chapter we have carefully created for you, the reader, a picture of how the TLS Continuum methodology works in your organization. Comparing the methodology to the scientific method we all learned in our high school science classes, we have shown that there is a discipline that is followed to explore how our delivery to the end user is either flawed or not meeting the needs of the customer. A point that we will visit again in later chapters is that this entire effort is not people oriented, meaning that the reason that we have a problem is never that the human capital messed up. If there is a hiccup in any process, it is the process that is the cause of the error. The purpose of the methodology is to identify the obstacle, remove it and ensure that we follow the standard of work going forward. Anytime we deviate from the standard of work we are creating waste.

In Chapter 8, I will take the lessons we have discussed and provide real-time examples of how the TLS Continuum works in HR. The basis for this discussion will be the Human Resource Certification Institute's Body of Knowledge for the Senior Professional in HR examination.

Notes

1. From the training materials for the Black Belt Training from St. Petersburg College.
2. Mikel, Harry and Richard Schroeder. *Six Sigma: The Breakthrough Management Strategy Revolutionizing the World's Top Corporations.* New York: Crown Publishing, 2005. Page xii.
3. Image found at http://haleysmaps.blogspot.com/2011/04/histogram.html
4. Yang, Kai. *Design for Six Sigma for Service.* New York: McGraw Hill, 2005. Pages 42–46.
5. Human Resource Executive Magazine. *Lean and Mean.* LRP Publications, March 16, 2009. http://www.hreonline.com/HRE/story.jsp?storyid=18721619& query=GE Healthcare

Chapter 8

HRCI Body of Knowledge

Introduction

I need to summarize where we are at on the journey to HR excellence. I began our journey with a look at how we establish HR excellence and Centers of Excellence in your organization. From there I took you on a trip down memory lane as I tracked the development of the continuous process improvement movement from the time of World War II to the present.

The first part of reaching our current point was to discuss, in Chapter 3, the concept behind the powerful improvement tool called the TLS Continuum, which combines the Theory of Constraints, Lean and Six Sigma. Using this concept, I discussed how to create cross-functional teams and the basics of project design. One outcome from that discussion was that as an organization you need to understand the importance of the voice of the customer. Along with that I discussed the nine types of organizational waste that detract from the voice of the customer.

Our process obstacle in writing this book was what was the single clear playing field that we could utilize that answered two questions? The first question is what are the Key Performance Institute categories which, regardless of the level of experience, would be understood by most professionals in the field? In the last chapter I demonstrated how the problem resolution process works as we proceed to discover the problems and potential solutions.

We answered the first question by turning to the material used by those professionals seeking to earn their certification as HR professionals (PHR, SPHR and GPHR) and what areas of study they have to master to pass the examination. To do this we turned to the functional areas established by the

Human Resource Certification Institute. Before we begin, I need to digress a moment and talk about the reasoning behind my approach. There are currently two competing certification vehicles within the HR community. The one presented by the Society for Human Resource Management is the newer of the two. And while my preference is not to use this one, I do need to at least acknowledge its existence.

The second one, which is the older of the two, is conducted by the Human Resource Certification Institute (HRCI). HRCI®, headquartered in Alexandria, Virginia, is the premier credentialing and learning organization for the human resources profession. For over 45 years, they have set the global standard for HR expertise and excellence through their commitment to the development and advancement of businesspeople in the people business. HRCI develops and offers world-class learning, as well as the administration of eight global certifications, and is dedicated to helping professionals achieve new competencies that drive business results.

The discussion in the remainder of this chapter will be based on the HRCI Body of Knowledge because I believe it is more encompassing than the SHRM Body of Knowledge.

In this part, Part 2, we take that roadmap and begin to apply it to what you and I do every day within our organizations. Beginning with Chapter 6 we return to our discussion from Chapters 4 and 5 and look at how organizations have directly applied the Six Sigma methodology to the HR arena. In each case we will show how the DMAIC process can be used to solve real-time examples of process obstacles found in the areas we deal with every day.

The HRCI Body of Knowledge

Taken from the HRCI Website information for the SPHR exam,[1] the HRCI Body of Knowledge consists of five (5) functional areas: Leadership and Strategy, Talent Planning and Acquisition, Learning and Development, Total Rewards and Employee Relations and Engagement. To better understand these functional areas, I will below take a deeper observation of each of the areas.

HRCI Body of Knowledge: Leadership and Strategy

The Leadership and Strategy functional area contains the typical management tasks such as the development of business plans, budgets and technology. It also includes compliance activities with state and federal laws. Increasingly

HR is called upon to interpret the various data point and metrics that rises out of HR and the organization as a whole; it is the beginning of HR needing to understand the language of business. It means that HR needs to assist in establishing the credibility of outside information in decision making. HR is the gatekeeper for human capital management of the organization.

As human resource professionals we are constantly trying to justify why we deserve a seat at the table when decisions are being made regarding the organizational strategic objectives. It is this functional area that provides you with the evidence-based reasoning for why you should be there. It shows the organization that as HR professionals we can demonstrate that we know and understand the language of business.

Mergers and Acquisitions

Remember the methodology is a problem-solving method to resolve issues within the organization. One of the areas that this can come to play is the area of mergers and acquisitions. Whether we are in the qualms of a recession like we have been or in a bull market where everything is coming up roses, human resources has a vital role in the due diligence effort to determine whether the merger is in line with the overall organizational strategies.

Part of the due diligence process is the determination of whether or not there is a cultural match between the organizations involved. The TLS Continuum methodology provides us with several tools that will aid in this effort. Think back to our discussion during the define stage of the process in which we completed a process map of your recruiting function. We can take the same process and use it in this situation. In the merger and acquisition process we would begin with a process map of your current operations. It is your call as to whether you want to take the eagle's view and do a process map or come down to the ground level and complete a value stream map. In either case we would begin with a mapping process of the current state of your operations. This will provide you with a picture of the demands of your organization here and now. A second mapping exercise is done on either the organization you are buying or are merging with. Once again this provides you with a picture of the current state of the organization. In order to complete the process, we would create a third process map, which lays out the future state of the process after the merger is completed. The process map can also be used to introduce new procedures in the organization so that the talent base gains a clear picture of what is expected of them.

An additional tool that can be used is the spaghetti diagram which would show the workflow with each organization. In our discussion about the

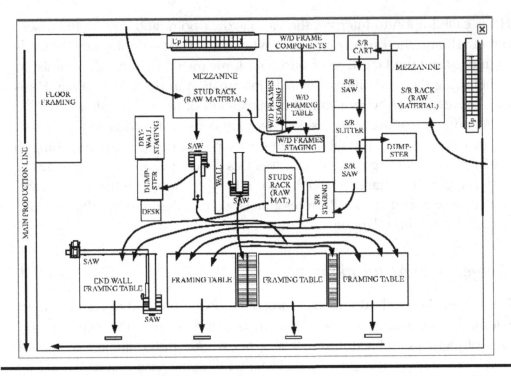

Figure 8.1 Office spaghetti diagram.

wastes we discussed the idea of unnecessary movement of materials and people. By taking an in-depth view of the way we move through the two parts and the final organization we can design the workplace in such a manner as to enhance the operative effectiveness of the organization. The spaghetti diagram will clearly trace the path of people and materials through the office. It will further show such things as how to reach a particular point in the office that your employees are required to take, which requires out-of-the-way steps to get there (Figure 8.1).

Human Resource Audits

Robert Mathis, in his book *Human Resource Management*, defines HR audits as a formal research effort to evaluate the current state of HR management.[2] While HR audits are probably utilized by less than 50 percent of organizations and usually only for a small segment of the operation like I-9 verification, we would contend they have a far more, greater impact on your organization. These efforts are centered on determining whether your organization is in compliance with the required regulatory issues. We would contend that there is a more important, if not concurrent, value to the completed audit.

The ultimate outcome of an audit is the identification of existing problems within your HR processes, problems whose presence is causing even minor problems for your organization. They can be as small as the lack of required posters to serious problems in the facility which could lead to serious injuries. As a result, instead of being used solely for the review of compliance issues it can also be used as part of the define stage to identify the process obstacles that are facing your department. With the use of the data from the audit we can begin to identify the problem we are trying to solve.

In the beginning of this chapter, we stated that the purpose of this part of the book in front of you was the demonstration that the discussions within the book were not just theory but that there were organizations who had utilized the methodology successfully.

Presented below are the first of the case studies which speak to this point. The case studies are from the Topazine and Lee Consulting firm of Canada. This firm discusses a completed TLS Continuum project which saved their client $1,250,000 from redesigned processes within the HR function.

CASE STUDY: ELIMINATION OF NON-VALUE-ADDED HR TASKS WILL RESULT IN 1.2 MILLION DOLLARS IN SAVINGS[3]

BACKGROUND

The back-office function we worked with was responsible for the delivery of Human Resource (HR) support and planning for more than 10,000 employees. The process consisted of back-office functions and relied mainly on paper-based and manual processes. On-boarding HR processes took 4 to 5 months from start to finish, and position management was even longer. HR processes were not standardized, and internal clients found the process to be labor intensive, long and confusing. The HR function was facing significant budget reductions, and we were asked to examine the HR on boarding and position management processes and identify a new more cost-effective process.

CHALLENGE

The greatest challenge was change management. HR employees felt that they were delivering an adequate service and that defects and inefficiencies in the process were a result of non-compliance from their clients. This was further complicated by a process that was non-standardized across the organization that relied on several manual activities.

SOLUTION

A multi-dimensional assessment was conducted, which included an assessment of the voice of the customer, systems, people, organizational structure, skills, competencies and tools. We learned that there were $1,250,000 in non-value-added and wasteful activities, inefficient organizational structure and a lack of change management; the process was managed in silos; and there was no visibility by the process owner across the value stream. Furthermore, there were a lack of measures to manage and improve the process, insufficient competencies to manage the end-to-end process and low client satisfaction.

We designed the standard process; automated all non-value-added activities; developed a prototype HR portal system that self-populated all forms, dynamically built recruitment, assessment and position management tools; tracked requests through the use of workflows; and rebalanced workloads automatically. We further designed a balanced scorecard performance framework and dashboards that cascaded from the most senior levels to frontline employees and developed and linked a continuous process improvement process to the scorecard. Finally, we designed a new service delivery model; an organizational structure that aligned the structure with the process, people and tools; and a mature process owner model.

BENEFITS

Our recommended solution will result in a $1,250,000 annual savings and more time for the HR function to focus on strategic management and expedited processes.

HRCI Body of Knowledge: Talent Planning and Acquisition

Human capital and their role within our organizations is a critical factor which indicates how successful our organizations are. The determination of this role can be very complex in nature, but as we will see in the case studies that follow, they can have a dramatic effect on the whole organization.

According to the Human Resource Certification Institute, the workforce planning area deals with developing, implementing and evaluating sourcing, recruitment, hiring, orientation, succession planning, retention and organization exit programs necessary to ensure the workforce's ability to achieve the organization's goals and objectives.

The workforce planning spectrum runs the gamut from the sourcing of new talent to their promotion or exit from our organizations. In between there are a vast number of areas where the methodology can be applied on road to HR excellence. Some of these projects can be seen below.

Accurate Tracking of Family Medical Leave

If you ask anyone in the trenches tracking FMLA can be a hard thing to do in certain situations. However, if we use visual management tools, we can construct a whiteboard with the various stages of FMLA and move the names of employees through the stages of the process via sticky notes. As an employee finishes one stage, their tag is moved to the next stage of the process. This provides HR with a clear picture of where each of your employees is in the FMLA process. We can also create control charts based on the numerical data to show whether the instances of FMLA requests are growing or lessening over time.

Frequently Asked Questions in the Employee Handbook

One of the tools we discussed in our review of the DMAIC process was the dependence on the voice of the customer. One tool in the Six Sigma toolbox is the use of surveys to determine what employees are concerned about. You can then transform the FAQ section into content within your employee handbook.

Job Posting Rates

In today's global workplace we are more than ever concerned with metrics to demonstrate what is going on within our organizations. An area of concern is the hiring process, and the toolbox can be used to create a control chart showing the variation in posting by job openings, by department or even by month. The resulting chart will give you a picture over time of your posting activity.

Increased Retention

One of the keys to having an excellent organization is one in which employees do not want to leave. We do that by creating an environment where employees are valued as the asset that they are. We can use the toolbox to track the retention rates in any number of ways ranging from pay grade, departments to duration with the company. The control charts will graphically provide you with a clear picture of the changes over time.

Application Response Time

Every day we hear about applicants who say they never hear from organizations where they have filed applications for positions. There are a number of tools within the toolbox that can be used to assist in this area.

Like we did with the FMLA process we can use visual management to track the process. According to the *Human Resource Executive* magazine[4] GE Healthcare created a large white board, which was the size of one wall. The board was divided into each stage of the process. Once again through the use of sticky notes, an applicant was moved through the hiring process. Checked on a daily basis it would clearly provide notice if a sticky note stayed within one stage for an indeterminate length of time.

Another tool that is invaluable in this part of the process we call HR is the use of Pareto Charts. Pareto Charts, as we discussed earlier, graphically over time show us how we are performing compared to the mean or average response time. By plugging in the response time by department, function or organization overall we gain a clear picture of where we are taking longer in responding to applicants on the status of their application. This will help in ensuring that errors or defects in the interview process or not carried forward.

Removal of Unnecessary Steps in the Process

One of the outcomes of the value stream mapping and process mapping exercise we discussed earlier in the material was to identify steps that are not required to achieve the voice of the customer. Remember any step which extends the hiring process is a waste to the organization. In a recent facilitation of the two-day seminar on which this book is based, one of the teams had a disturbed look on their faces. When I walked over to the team to find out what was the problem, they said that when they completed the value stream map they discovered that in the process of sourcing and hiring a new employee, the job requisition was reviewed three times by the same person. When quizzed as to why, they had no idea. Would that one step have caused a major obstacle? Can't say for sure, but it was a non-value-added activity since unless someone changed the wording of the job requisition then there is no reason to have the requisition reviewed again.

One of the other tools we discussed early on was the cost of quality (COQ) worksheet. The worksheet provides the organization with an idea of what its program is costing the organization.

The premise of the COH worksheet is you take each step from your value stream map and plug in each stage into the worksheet. For each stage you then multiply the length of time it takes to complete the step by the time expense of the FTE who is responsible for the step. The result is the total cost of that step to the organization. In the example given in Figure 8.2 if it takes 36 hours to get corporate approval on the job requisition and the recruiter assigned can't begin to source candidates until the position is signed off, then the cost of the 36 hours to the corporation is $1,512.00, which if carried out over say 50 new hires per year means any delay in approval could cost the organization approximately $75,000 annually. The worksheet is developed as an excel worksheet so as you change any of the data your overall number change. In our example we showed that the total cost of recruitment on a single position from beginning to end was $24,108. If this was once again carried out over 50 hires the ultimate cost to the organization would be $1,205,400. By eliminating non-value-added steps or time sequences we can lower the overall cost to the organization.

Cost of Recruiting Worksheet

Problem Description: **Recruitment of new talent**   Type: External

Tasks	Average Hours/ Task	Hourly Rate	Cost of Task	Cost of Materials	Other Failure Costs	of Non-Conformance
1. Position Requisition	36.0	$42	$1,512.00	$0.00	$0.00	$1,512.00
2. Attract Candidates	90.0	$42	$3,780.00	$0.00	$0.00	$3,780.00
3. Sourcing candidates	200.0	$42	$8,400.00	$0.00	$0.00	$8,400.00
4. Interview candidates	40.0	$42	$1,680.00	$0.00	$0.00	$1,680.00
5. Management Time	20.0	$63	$1,260.00	$0.00	$0.00	$1,260.00
6. Background checks	72.0	$42	$3,024.00	$0.00	$0.00	$3,024.00
7. Onboarding	16.0	$42	$672.00	$0.00	$0.00	$672.00
8. Training	36.0	$42	$1,512.00	$0.00	$0.00	$1,512.00
9. Career Coaching	36.0	$63	$2,268.00	$0.00	$0.00	$2,268.00
Total Cost Per Hire						$24,108.00
Hires/year						20
1. Lost Opportunity Costs					$100,000.00	$100,000.00
2. Lost Acquisition Costs	($50,000 x 175%)				$87,500.00	$87,500.00
3. Lost Business Costs					$15,000.00	$15,000.00
Additional Costs						$202,500.00
Annual Cost of Hire						$684,660.00
Basic tasks to fix the problem	Average min/6C	Loaded rate	Calculated cost	Expenses	Customer or Employee found	Total

Figure 8.2 **Cost of hire worksheet.**[5]

I have found in the literature, several case studies that support this idea. The first is from Lean Methods Group that looks at Reducing Employee Turnover in a Hospital System.[6] The second case study is from the Guidon Consulting on their efforts to Using Lean Six Sigma to Improve a Recruiting Process.[7] The third case study is from the Ceridian Corporation on their efforts to Using Lean Six Sigma to Improve a Recruiting Process[8] The fourth case study is from an Electronics firm who took our two-day class upon which this book is based, on reducing the time to hire in their organization.

CASE STUDY: REDUCING EMPLOYEE TURNOVER IN A HOSPITAL SYSTEM

THE CHALLENGE

A three-facility hospital system was facing a challenge with employee turnover. Statistics showed that almost 50 percent of terminations were employees in the first year of their employment, a number that was more than 20 percent higher than the national average. The hospital system estimated that terminations cost as much as $2.2 million annually and that reducing terminations could have a significant impact on the bottom line by eliminating rework inside the hospital's HR department.

A Six Sigma team was brought together to examine the situation. After deciding this was a top priority for the organization, the team began work on a DMAIC project to see how they could save the company time, money and effort by reducing employee turnover.

THE PROCESS

To scope the Six Sigma project, the team first reviewed the path that the hiring process follows by examining how employees were being interviewed, selected, hired and trained. The goal was to determine where the major problems could be stemming from and what may be the causes.

An Attribute Gauge R&R identified that human resource recruiters often considered applicants they would have otherwise considered unqualified due to a low applicant flow. Also, managers were often selecting candidates against HR's recommendation because they felt pressure to get the jobs filled rather than to find the most qualified person.

Lastly, the team found a number of hidden factors such as recruiters, keeping the "best applicants" in their offices for future openings rather than filling them immediately. These issues indicated to the team that there was not a good process in place for pooling qualified candidates when openings became available.

During the analyze phase, the project team used FMEA and survey analysis tools to narrow the project focus to four key areas: manager interviewing techniques, job preview, cultural fit assessment and HR screening techniques and knowledge of the jobs to be filled.

Analysis work indicated a number of key statistical differences in the retention rate between different types of jobs and even between different recruiters. Surveys and interviews indicated to the project team that job shadowing was a practice some departments used to give candidates a realistic picture of the job and that this practice had a significant impact on reducing job turnover.

In the improve phase, the team made a number of recommendations to improve the hiring process including:

Modifying HR recruiter performance evaluations to include ratings related to prescreening, learning more about the jobs for which they are recruiting and turnover

An applicant screening sheet to minimize the number of unqualified applicants and to more clearly define each candidate's qualifications

An interactive workshop for managers to show them how to use proper interviewing guidelines and screening criteria for all vacancies

A standardized list of "cultural fit" questions

The organization also decided to implement job shadowing in the department where there was the highest turnover rate a case study to support the future recommendation of job shadowing across the organization.

THE RESULTS

After an initial five-month adjustment period, the team found that the first-year employee turnover rates decreased from 50 to 35 percent as a result of the organizational changes. Financial savings were calculated to be upward of $42,000 after just a few months and are projected at $300,000 annually for each year thereafter.

CASE STUDY: USING LEAN SIX SIGMA TO IMPROVE A RECRUITING PROCESS

Hiring talented employees is essential for financial services companies, especially in competitive and challenging economic environments. However, one major financial services company was experiencing lead times averaging between four and five months between the date of requisitioning a new hire and the date an offer was made to the prospective employee. This left important roles unfilled for months before a new hire came on board for training. At the same time, the human resources team was convinced that the problems lay in their software system. Most of the management team believed that inefficiencies in hiring were due to a lack of system upgrades and features.

Guidon's experts helped the company assemble a 20-person cross-functional team of subject matter experts, business process management team members and two high-performing employees who were not part of the human resources function. The director of human resources was also involved. During a week-long Kaizen event, these diverse viewpoints reviewed the hiring process, from beginning to end. They discovered that less than 10 percent of the delays were due to the software. Instead, of the 71 improvements that were identified, most were related to the process itself.

While the process of recruiting was straightforward, the team found ways to streamline the workflow and the distribution of work across recruiters. An enthusiastic group, they reviewed every component of the process to determine which steps added value and which didn't. The biggest obstacle they discovered was a requirement that senior leadership approved all new hires. This led to a four-day delay in the process. And while it was an effective deterrent to hiring unnecessary employees, it was also a significant impediment to the hiring process overall. By removing that requirement for some hires, especially those at lower levels whose skill sets did not need the senior management input, the company could significantly reduce lead time for any new hires.

Other process improvements identified included:

Create more visual queue boards to keep participants apprised of the hiring progress

Move from having a single recruiter responsible for all hires to an approach where work is spread evenly among recruiters

Reduce hand-offs and decision-making requirements

While the firm has not implemented all of the 71 improvements, it has made major strides and reduced its hiring time for various positions. Prior to the improvements, the timeline from requisition to hire averaged 132 days (which included 27 days prior to HR recruiter action and 95 days of processing after requisition, as well as other delays)—to within the stated goal of 54–70 days. Better communication eliminated many of the delays and roadblocks, including a lack of transparency about the process and the status of each new hire. Ultimately, the organization achieved its goal of getting new talent in the door in approximately half the time it used to take, putting new employees to work that much more quickly.

THE CHALLENGE

A major financial services company was having people trouble. The company wanted to scale and add services without adding more complexity to its human resources department. However, its hiring process had several inefficiencies, including:

Excessive lead time required to hire new people

Incorrect focus on hiring system as the cause of delays, inhibiting the staff's ability to find the real problems and solutions

Uneven distribution of work among human resources recruiter

THE SOLUTIONS

Through a four-day Kaizen event, Guidon Performance Solutions helped the client create more effective workflow solutions with consistent demand on recruiters and streamlined the entire hiring process, reducing the number of decision-makers involved in many hires and refocusing attention away from software issues—which actually represented less than 10 percent of inefficiency—and redirecting it to streamline the hiring process.

THE RESULTS

Through the event and its finding Guidon helped the client:

Uncover more than 70 opportunities for hiring process improvement

Reduce new hire lead time from an average of 132 days from initial requisition to hire date to the goal of 54 to 70 days

Confidence to take the approach into other business areas

In the Ceridian Study they implemented the TLS Continuum methodology to review and revise their talent acquisition processes. As you will see from the case study the DMAIC process resulted in a dramatic increase in the bottom line of the corporation.

CASE STUDY: HOW CERIDIAN IMPROVED HIRING PRACTICES AND INCREASED PRODUCTIVITY BY AN ESTIMATED $28,000,000

Most U.S. businesses spend 35 percent of their total expenditures on people. Between compensation, benefits and human resource operational costs, your workforce is your most significant investment and important asset. And because your human resources are the key to your company's success, finding, training and retaining the best possible people is of critical importance.

From 2008 to 2009, Ceridian began a detailed review of its employee recruiting, hiring, and training policies and procedures. Using key business process improvement methodologies, Ceridian examined, measured and ultimately improved its talent acquisition efforts.

THE BOTTOM LINE

From 2009 to 2010, Ceridian:

Improved its hiring cycle time by 48 percent (from 77 to 40 days)

Increased gross revenue production by $31,302 per new hire—or more than $28 million for 90 new hires (average number of new hires hired each year)

Improved its time to hire by 23 percent (from 35 to 27 days)

Improved its 90-day employee retention rate by 3 percent (from 95 to 98 percent)

Increased hiring manager satisfaction with the recruiting process by 15 percent

Freed up recruiters' time so they could engage in more highly valued forms of recruiting

THE PROCESS

Ceridian uses a variety of tools and techniques to help customers get the most out of their HR processes and solutions. Some of the tools Ceridian uses include Six Sigma, DMAIC (define, measure, analyze, improve and control), Lean and Business Process Management Systems (BPMS) methodologies. Ceridian's quality tools and techniques provide a structure through which Ceridian listens to customers, works with them to prioritize strategies for making improvements to processes or solutions, executes and measures those efforts and periodically checks on implemented improvements to make sure they are still effective.

Integral to the use of Six Sigma is the DMAIC framework. As applied to Ceridian's talent acquisition process, the steps included the following:

Define—Identify the problem to be solved, aligning it with organizational objectives.

Measure—Measure baseline process performance and validate the accuracy of the measurement system.

Analyze—Establish current process capability, define performance objectives and identify sources of variation.

Improve—Define the future process, removing current sources of variation; establish operating procedures; and implement improvement.

Control—Define and validate the measurement system on the new processes, measure new process capability and implement the system for ongoing control.

DEFINE CERIDIAN'S RECRUITING AND RETENTION PROCESS ISSUES

In 2008, Ceridian's Talent Acquisition team surveyed and interviewed more than 75 Ceridian leaders and hiring managers to identify departmental strengths and weaknesses. The team also performed an internal audit of their existing processes and services. Their surveys, interviews and audits resulted in a variety of suggestions on how the talent acquisition process and practices might be improved. The key idea was to create a recruitment structure that better aligned with the organization's needs. In other words, create recruiting and hiring practices that were easy to partner with, streamlined, reliable, repeatable, scalable and cost-effective.

One of Ceridian's key business process improvement methodologies begin with an in-depth audit. In the case of Ceridian's Talent Acquisition team, key members decided they wanted to examine their overall recruiting and hiring practices to see if these could be improved. In this instance, a Ceridian quality expert worked with the Talent Acquisition team using a process known as Lean. The Lean process consists of an in-depth five-to-ten-day group meeting in which the team members work with a Ceridian quality expert to identify key metrics and processes. One of the outputs of a Lean event is a *value stream map*. The value stream map is a visual representation of the process to be addressed. It contains process steps, cycle times, systems and people involved. The purpose of the value stream map is to determine where process improvement opportunities exist.

In the case of Ceridian's Talent Acquisition team, a Lean event took place in the first week of 2010. During this event, the entire team outlined, analyzed and measured their current practices before beginning to strategize possible improvements in the way they recruited, hired and trained new Ceridian employees. Some of the key metrics the team examined included hiring cycle times, time to hire and Ceridian's 90-day employee retention rate. The ultimate result of the Lean event was an itemization of the Talent Acquisition group's workflow into a value stream process flowchart.

MEASURING CERIDIAN'S RECRUITING AND HIRING PROCESSES

While a value stream map can describe very complex processes and systems, some of the map's explanatory collateral articulates key measurements in the Talent Acquisition team's processes. In particular, according to the group's old processes, key hiring metrics included the following:

New hire process took 28.5 hours.

The recruiting-to-hire cycle took 77 days.

Average time to hire (from initial offer) took 35 days.

The entire recruiting-to-hire process contained 60 work stops.

Proactive hiring, in which Ceridian recruiters proactively search for talents as opposed to waiting for a candidate to respond to a job advertisement, was not always used.

The offer letter defect rate was 50 percent.

There was a significant amount of waste time screening resumes.

The average cost per hire was $3,428.

The average hire per recruiter was 82.

BENCHMARKING CERIDIAN'S RECRUITING AND HIRING PROCESSES

Ceridian analyzed its recruiting and hiring practices and compared them to the marketplace and industry trends. Understanding recruiting and hiring trends was an important component of making potential changes to Ceridian's practices. Ceridian's primary goal is to make sure its practices are as efficient and cost-effective as possible. Benchmarking Ceridian's practices against industry and peer practices provided another important perspective about potential Ceridian recruiting processes that could be changed.

Leaders in Ceridian's Talent Acquisition group reached out to peers and colleagues, as well as professional organizations and analysts, and obtained a variety of benchmarking statistics. Some of the statistics were provided by other corporations, and others were provided by analysts. In summary:

The number of hires per recruiter ranged from 35 to 200 depending on exempt (35–100) vs. non-exempt (60–200),

The average number of hires per year per recruiter was 89.

External recruitment only vs. both internal and external: Recruiters who managed both internal and external hiring filled 50 percent more positions than those who recruited only external recruitment.

The time to fill a position ranged from 30 to 51 days, with an average of 46 days.

The cost per hire ranged from $3,500 to $7,500, with an average of $4,427.

IMPROVING CERIDIAN'S RECRUITING AND HIRING PRACTICES

The Lean event was important for several reasons—not the least of which was the resulting value stream map. During the process of mapping the Talent Acquisition team's recruiting and hiring practices, several key improvement initiatives surfaced and began. Each of these key initiatives was designed to address problems in the team's various processes from creating more accurate job descriptions to improving new hires' first days and weeks on the job (typically referred to as on boarding).

During the process of implanting the preceding improvements, the Talent Acquisition team continued to monitor results. By the time all or most of the improvements were implemented, the team saw a dramatic improvement in many of their key process metrics.

THE RECRUITING CYCLE TIME GROSS REVENUE DOLLAR IMPACT

While the preceding metrics demonstrate measurable improvements, there is also a demonstrable dollar value to the improvements, usually identified as an opportunity cost. In essence, if Ceridian can recruit, hire, train and get new employees operating at full productivity using a more stream-lined, faster process, these employees will be that much more productive sooner. Judging from the improvements made in Ceridian's recruiting cycle time process (Table 2), it appears that new employees are recruited, hired, trained and made productive 37 days sooner today than they were in 2009. The formula for determining the opportunity cost is as follows:

Company annual revenue/#employees/220 workdays per year = average daily revenue production per employee

For example, in a 1,000-employee company with $100 million in gross revenues, the average daily revenue per employee would be:

$100,000,000 / 1,000 / 220 = \$454.54 gross revenue per employee per day

Using this example, if the company reduced its recruiting time to hire from 40 to 20 days without sacrificing the quality of the hire (hopefully improving it), then this company's gross revenue production would increase. The per-employee increase in revenue production for 20 days would be 20*$454.54 = $9,090.90.

The total impact to the company of the improved recruiting cycle time would be the revenue production improvement by employee multiplied by the number of new hires each year. For instance, if the 1,000-employee company has a 20 percent annual turnover, it is hiring approximately 200

Table 8.1   Eleven Key Recruiting and Hiring Practice Improvements Implemented in 2010

Activity	Purpose
Roll out the Recruiting Strategy Discussion (RSD) form to all recruiting personnel	More accurate job description/sourcing strategy discussion leads to more accurate, targeted recruiting
Roll out a Standardized Pipeline Process and Request form to team and business units	Efficiencies result from all business units using the same form/process results in an improved ability to be a consultative partner, a more streamlined process, etc.
Establish and roll out a database for proactive lead management	Place for the team to track leads and share information—leads to quicker sourcing when a talent need is identified
Develop a process and teach the auto screen functionality to the team for use with mass hires	Results in faster prescreening to get quality candidates in front of managers quicker
Train the team on paperless background check storage	Leads to easier access and real-time information for recruiters to better manage the post-offer process
Roll out a revised hiring manager and New Hire Survey	Leads to an increased response rate and more accurate net promoter scores (NPS)
Develop Lead Generation/Social Media Role for the department	Leads to consistent branding and modern candidate generation
Standardize and brand Interview Confirmation document for each site	Leads to better candidate experience with less confusion and rescheduling of interviews by the team
Change Val U Welcome Call facilitators	Consistency leads to a more positive, accurate delivery of information and a better on-boarding experience
Develop Background Check Service Level Agreements with choice point	Results in more cost-effective, efficient and timely background checks
Streamline offer process to deliver employee ID numbers earlier in the process	Provides more lead time for new hire systems setup and a better and faster on-boarding experience

Table 8.2   Key Metrics Based on Process Improvements Made by Ceridian Talent Acquisition Team: Late 2009–Mid-2010

	Baseline pre-AVO[a]	*New (February 28)*	*60 day (March 31)*	*Target (June 30)*	*Improvement (Target)*
Cycle time (Days)	77	72	64	40	48%
Time to hire (days)	35	32	24	27	23%
Retention (90-day retention)	95%	NA	97%	98%	3%
NPS[b]	NA	NA	51%	60%[c]	15%

[a] Action workout, or the process before the targeted waste, was worked out of the system.
[b] Implemented revised NPS questions on January 1, 2010.
[c] 40 percent is world class.

people per year. If each new employee hired is contributing $9,090.90 more each year, the opportunity cost of improving the recruiting cycle time process is $1,818,181.81 per year—dramatic and significant.

Ceridian's estimated opportunity costs from improvements made to its recruiting cycle time process are more dramatic ($28 million) for four reasons.

Ceridian has approximately eight times the number of employees as a 1,000-employee company.

Ceridian's recruiting cycle time improvements were more dramatic: 37 days instead of 20.

The figure used for Ceridian's gross revenue was $1,489 million.

Because Ceridian is a larger company, it hires approximately 900 new employees per year.

Using the stated formula, Ceridian's overall revenue production improvement from its dramatically shortened cycle time is estimated at $28 million.

Table 8.3   Full Equation of the Recruiting Cycle Time Dollar Impact Opportunity Cost

Annual Revenue		Employee Count		Workdays per Year		Recruiting Cycle Time Improvement (days)		Hires per Year		Productivity Improvement
100,000,00	/	1,000	/	220	X	20	X	200	=	$1,818,181.81

CONTROL—FOLLOW-UP AND REVIEW

The DMAIC process, referred to earlier in this best practice study, provides for a periodic follow-up and review of Ceridian's Talent Acquisition processes. Historically, Ceridian has made several changes to its recruiting and hiring practices in order to take advantage of new technologies, tools, laws and regulations and so forth. Ceridian will make certain its talent acquisition efforts continue to reflect industry best practices as well as being cost-effective and efficient.

Ceridian is an HR services company with significant expertise in all areas of human resource management. Ceridian constantly uses its knowledge of best practices, process improvement methodologies and industry benchmarks to focus on its employee programs. The review of and changes made to the company's talent acquisition processes is just one way Ceridian better manages its overall HR costs.

CASE STUDY 2: REDUCTION IN THE
EFFECTIVE TIME TO HIRE

THE ORGANIZATION

A provider of complex and sophisticated electromechanical devices with capabilities that include concept development, industrial design, design and manufacturing engineering, production, distribution, and field service. The primary market classifications served are Navigation & Exploration, Defense & Security, Medical, and Complex Systems. Headquartered in Schaumburg, IL, the business was founded in 1900 and offers its customers' development, design, manufacturing, and distribution capabilities in a highly collaborative environment.

THE PROBLEM

At their Brooksville, Florida, location the organization was witnessing an extended hiring process. The problem was that this process cost the organization monies in the way of productivity, overtime, management being taken away from the delivery of end products to customers and costs associated with agency usage (Tables 8.4 through 8.10).

PROJECT CONCLUSION

After analyzing the data collected, items from the pick list were implemented and a new process flow chart was developed. During that time, the time-to-fill metric was changed to stop the clock at the signing of the offer letter rather than the actual start date. Taking into consideration the reduced target time to fill from 71 to 59 days, 59 days became the new goal. To effectively measure their improvement, the team adjusted the original actual time to fill from 111 to 97 days.

Since the implementation of the new process and the writing of this document, the company has filled seven (7) salaried positions. The result is an average time to fill of 40 days and average cost of hire at 2.54 percent—a 58 percent improvement in time to fill and an 81 percent decrease in hiring costs.

As can be seen from the four case studies, the TLS Continuum methodology and related toolbox can have a profound influence on the talent management aspect of your human capital management area.

Table 8.4 Project Charter Statement

Black/Green Belt Lead	Quality Manager	Business Unit/Location			Brooksville
Process Owner	HR Manager	Project Start Date			April 15, 2014
Conf. Call info		Target Completion Date			September 30, 2014
Champion	Lean Master				
Estimated opportunity	TBD				

Element	Description	Team Charter			
1. Process	Define the process in which opportunity exists.	The recruiting process for salaried positions can yield improved performance in the time to fill and cost per hire metrics.			
2. Project description	Describe the project's purpose and overall objective.	This project seeks to reduce the average time to fill for salaried positions from 111 to 71 days. This represents a 36 percent reduction which brings the Brooksville facility in line with the corporate time to fill plan. In addition, we seek to reduce our cost per hire from 13.5 to 9 percent, representing a 33 percent improvement also in line with the corporate plan.			
3. Project scope	Define the part of the process that will be investigated. Include both in-scope and out-of-scope aspects.	In scope—salary exempt and non-exempt positions Out of scope—hourly, temporary and contract labor positions			
4. Objective	Define the baseline, the theoretical target, and the goal for improvement on the primary metrics: Rolled Throughput Yield, Cost of Poor Quality and Capacity/ Productivity. Metrics *may* be changed to suit your project.		**Baseline**	**Entitlement**	**Goal**
		Time to fill	111 days	–36%	71 days
		Cost per hire	13.5%	33%	9%

5. Opportunity statement	Summarize the project description and objective in specific terms. Include the Key Process Output Variables, their current baseline, the target level for improvement and the financial impact.	The opportunity exists to streamline the recruiting process and improve our time to fill metric. Our current average time to fill for salaried positions is 111 days. This project seeks to improve that time by 36 percent, thereby averaging 71 days to fill salaried positions. In addition, we seek to improve the cost per hire from 13.5 to 9 percent. The financial impact will be determined in the measurement phase of the project.	
6. Team members	Define the team members (number and area represented).	HR Manager, Data Analyst, HR Generalist, Black Belt/Customer, CI Lean Master, Administrator.	
7. Benefit to external customers:	Define the final customer and describe their most critical requirements and the benefit they will see from this project.	Our customers will receive an improved level of service in quality and response time when we are a fully staffed workforce. The hiring managers will have less downtime for vacated positions, allowing for department responsibilities to maintain performance levels. Peers of the position will have a shortened period of time to carry the extra workload.	
8. Schedule	Key milestones/dates	**Project Start**	4/15/14
	Define scope of project	**"D" Completion**	4/30/14
	Measure current state and metrics	**"M" Completion**	5/23/14
	Analyze data, gap analysis	**"A" Completion**	6/6/14
	Implement Improvements	**"I" Completion** (delay in hiring has pushed back implementation date)	9/15/14
	Control new process & adjust	**"C" Completion**	9/30/14
		Project completion	9/30/14
		Safety review	N/A
9. Support required	Define any exceptional anticipated needs: equipment, hardware, trials, access, travel, training, etc.		

Table 8.5   SIPOC Diagram

Suppliers	Input	Process	Output	Customers
Hiring manager	Job requisition	**Start:**	New hire	Corp human capital
Stakeholders	Skills/ knowledge	Job posting	Increased organizational skill levels	Managers
Employees	Referrals	Candidate screening	Innovation into the organization through new ideas	Customers
Electronic job boards	Candidates	Interviews	On-boarding	Hiring managers
Recruiters	Job requirement	Background checks		
Social media		Request to extend offer		
Managers		Offer letter		
Professional organizations				
		END:		
		Hiring metrics		
		Reduced time to hire		

Table 8.6   Ishikawa Diagram

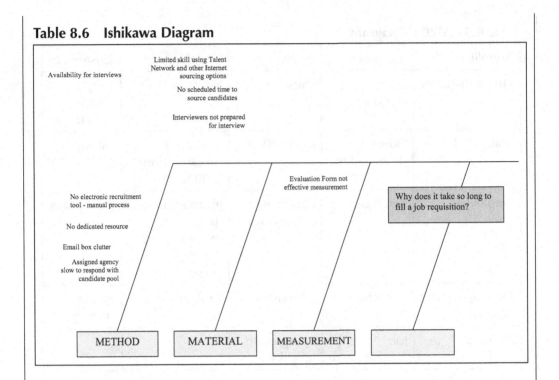

Availability for interviews

Limited skill using Talent Network and other Internet sourcing options

No scheduled time to source candidates

Interviewers not prepared for interview

No electronic recruitment tool - manual process

No dedicated resource

Email box clutter

Assigned agency slow to respond with candidate pool

Evaluation Form not effective measurement

Why does it take so long to fill a job requisition?

METHOD   MATERIAL   MEASUREMENT

Table 8.7   Pick Chart: Recruitment Process Improvement

	BIG payoff	**SMALL** payoff
EASY to implement	Work from home on recruiting Set dedicated recruiting time Review agency performance Establish time limit for manager review Establish time limit to send to agency	Separate resumes into their own job folder Meet with Danielle - Tips and Tricks Flag resume submissions mgr Follow-up email to mgr after 48 hrs
	Implement Challenge	Possible Kill
HARD to implement	Create talent pool of candidates Go to Agencies Sooner Use Talent Network-internet connection inhibits Build Network Use Social Media Review outlook capabilities	Referral Bonus for external people

Table 8.8   Electronics Firm Detailed Activity Sheet

Action	Time Requirement
Post job internal	10
Post job external	15
Source resumes	2 each
Forward to manager for review	
Pre-screen interview	30
Schedule phone interview with manager	2
Schedule on-site interview	10
Email candidate confirmation	5
Airline reservations	45
Interview	90
Plant tour	30
Debrief meeting	15
RTEO	5
Contact candidate with offer	15
Prepare offer letter	3
Email candidate offer	2
Offer letter received	
Schedule drug screen	15
Background check request	10
Pull results	2
Assign ID#/email manager and trainer	1
New hire notification	1
Candidate starts Close job folder Record affirmative action data	

Table 8.9   Time Electronics Firm Candidate Activity Sheet

Candidate	Date/Time to Hiring Manager	Response Received
Candidate 1	6/20/14 11:38 am	6/27/14 6:38 pm
Candidate 2	6/23/14 11:46 am	6/27/14 6:38 pm
Candidate 3	6/20/14 8:55 am	
Candidate 4	6/18/14 8:38 am	6/27/14 6:38 pm
Candidate 5	6/16/14 8:38 am	6/27/14 6:38 pm
Candidate 6	6/12/14 5:36 pm	6/27/14 6:38 pm
Candidate 7	6/12/14 10:39 am	6/27/14 6:38 pm

Table 8.10 Human Resource Process for Filling Open Positions

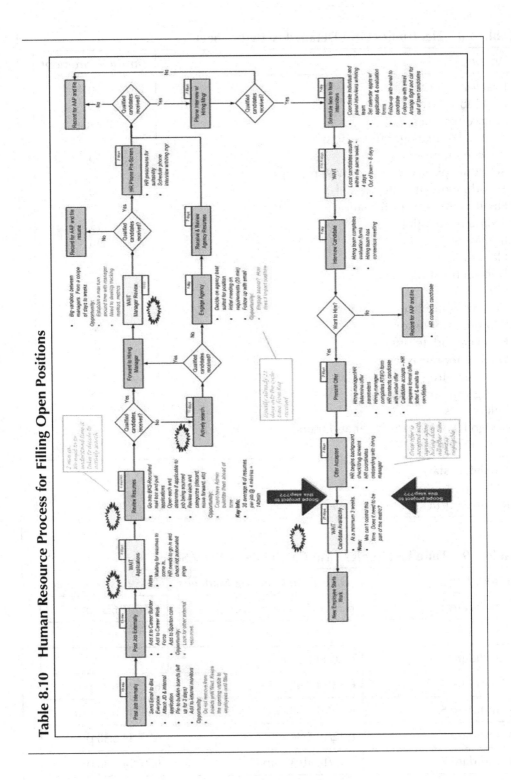

HRCI Body of Knowledge: Learning and Development

HRCI indicates that the Learning and Development function is charged with identifying the opportunities for improving the education and training of the organization. It is further responsible for developing succession plans for key human capital assets and evaluating employee retention strategies in order to maintain the corporate knowledge base.

According to *Workforce Management* magazine[9] the amounts invested in providing training to the American workforce by various corporate enterprises amounted to $56.2 million in 2008. The nature of the marketplace has changed over time on a global basis, and many of our organizations are not prepared for the change. This change fundamentally altered the way the human factor was viewed within the business community. Our FTEs were now an asset. They are a non-owned asset rather than an expense. And yet as the market entered the doldrums of the current economic times, we find that corporations cut the training expense first. However, as the generational make-up of our organizations changes, the remaining generations were vitally interested in enhancing their career portfolios. This left our organizations with a dilemma.

Whether your organization is a part of the Fortune 1000 or a small- to medium-sized enterprise, when we look at this functional area, there are several critical issues we need to consider. First, is the cost of the training an effective use of corporate funds in light of other economic requirements? The second issue is whether we are providing the right kind of training to our workforce (Training vs. Education[10]) that will enable our organization to be more innovative and thus more competitive in the marketplace. The final issue is whether or not our training offerings are effective based on the dollars spent. The Six Sigma methodology can assist us in finding the answers to each of these issues.

The functional area of human resource development is responsible for the development, implementation and evaluation of activities and programs that address employee training and development, performance appraisals and talent and performance management to ensure that the knowledge, skills, abilities and performance of the workforce meet current and future organizational and individual needs. As a result, there are a number of tools within the methodology that will assist you and your organization to reach these goals.

One of the potential tools that can be used is the Quality Function Deployment (QFD) matrix, as shown in Figure 8.3. Its purpose is to

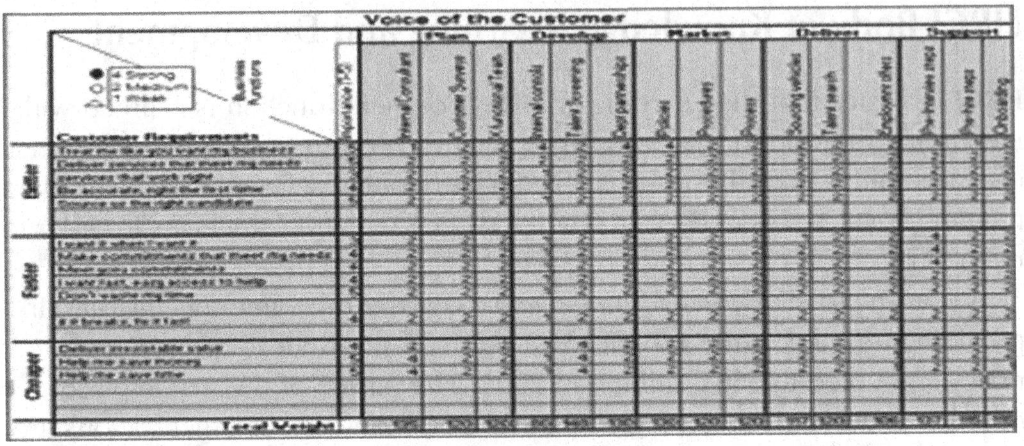

Figure 8.3   Quality Function Deployment Tool.[11]

graphically show the voice of the customer. In the above example in the side bar the responses from the employees and the managers would show their preferences for the delivery of training under the three outputs of training and process improvement. How can we, based on the voice of the employee and managers, make the training better (high level of quality), faster (quicker) and cheaper (at less cost to the organization). Each of the responses is given a number value on a scale of 1–4, with 4 being the strongest desire. Once we have established the criteria the QFD contains both a number value for each desire and an implication step but is weighted in value. At the conclusion we have a clear picture of what the low-hanging fruit is so that we can begin to deliver the customer expectations. Some of you may remember that we used the QFD tool during our discussion of the voice of the customer, as seen on page 94 in Figure 5.3.

Another tool that can be used is control charts that can back up the QFD through an analysis of the data to identify trends in the delivery of training. This can be looked at from the aspect of the frequency of the programs, the method of delivery and location just as examples.

Talk to a number of trainers, and they each have their preferred facility set up for the delivery of training. Through the use of process maps and even value stream map, we can produce graphic views of the flow through the training facility.

Further through the use of statistical analysis forms we can determine how effective our training programs are. One of the hardships within the training field is how to determine the outcomes of the programs you offer. Most organizations evaluate the training, using what the industry refers to as "smile sheets," which were developed by Kirkpatrick in his evaluation method. These are actually a form of surveys that are discussed in the define stage'; however, many organizations do not go further than asking the participant to answer these series of questions.

One of the tools that organizations use in their human development space is what is referred to as a 360-degree performance review. In these exercises, both managers and their staff are asked to rate each other on a numerical scale. We can use data collection tools from the toolbox to assess the results of the analysis and then move the final results to a Pareto chart to see if the results tell you that we are within the mean scores of the results.

The case study shown below is the result of my Six Sigma Black Belt training. The project was an attempt to answer an old-age question of whether we are getting our monies worth out of the training we provide to the organization.

CASE STUDY: TRAINING: IS THE COST JUSTIFIED? A SIX SIGMA BLACK BELT PROJECT RESULT

PROBLEM

In today's competitive talent market, one attribute most sought after by the generation coming into the marketplace is the ability to enhance their career portfolio. The question for training providers and senior management is whether the training they provide is the right type (training versus education) to meet their needs. In order to determine this, we must investigate the availability of the correct tools to properly calculate our return on the investment of the various training being delivered.

SCOPE

The goal of this project will be to create a visual dashboard, which will enable the trainer provider to quickly determine by analyzing the selected evaluation methods and how they are doing with the training programs and from there calculate the return on investment of the said programs. After selecting the best venue for the evaluation, the strategies from that training will be embedded into a Kaplan and Norton Balanced Scorecard vehicle for future training development.

METHODS

Daniel Bloom & Associates, Inc. utilized an array of tools to construct the data for this evidence-based study, including the DMAIC process, focused surveys, stakeholder analysis using a SIPOC and the Ishikawa Fishbone Diagram.

MAJOR RESULTS

With the understanding that there is a reluctance of organizations to fully implement a training assessment effort, Daniel Bloom & Associates, Inc. developed an evaluation tool based on different criteria than the Kirkpatrick Models or the other often-used vehicles. In order to facilitate the evaluation, the entire process is based on the voice of the manager.

PROJECT IMPACT

Based on the selection of the evaluation methods of training, we should be able to demonstrate the best practices in designing training programs for the corporation, which will enhance the career portfolios of the involved FTEs and, at the same time, through increased employee engagement have a direct impact on the corporate bottom line by getting the most for the dollars spent in providing the training programs.

It was our findings that, first, a majority of corporations are globally not carrying evaluations out to the point of being able to determine the economic impact of their training programs on the corporate bottom line. Further, the majority of corporations globally basically confine evaluations to determining the FTE Reaction to the training presented (Kirkpatrick Level 1). It was our belief that corporations need to find a new method to accurately evaluate the impact of the training process, faster, cheaper and better. We understand that the same methods are not going to complete the tasks required because of the time constraints in today's workplace.

Based on Microsoft Excel, Daniel Bloom & Associates, Inc. designed a five-level worksheet to evaluate the training opportunities. Each succeeding level is interdependent on the data from the preceding page to arrive at an answer to the dilemma faced by management.

Worksheet 1: Training Attributes

The level 1 worksheet asks the manager to review the human development needs from three perspectives. These perspectives are the current performance of the department, the corporate goal of where they would like the department to be at and finally what is the priority for the

Corporate Tactical Improvement Areas for 2009		Current Performance (1 to 10)	Corporate Goal (1 to 10)	Business Priority (1 to 10)	Improvement Goal %
1.	Individual's Performance Level	3	10	10	333
2.	Increased Peer Pressure - to do a good job	Data Limits Ener a whole number from 1 to 10.	7	1	175
3.	Employee Motivation - to go up and above		7	1	350
4.	Meaningful Performance Assessment (good / better / best)		8	10	400
5.	Incorporating Process Improvement as a corporate culture	5	10	1	200
6.	Achieving Bottom Line Results	3	8	8	267
7.	Respective of our Corporate Values	5	8	1	160
8.	Increasing our Competitive Advantage	6	7	7	117
9.	Maximizing Employee Loyalty	5	8	1	160
10.	Employee's Perceive our Compensation Benefits to be fair	5	6	1	120
11.	Building Trust through out the organization (between levels)	4	6	1	150
12.	Relationship Building (between levels, across levels)	4	6	1	150
13.	Networking within the organization - team building efforts	3	5	1	167
14.	Open and Honest Coaching and Feedback	4	5	1	125
	Ranking		Corporate Goal	Business Priority	Average Improvement

Figure 8.4   Training Effective Attribute Assessment Tool Level 1.

organization to achieve this future state. The worksheet also provides a list of 14 corporate impacts that are desired in the organization. These impacts are not set in stone and can be unique to your own organizations. Figure 8.4 shows you the structure of the worksheet.

For each of the corporate tactical areas, the manager is requested to evaluate the areas on a score of 1–10, with 10 being highly desirable. As we stated above, the manager begins by determining the current performance levels of the department staff. Once they have done that, they do the same for the corporate goal. This corporate goal represented the anticipated outcomes from the training expected by management. The final step in the process is to determine how important the corporate impact is to the total organization. It is critical that this is in conjunction with the overall corporate strategic initiatives.

Built behind the worksheet are formulas for carrying the results to the next appropriate levels within the tool.

Worksheet 2: Training Attributes Micro View

In the second level of the tool the corporate impact areas are broken down into the Key Performance Indicators of each area. Once again, these KPIs are totally subjective on the part of the manager involved.

The level 2 worksheet can be found in Figure 8.5:

The manager begins with the response to the question of whether, based on their observations of their staff members, the training impacted

Training Attribute Tool					
Attribute	Did Training Positively Impact the Corporate Improvement Area (?)	If yes - how long will it take to see tangable Improvements (?) Short Term (≤ 3 mo.) Mid Term (3 to 6 mo) Long Term (12+ mo.)	How Effective was the training in meeting the Corporate Goal	Targeted Corporate Improvement Percentage(%)	Training Effectiveness Calculation Projected Improvement Results
	select Yes or No	enter a 3, 6 or 12	Scale (1 to 10)		
Performance Levels				333	50
Increased Process Efficiency	Yes	6	2		
Increased Productivity	No	3	2		
Increased Team Performance	No	3	2		
Increased Peer Pressure				175	87
Increased Team Participation	No	3	5		
Increased Peer Pressure	No				
Employee Motivation				350	70
Increased Pride of Job Ownership	Yes	6	5		
Increased Employee Engagement	Yes	6	5		
Increased Career Portfolio	Yes				
Increased Status and Promotability	Yes				
Increased Morale	Yes	3	3		
Built Team Spirit	Yes	3	3		
Performance				400	[not effective]
Identified Top Performers	No				
Assessed Employee Performance	No		0		
Focused Process					

Figure 8.5   Training Effective Attribute Assessment Tool Level 2.

positively the corporate improvement areas from the level 1 worksheet. The response is a close-ended yes or no.

Next the manager is asked to determine how long it will take to see tangible improvements in each of the areas on a 3-, 6- or 12-month basis. Once again, the worksheet requests them to enter 3, 6 or 12 in the appropriate box on the worksheet. In the beginning they were asked closed questions, to respond whether the training impacted the department. Now we are asking them to rate the impact on a scale of 1–10, with 10 being highly impactful.

Once again, the worksheet contains built-in formulas which take the data forward to higher-level worksheets.

Worksheet 3: Return on Investment Calculator

We can't get away from management the question about the return on investment of training programs. This level of the tool is a fairly standard return on investment calculation based on a 75 percent level of confidence that our numbers are correct. The worksheet is shown in Figure 8.6.

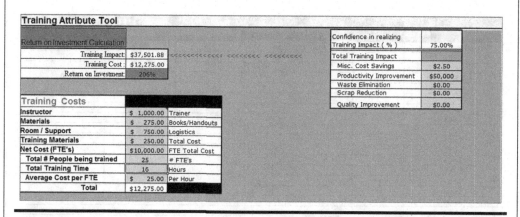

Figure 8.6   Training Effective Attribute Assessment Tool Level 3.

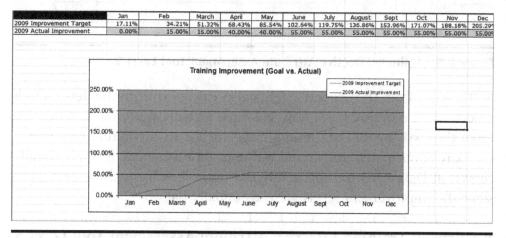

Figure 8.7   Training Effective Attribute Assessment Tool Level 4.

It should be noted that the instructor's time is based on the hours that they are actually facilitating training, not on their annual compensation.

Worksheet: Training Effective Attribute Assessment Tool Level 4

Using the control chart tool out of the toolbox and the built-in formulas from the lower-level worksheets, we are able to assess how we are doing on reaching our goals. Remember that we said in the discussion of the responses on the first worksheet that the data was carried forward to a higher level within the tool. It is on this worksheet that the data is carried forward. The first worksheet inputs the anticipated training improvement over a 12-month period calculated on a monthly basis as shown in Figure 8.7.

2009 Course Offerings	Location	Instructional Method Utilized	Number of Instructional Hrs	Number of FTE Involved	Total Instructional Hrs
Sexual Harassment	Corporate	Instructor Led	8.0	20.0	160
Sales					0
Sales					0
Sales					0
Sales					0
Sales					0
Sales					0
Sales					0
Sales					0
Sales					0
Sales					0
Sales					0
Sales					0
Sales					0
Sales					0
Sales					0
Sales					0
Sales					0
Sales					0
Sales					0
Sales					0
Sales					0
Sales					0

Figure 8.8   Training Effective Attribute Assessment Tool Level 5.

The data from the second level is also carried over to this level, but it reflects on a monthly basis how we have actually performed. When we input the two sets of data points it creates for us a control chart which compares anticipated and actual training improvements. In the example shown in Figure 6.8 we apparently did not follow through on our goals since the improvement levels were essentially flat.

Worksheet: Training Effective Attribute Assessment Tool Level 5

The last worksheet in the Assessment Tool is a record of the actual training programs offered, as can be seen in Figure 8.8, and the attributes of that training.

It provides you with a location to record first the topic being trained and where it was given. One critical factor in assessing the quality of the training programs is the method used to facilitate the training. The manager is given the options of Instructor Led, Web Based, Computer Based or Blended Learning. If you have additional ways to deliver the content, you can add them to the drop-down menu.

HRCI Body of Knowledge: Total Rewards

From achieving HR excellence perspective what is the role of compensation and benefits? It is critical that we understand just what role this plays in the total picture. I turned to our service partner, Effective Resources and Angel Rao-Brown, for the answer. Her response was that in its simplest terms compensation and benefits are the vehicle for organizations such as yours to attract and then retain quality employees.

Thus, the question of compensation and benefits is a critical area for many organizations. What is too little? What is too much? Is there a component that our human capital assets are demanding, and we are not offering? This functional area therefore looks at the process of developing/selecting, implementing/administering and evaluating compensation and benefit programs for all employee groups (exempt, no-exempt, rank and file, management) in order to support the organization's goals, objective and values.

The level of engagement by your organizational human capital is going to be tied directly to its level of satisfaction with the way the organization takes care of its needs through your benefits package and compensation program.

There are many areas within this functional area that can present project opportunities within the compensation and benefits arena:

Benchmarking Other Organization's Programs—If you think back to our discussion of the Six Sigma toolbox in Chapter 4, we mentioned that benchmarking was one of the available tools during the analyze stage. As HR professionals we have used this tool for many years without realizing it was tied to the Six Sigma process. However, it is a good way to identify what others are doing in the process of implementing their compensation programs. It enables us to gain a clear picture of what is working and what is not in the global workplace.

Control Charts—We have at every step of the review of the process discussed the use of control charts as a tool for verifying the results of our efforts. In the compensation effort, the control charts can be used to track when employees take advantage of the enrollment period to sign up for continuing or new benefits. What we are trying to accomplish is the identification of the optimum time to have employees take care of the enrollment open in an efficient time frame.

Histograms—Like the control charts, the purpose of histograms is to identify the point of most usage. As we plot the data points the histogram will show us a view of the data as to the frequency of certain data criteria. By seeing where the largest data point is, we can find where the most frequent usage and time consumption take place in the enrollment process.

Process Maps—We used the process map earlier to demonstrate how the recruitment process worked. The same steps can be shown to lay out a graphical view of the steps that are required in the enrollment process.

Pareto Charts—The data points entered into the Pareto chart will graphically show over time the spread of pay for various functions within the organization. You have benchmarked your compensation for any function, and now through the use of the Pareto chart you can use the data to observe the spread of pay as you received from the benchmarking effort. If your spread indicates that your organization is worse than the benchmark, then you have the evidence-based data to make the argument for changes to the program. Likewise, if the data show your organization is better than the benchmark data, then you are left with the decision as to whether you need to make some changes in the other direction.

Visual Management Queue Boards—Taking the compensation and benefit program details it's possible for the organization to create a visual system for tracking the process of benefits enrollment for each department or, even if the number is small enough, by the employee.

An organization determined that the TLS Continuum methodology was the best vehicle to explore the level of abuse in the Family and Medical Leave Act benefits.

CASE STUDY: "FMLA ABUSE-SIX SIGMA SOLUTION" BY ANDREA MATEER

In today's complex business world, companies welcome simplified solutions to difficult, vexing problems such as those involving the Family Medical Leave Act (FMLA). Breaking with previous piecemeal approaches, an innovative strategy now addresses compliance issues while implementing a tightly controlled solution that dramatically reduces FMLA abuse.

The FMLA was enacted on February 5, 1993, "to generally require private sector employers of fifty or more employees, and public agencies, to provide up to twelve work weeks of unpaid, job-protected leave to eligible employees for certain specified family and medical reasons." Let's examine how that ties in with a large, multi-state, unionized company with over 75 percent of its employees working various shifts, weekends, holidays and quite often on call.

Initially under the act, requests for leave were few and infrequent and for catastrophic reasons. However, the usage increased, and reasons became more ordinary and less catastrophic. Compounding the problem, the leave process was fragmented and lacked communication with the manager. Additionally, the administrator usually approved each request without question. Many employees would ignore denial letters and continued using FMLA. Also, with no accountability as to entitlements, many employees were using more than 12 weeks in a 12-month period.

Meanwhile, employees felt no obligation to notify managers of their approval and managers felt that they could not question an employee who took FMLA. Consequently, by 2004, management concluded that the company was at a critical point on FMLA abuse, with jobs going unfilled or worked at an overtime rate, and in management's opinion (at the time) FMLA abuse was the cause.

SIX SIGMA SOLUTION

The solution? First, the company looked at outsourcing but opted for a Six Sigma strategy and new software. The former seeks to identify and remove causes of defects and errors in the manufacturing and business processes by using a set of quality management methods with two methodologies: DMAIC and DMADV, both inspired by Deming's Plan-Do-Check-Act cycle.

This company had already been realizing huge time/cost savings benefits regarding other issues through Six Sigma. Therefore, management decided to apply DMAIC to see if the FMLA problem could be quantified and controlled. Implementing DMAIC's steps, the company first developed the ARMI (Approver, Resource, Member and Interested Party), project stakeholders and their roles. The team must have a champion, sponsor, resources, a Black Belt and members. In this case, the champion was the Sr. VP, Human Resources, as the team business leader who allocated the resources. The function would reside in the Labor Relations department because the company's contract-covered employees were using most of the FMLA and Labor Relations was their primary HR contact. Three full-time positions (director and two managers) and two temporary positions were added to implement this change. The Vice President of Labor Relations was the sponsor and also available to allocate resources.

Members from the Law Department and the IT staff were team resources on an ad-hoc basis, with the director and two managers being the team members who would actually do most of the work.

Once the ARMI had been defined, the company developed a charter, which included a problem statement to clearly define and measure the problem. The goal was to increase productivity by managing the FMLA process, building internal and external controls and measurements and reducing abuse by 5 percent by December 31, 2005. Meeting these goals would be critical to the quality (CTQ) of the Six Sigma project. Specific customer and organization benefit commitments were identified and quantified. These benefits included educating employees as pertains to FMLA, FMLA-trained managers and compliance with the federal regulations. In addition, there were the elimination of the two temporary positions, a reduction in the replacement cost, improved availability and a 5 percent reduction in abuse, resulting in a gain in productivity. There was also the cost avoidance of in-sourcing rather than outsourcing the function. The commitments were measured and quantified as part of the Six Sigma rigor.

GAME-CHANGING SOFTWARE

Technical issues were first addressed by contracting with a vendor to image documents. Then, the company shopped for an FMLA computer system because the FMLA module was "lacking" and an external technology solution looked more viable than an internal one. After talking to different companies, LeaveLink® enterprise software was selected. Designed to administer federal and state leave laws, employer authorized leaves and employee attendance policies for mid-size to large multi-state employers, its implementation was fast and painless. The vendor, Chattanooga, Tennessee–based Absentys LLC, was (and remains) excellent to work with. Prior to LeaveLink the process was manually driven. Upon introduction, the software made it possible to immediately eliminate two temporary positions and manual letters, while significantly reducing the possibility of administrative errors.

The system calculates leave eligibility and entitlements. Hours worked and FMLA time used are sent nightly to the vendor for importing into the software, which creates tasks and reconciles lists for the FMLA managers; users can also add tasks. LeaveLink administers the federal FMLA and automatically applies state leave laws based on an employee's work state.

If a law changes, the vendor immediately updates the software and notifies their customers. Essentially, the company made the transition from being reactive to proactive by managing the FMLA usage rather than just administering the leave.

Next, communication was addressed, beginning by reviewing policy, making changes, posting to the employee home page and mailing a copy to each employee's home. Also, a manual titled "What You Need to Know about the Family Medical Leave Act" was developed and mailed with the policy and posted online. Weekly, electronic communications are sent to managers, e.g., recognizing and reacting to signs and situations possibly developing into an FMLA event and how to ask the right questions. Managers and employees were field-trained on rights and responsibilities, and company reps also met with union leaders and reps. Letters to employees are regularly revised as is the medical certification form to continually ensure that the company best meets employee rights and employer responsibilities.

Three levels of review were developed:

Med cert was reviewed by an FMLA manager.
If there is a legal question, legal counsel was included.
If there is a medical question, the medical department was included.

Employees' FMLA usage was monitored. If the condition was chronic and something had evidently changed, the employee was asked to recertify. If a pattern of unusual absence behavior was detected, additional questions, as described in the DOL Opinion Letter FMLA2004-2, were asked and employees were notified when they exceeded entitlements. Finally, the company began disciplining employees when the evidence indicated that they had falsely stated the reason for certain absences. At first there was disbelief, but slowly the employees began to more carefully read FMLA-related letters and managers began to come in for advice, seeing a resource rather than just an administrator.

In most cases, the arbitrators and the DOL have supported actions taken. When they have taken exception, some modifications in the process have been made. Data indicates that the abuse began to significantly decline after the company began managing the FMLA process. The abuse began to drop around July 2005, especially after employees were sent for second and third opinions and were asked to recertify their leaves if the data indicated that something had changed.

Since 2005 processes have been continually tweaked. When weaknesses in letters and forms have been determined, revisions have been made. Upon the implementation of FMLA Self-Service and FMLA Manager Self-Service, employees can apply for FMLA, request their employer packet, download all their forms and letters and check on their usage and entitlements online. The manager can also get the information they need online. A monthly dashboard report with control limits is generated to ensure the ability to immediately react if the abuse begins to go out of control. This has not yet happened in the three years since deciding to take control.

DRAMATICALLY REDUCING ABUSE AND COSTS WITHOUT CORNER-CUTTING

The company's savings have been more than anticipated. After implementing LeaveLink, educating employees and managers and assuming responsibility for managing FMLA while insisting on total compliance, FMLA staff has been reduced from five to one. One manager can now do the job that required two managers, a director and two temps. The software has also helped to significantly reduce cycle time and to meet the important CTQs.

Over the past 3 years the abuse has consistently decreased. While the company continues to hire and its workforce has increased, the available days lost to FMLA abuse have decreased by approximately 63 percent.

Most importantly, the company insists on total compliance with the regulations. No employee who has a need for FMLA and is eligible is ever adversely affected. Rather, the company has become a resource for managers and employees. At times employees have a need but are not eligible. In these instances, the company has worked with managers and union reps to assist in other ways. This includes developing opportunities to partner with the Department of Labor and unions to help address certain issues. Ultimately, the company has shown that FMLA abuse can be effectively managed with less people and without sacrificing compliance.

HRCI Body of Knowledge: Employee Relations and Engagement

The functional area of Employee Relations and Engagement including the keys to employee satisfaction and performance management. In addition, this area looks at the requirements from the government agencies on workplace safety and risk management. The final area of concern is the organization-union interactions.

We do not have to explain to you as HR professionals that the demands on your time have become more complicated as the years pass. Whether we are looking at increased scrutiny from regulatory agencies on our operations or demands from our human capital assets, we are faced with the task of creating more and more complex processes to run our HR function.

This functional area is given the duties to develop, implement/administer and evaluate the workplace in order to monitor relationships and working conditions that balance employer/employee needs and rights in support of the organization's goals and objectives.

The Six Sigma methodology can be used to make the processes more easily understood by both management and the rank and file within the organization. Let's look at some of the ways we can do that.

Complaint Procedures

It would be ideal if we could run an organization with no problems. But you and I both know that is probably just a pipe dream. Complaint processes take up an enormous amount of time, partly because you need to have all your "I's" dotted and your "T's" crossed in order to be compliant with the complaint procedures laid out by either internal or external influences. One of the easiest ways to lower the stress level is to create process maps, as we have done in other areas of this book, to prepare a graphic view of the steps required during the process. While the process map does not have to be as detailed as a value stream map, it still needs to include every step of the process from creation to resolving the issues within the complaint.

Incident Reports

Every year you are required to complete and file a form with the Occupational Safety and Health Administration (OSHA) reporting all accidents in the workplace. You also have other incidents that occur within the workplace, which may not be part of the annual report. Incidents such as theft, drug abuse or even domestic violence are among these other areas. Control charts allow us to track on a monthly basis the rate of occurrence in each of these areas. The control charts will allow you to set a level of acceptable occurrence and from the data points see if you are within that tolerance level. This is not to suggest that any occurrence of these types is acceptable, but we are dealing with human interaction so these things may occur whether we want them to or not.

Control Charts to Show What Benefits Are Most Effective for the Employees

As we have stated previously, control charts are a graphic method of demonstrating how the data points are performing within the organization. If we collect data points for each segment of the benefits package based on a set criterion such as the number enrolled, the control chart will show us which benefits are being used the most by our human capital. From this we can use the data to make future changes to the benefits package we offer to the organization.

Control Charts or Pareto Charts to Show the Variation between Work Time and Leisure Time

One of the major issues confronting our profession is the balance present between the demands of the organization and the demands of the human capital assets for leisure time to unwind from the stress of the work environment. We can use the tools within the toolbox to plot data points comparing the workload to the amount of time off by function, pay rate, longevity within the organization, etc. The result is a visual management tool that allows us to see whether there really is an off the balance between the time expected to be on the job and what the human capital assets have at their disposal for other activities.

Tracking Complaints That Most Likely Will Lead to Employee Assistance Programs

We have all heard the proposition that we should leave our personal lives outside the workplace. We are so very cognizant of the fact that it is impossible to do that on a regular basis. It is therefore critically important that we keep track of the frequency and types of problems being referred to your Employee Assistance Programs. Through the Six Sigma toolbox there are a number of tools that can be used for this purpose.

Begin with control charts where the data can be constructed around the types of complaints and the frequency of the occurrence on whatever time period you want, although for the strength of the data we would not go less than a month at a time. The control chart would then in graph form show the rate of increase or decrease in the frequency of the complaints. It would also be possible to set up a control group of all the complaints compared to the rate of a single employee to determine if the rate of occurrence was out of sync with the rest of the organization. Following this, we would move the data points into a Pareto chart, which would graphically show whether the frequency rate was in sync with the rest of the organization.

CASE STUDY: DEVELOPMENT OF A CORPORATE POLICY MANUAL AND THE ASSOCIATED MANUALS

THE PROBLEM

We were contacted by a nonprofit organization which was growing their employee base dramatically to the point where they were now coming under the scrutiny of a number of major federal laws that governed organizations with at least 50 employees and to complicate the situation further they were federal contractors. Further the policies had not been reviewed in over three years.

THE PROCESS

Over a six-week period we reviewed 90 different policies that were in place and based on the applicable federal law we updated the wording of each one. We also added in the wording for the new laws that were now influencing the organizational decisions.

At the same time the organization acquired the license to implement an online version of the policy manual rather than distributing copies to each member of the staff.

As we were reviewing the current policy manual, based on benchmarking other similar organizations we were able to remove about 20 of these policies that either were not needed or combine them with other equivalent policies.

THE SOLUTION

As we finished the process of creating the new policy manual, we created for the client four separate but interdependent manuals for their staff, each of which was placed into the electronic format.

The first manual was the overall Policy Manual, which covered the normal areas of concern. Each of these policies was hyperlinked to archived versions of the policy in question, along with links to further explanations of the details.

The second manual was the Employee Handbook, which was the guide for the staff as to the expected behavior of staff in the workplace, along with the vision and mission statements.

The third manual was a procedures manual, which outlined for the staff what the steps were if they had a complaint that needed to be filed. It explained step by step what their responsibilities were and concluded with a process map of the complaint procedures.

The final manual was a process manual designed for management of the organization, which was the procedures manual with the addition of what management's responsibilities were following the filing of a complaint. It included a process map, which took it from the employee the process map and added what the manager's steps were to a conclusion.

There are several areas where the methodology can play a part within the Employee Relations space.

DATA ANALYSIS REGARDING ACCIDENT INCIDENTS

When we become aware of potential risk management issues, one of our first concerns is if this is an isolated issue or an ongoing critical factor that must be dealt with on an immediate basis. One of the ways to determine this is through the use of data mining charts, where we can establish the frequency by comparing the types of incidents on a monthly basis using several departments. The purpose is to show where the real problems are occurring. The data can then be placed in a Pareto chart to further delineate the frequency issues.

CREATING A KANBAN SYSTEM WITHIN THE WORKPLACE

One area of risk is what happens when an employee goes to pull a needed part or chemical for a process and finding none grabs something else that most likely will do the same thing. If the substitute is not correctly utilized injuries can happen. The Kanban system allows a vehicle to minimize this event.

A Kanban system consists of a visual queue being placed in the workplace where when supplies get to a certain point the system automatically alerts purchasing to order replacements. For example, you know that the process before requires a certain amount of chemicals to complete the task. On this basis you will use up the current supply within five weeks. You further know that it takes two weeks to receive the completed order. Then the system would alert you to order new stock approximately 7 weeks out. This allows you for the stock you have left plus the replacement period.

KAIZEN EVENTS TO CORRECT WORKPLACE ISSUES

Kaizen events are designed to correct problems in a rapid series of events. One of the participants within our Driving HR 500 seminar used this to correct back injuries that arose out of employees throwing heavy, large pallets for storing inventory. Through the process they were able to modify the process to lower the rate of back injuries.

CASE STUDY: ERGONOMICS CASE STUDY: THE DOW CHEMICAL COMPANY'S USE OF SIX SIGMA METHODOLOGY[12]

THE PROBLEM

Reducing Musculoskeletal Disorders

Ergonomics-related injuries, including musculoskeletal disorders (MSDs) caused by repetitive strains, continue to be a serious problem for employers. In 2002, ergonomics-related injuries accounted for a third of all workplace injuries involving missed work time, with an average absence of nine days per injury.[13] The resulting worker injury claims and loss of productivity are estimated to cost $13 million to $20 million per year for U.S. employers.[14] As computer workstation users spend more and more time at desktops, the risk of MSDs occurring has increased. Yet, as illustrated below, in many companies there are inherent difficulties and concerns associated with addressing this increased ergonomics risk.

For example, Tricia, the Environmental, Health and Safety (EH&S) Leader for the Specialty Chemicals Business of The Dow Chemical Company wants to reduce MSDs among computer workstation users throughout her business's various divisions and operations. Before she can understand what changes to make in either the workstations or the work practices in those divisions, she must identify the root causes of

MSDs among the operators. Although she has some theories, Tricia does not know for sure what factors are causing or contributing to the employees' MSD complaints. Only by knowing the root causes can she implement with confidence controls that would achieve positive results.

Tricia also suspects, but is not sure, that many of the root causes of MSDs are the same across the different operations and divisions in her business. Because of constraints on both her budget and time, Tricia would like to design one basic program that is flexible enough to implement company-wide. She also knows that any reductions achieved under the new program must be sustained over the long term, and she is concerned that over time employees and managers will "backslide" on their commitment to the program and return to their ergonomically risky behaviors.

Fortunately for Tricia, she could refer to a similar project successfully undertaken by the Design and Construction function of The Dow Chemical Company, which is discussed in the case study below. This project, which utilized a problem-solving methodology called "Six Sigma," offered an innovative way to address Tricia's concerns for the development and implementation of a sustainable program to reduce MSDs throughout her business.

THE SOLUTION

The Dow Chemical Company's Innovative Use of "Six Sigma"[15]

Avoiding ergonomics-related injuries is an important component of The Dow Chemical Company's ("Dow" or "the Company") overall emphasis on safety and health. Dow is a science and technology company that develops, manufactures and provides various chemical, plastic and agricultural products and services for customers in over 180 countries. In 1994, Dow adopted a set of voluntary 10-year EH&S goals to dramatically improve the company's performance by 2005. These goals call for a reduction in the company's reportable injury and illness rate by 90 percent to 0.24.

In 2000, the company identified an opportunity to improve its injury rate within the Dow Design and Construction business unit. Dow Design and Construction ("DDC") is responsible for managing the design and construction of Dow's facilities worldwide. Because DDC's approximately 1,250 workers (including employees and contractors) work primarily at desktop workstations, where they spend the majority of their time working at computer keyboards, they were increasingly susceptible to ergonomics injuries. While the rate of ergonomics-related injuries among the DDC workers was low (only three were reported in 1999), the company chose to make proactive improvements before ergonomic injuries increased in number or severity.

Dow's EH&S function decided to address ergonomic injuries at DDC using the "Six Sigma" problem-solving methodology. Six Sigma is a disciplined, process-oriented approach to problem solving, adopted by Dow and many other companies, which emphasizes the reduction of defects in processes, products and services by applying a four-step improvement methodology. Because Six Sigma emphasizes sustainable results over short-term fixes, Dow has found it particularly useful for EH&S projects. Following the steps prescribed under Six Sigma, Dow developed a Six Sigma project team, which first defined the primary contributing factors to MSDs in the DDC function and then sought to reduce those factors by 70 percent. While each of the four steps of the Six Sigma project is outlined below, a more detailed discussion of the Six Sigma methodology appears at the end of this case study.

Step 1: Measure

Once the Six Sigma project team developed its charter and defined its task, it then began by defining the current process. First, the team outlined the sequence of events from workstation assignment to task performance and potential injury. They next identified a series of key variables affecting the process outcome that included:

- User attributes (such as daily time at workstations)
- User behaviors (including posture, force and duration of use)
- Environmental factors

In this phase of the Six Sigma method, the "defect"—a measurable outcome of the process for which improvement is desired—is defined. While the true "defect" for this process would be the occurrence of an ergonomic injury, there were so few at the start of the project that measuring a statistically significant improvement was going to be difficult. Therefore, the key process variables identified were taken as the "defect," and a goal of 70 percent improvement (reduction) in the baseline level was set for the project. Scored surveys of DDC workstation users were developed and conducted on the variables identified and used to measure the baseline defect level.

Step 2: Analyze

Accurately identifying the root causes of a problem, which in turn leads to more effective improvements, is an essential function of the Six Sigma methodology. Therefore, the project team next analyzed the collected survey data to determine differences in the workstations, work environments, user training and behavior at the different DDC sites. The team then identified possible root causes underlying these variables using several of the Six Sigma tools and methodologies, including brainstorming, "fishbone" diagramming, a work performance matrix and Antecedent–Behavior–Consequence and Balance of Consequences analyses. After developing a list of possible root causes, the team used additional Six Sigma tools and methodologies to identify probable root causes and validate them. For example, one possible root cause identified was a failure of the employee to recognize the importance of ergonomics compliance to his or her personal well-being. This root cause was validated by the employee survey, in which many of the employees expressed an attitude of "it won't happen to me."

Other key root causes validated through this process were the lack of adjustable furniture at some worksites and a lack of "ownership" in personal safety on the part of the employee. The team also determined that ergonomics was not emphasized by DDC to the same extent as other, more immediate, safety issues such as the use of personal protective equipment in hazardous environments.

Step 3: Improve

After determining the most significant root causes through analysis and validation, the project team developed a series of improvements to correct the identified root causes, including both work-related and personal risk factors. Workstation deficiencies were easily addressed by implementing a workstation upgrade plan. Elevating workstation ergonomics to the same level of importance as other personal safety and health issues was a more challenging improvement. However, the team elevated the focus on workstation ergonomics by improving awareness on the part of management and employees and by altering employee behavior and work habits through increased accountability.

The project team developed a novel approach to raising employee awareness by collecting a series of personal testimonials from other employees and posting them on the company's intranet site. These testimonials were supplemented by more traditional communications, including regular workgroup safety meetings, training and increased ergonomics resources. At each facility, the company also designated Ergonomic Focal Points and Ergonomic Contacts, DDC workers who volunteered to receive specialized training and be available as the first point of contact for ergonomic concerns and questions. The team addressed employee behavior by providing feedback to individuals, creating a specific channel for early reporting of discomfort and developing a health assessment program to address the early warning signs of potential MSDs. Employee personal accountability was addressed by implementing a "Safety First" mentality that stressed ergonomics as a key issue in personal safety and not a separate stand-alone topic.

These improvements are not static but are a part of an ongoing ergonomics safety and health process. For example, while furniture improvements have been implemented, it is understood that the workstations will continually evolve to meet the employees' changing needs.

Step 4: Control

After the immediate improvements were implemented, the project team developed a long-term control plan designed to sustain the achievements. The control plan took the sequence of events which might contribute to an injury, as outlined in the measure step, and added a series of performance standards, measures, responsibilities and contingency plans. For example, in the original sequence, an employee was instructed to attend ergonomics training when starting a job, but there was no control measure to ensure this took place. Under the control plan, the employee is now required to attend the training within 30 days of job assignment, and the designated Ergo Contact at the job site is alerted and follows up with the employee if the employee fails to attend within that timeframe. Each step in the sequence has a similar control, ensuring that the improved process is followed long after the conclusion of the project.

RESULTS OF THE PROJECT

DDC made immediate improvements in the identified risk factors, which have been reduced 64 percent since the baseline measurement and by more than 45 percent overall. These improvements have been well received by the DDC's management and workers, and employees are proactive in addressing discomfort and have a better understanding of the personal benefits of ergonomics. As improvements like these have been repeated throughout the company, the severity of ergonomics injuries has declined. In 2001, 53 percent of the company's ergonomic injuries resulted in lost work time or advanced medical treatment. However, in 2003, only 30 percent of ergonomic injuries were this severe; the remaining 70 percent of cases required only first aid or precautionary measures. This result, in turn, has contributed to Dow's 2005 goal of reducing the company's reportable injury and illness rate by 90 percent to 0.24. Moreover, by virtue of the Six Sigma methodology's emphasis on long-term control, the project has developed an ongoing process that will help the DDC sustain its immediate results and continue to improve. The positive results of this project have been shared with Tricia and other EH&S managers at other business units, leading to similar projects throughout the company.

Dow believes that using Six Sigma for EH&S projects such as these enables employers to develop program improvements based on measurement and analysis, rather than speculation, resulting in a more cost-efficient and sustainable fix that will yield benefits indefinitely. Rather than undertaking costly trial and error attempts at solutions, the company was able to identify the root causes of ergonomic injuries with confidence and make improvements to the ergonomics program in a systematic and sustainable way.

SIDEBAR: SIX SIGMA METHODOLOGY

The Greek letter sigma (σ) is used in mathematics to represent standard deviation or how much a process varies from its average value. Under the Six Sigma methodology, deficiencies are described in terms of "defects" per million opportunities, with a score of 6σ equal to 3.4 defects per million opportunities. Six Sigma uses the following four-step process known as MAIC (Measure, Analyze, Improve, Control) to significantly reduce defects in processes, products and/or services:

Step 1: Measure—clearly define the process to be improved and the "defect" for the project and identify a clear and appropriate measure for the "defect"

Step 2: Analyze—determine the root causes of the defect

Step 3: Improve—develop solutions to address the root causes and validate process improvement

Step 4: Control—implement a long-term strategy to ensure that the improvements are sustained

The methodology can be applied to any process that allows the measurement of benefits and improvements in defect reduction, whether in the manufacture of a product, the delivery of a service, the control of costs or management of injuries and illnesses.

Dow has adopted the Six Sigma methodology to accelerate the company's improvement in quality and productivity. Dow has expanded the use of the Six Sigma approach to help manage the aspects of the company's operations beyond production and quality, including the safety and health of its workforce. Some of the projects to which Dow has applied the Six Sigma methodology include:

- Reduction of repetitive stress injuries
- Reduction of motor vehicle accidents
- Improved safety for visitors (especially contractors)
- Site logistics risk reduction
- Off-the-job safety process improvement

These projects have been key components of Dow's 2005 Environmental, Health and Safety Goals, which include reducing Dow's reportable injury and illness rate by 90 percent to 0.24 percent.

As the example in our case study illustrates, Dow's Environmental Health and Safety (EHS) function has found the Six Sigma methodology particularly useful in identifying and validating root causes that are hard to discern because of their subjectivity and in focusing improvements to an ergonomics program in ways that caused measurable improvements. Moreover, since the Six Sigma process includes the implementation of controls to ensure that achievements are sustained over a long-term period, the company expects to realize the benefits of its efforts for years to come.

Notes

1. Human Resource Certification Institute. *SPHR Exam Content Outline at-a-Glance.* https://www.hrci.org/docs/default-source/web-files/sphr-exam-content-outline.pdf?sfvrsn=7fc44f61_22

2. Mathis, Robert L. *Human Resource Management,* 12th edition. Mason, OH: Thomson Publishing, 2008, Page 61.

3. Provided and reprinted with permission from Toppazzini and Lee Consulting of Ottawa, California. http://www.TLeecorp.com

4. http://hre.lrp.com/HRE/story.jsp?storyId=186721619

5. The Cost of Hire Worksheet was created with QI Macros. An editable copy can be found at https://drive.google.com/file/d/11tYneG_5nDiGnq3lxCxHfh bqfw01Mx5T/view?usp=sharing

6. Reprinted with permission of BMGI found at http://www.BMGI.com

7. Reprinted with permission of Guidon Performance Solution. http://GuidonPS .com

8. Reprinted with the permission of the Ceridian Corporation. The full case study with full documentation can be found at http://www.ceridian.com/www/co ntent/9998/15514/15571/16532/16869/ceridian_best_practices_recruiting.pdf

9. http://www.workforce.com/article/20090126/NEWS01/301269979

10. Training refers to those programs where we increase an employee's ability to complete a process, i.e., run a machine or utilize an applicant tracking system. Education refers to programs designed to increase an employee's career portfolio and enable them to become more engaged employees, mostly oriented around soft skills.

11. Quality Function Deployment Tool is a method of determining what both managers and employees expect out of the training programs. It shows each stage of the process and what the expectations are to deliver high-quality training quicker and less expensive.

12. Reprinted from http://www.osha.gov/dcsp/success_stories/compliance_assistan ce/dow_casestudy.html

13. March 2004 U.S. Department of Labor News Release Regarding Bureau of Labor Statistics Survey of Occupational Injuries and Illnesses.

14. A Critical Review of "Epidemiologic Evidence for Work-Related Musculoskeletal Disorders of the Neck, Upper Extremity, and Low Back," The National Institute for Occupational Safety and Health.

15. This case study was developed from the information provided by Karen Kearns, Industrial Hygiene Specialist, and Mark Spence, Manager, North American Health and Safety Regulatory Affairs, The Dow Chemical Company.

Chapter 9

How to Implement the TLS Continuum

Introduction

The question that remains is if the concepts I have discussed so far present some promise in assisting you in bringing HR excellence to your organization how do I do it? In this chapter I will walk you through the three pillars to accomplish that task (Figure 9.1).

Pillar #1: Voice of the Customer

I have stressed since the first pages of this book that the crucial factor in any continuous process improvement effort and in the TLS Continuum is the voice of the customer. They are the ones that tell us when something is wrong. When we look at the role of the voice of the customer and how we respond to their demands there are several strategies that contribute a major impact on the system constraint resolution.

Strategy #1: Walk the Walk, Talk the Talk and Do the Gemba Walk

As managers we can sit in our wood-paneled conference room around the big table and brainstorm all day long about the existence of problems, their potential causes and potential solutions. But all of that is anecdotal in

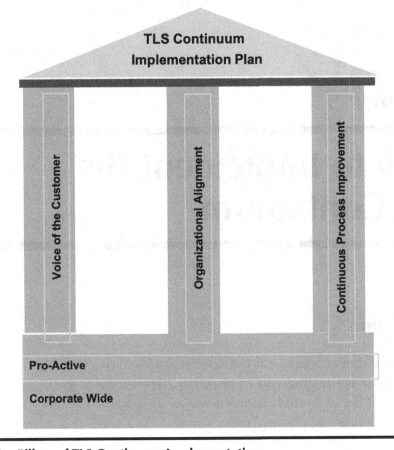

Figure 9.1 Pillars of TLS Continuum Implementation.

nature. That is based on someone's thoughts, not on evidence-based data. The solution is to get out of the office.

The Gemba Walk originated with the work of Taiichi Ohno at Toyota. He liked to take his managers and have them stand in a circle on the factory floor (Gemba) and observe the processes in action. Hye would stand there for half an hour at a time and watch. At the end of the period, Ohno would ask them what they saw, and if they could not find process constraints, he would send them back to the floor again. In essence a Gemba Walk means go and see.

In order to gain a clear picture, I suggest that you anticipate three separate Gemba Walks. The first walk is to choose any of your products and start at your receiving deck and follow a part, from the back door to the front door. Watch how each part moves through the process, and like Ohno's managers look for what may be holding up the process. At the same time, you need to recognize you are only looking at a third of the pie.

The second Gemba Walk is a backward one. Take that part that you followed through your process and track it back through your supplier's processes. See how that part came in their back door and follow it to your back door.

The final Gemba Walk is forward in nature. Follow your product or service from your shipping desk to the back door of the customer and follow the product through their processes. This will provide you with some insight into why the customer is finding issues with your organization.

The goal here is to see the problem, feel the problem and then take whatever steps are needed to create a new normal—removing the system constraint so that the process flows smoother until you find the next system constraint.

Strategy #2: Focus on the Process

I guess it is human nature to discover a problem and assume that it is somebody's fault it happened. When your organization has a process system constraint, it is never about a person. It is always something wrong with the system. It is the process flow that does not meet the needs of the customer. It is the process design that throws up system constraints to the timely response. It is the customer demands that throws up system constraints to the timely response.

Part of the TLS Continuum tells us that we need to focus our efforts on five areas within your organization. Eliyahu Goldratt in his book *The Goal* tells us that the five focusing steps to resolve the issue are (1) to identify the system constraint which we did as we walked through the TLS part of the process; (2) decide how to exploit the constraint; (3) subordinate everything to the constraint; (4) if necessary, elevate the constraint; and then (5) return to step 1. The overall goal is to identify the system constraint and take specific actions to remove it. You can't undertake that effort unless you understand the process. You can't undertake that effort unless you walk the walk, talk the talk and do the Gemba Walk.

Strategy #3: Do It Now

Human beings are known for their tendency to procrastinate. Just think back when you were in High School and College as to when you tended to try and work on assignments. At the last minute, right?

Corporate America is also known for its methods of arriving at a decision, usually by committee mentality. The direct result is that any attempt to reach a conclusion, regarding process system constraints, is to postpone indefinitely. The only way to resolve the tendency is to do it yesterday.

In the real estate field, we have a clause on the contract that states that time is of the essence. The idea behind the clause is that the contract requires prompt and timely fulfillment of the obligations under the contract. Continuous process improvement is no different. Your customer has a problem, and they want it resolved yesterday. It is your responsibility to attend to the problem now rather than yesterday.

Strategy #4: Gain Knowledge

I am totally cognizant that much of what I have presented to you so far is almost like trying to speak a foreign language for the first time. But there is a solution. Take whatever steps are necessary to better understand the concepts.

This knowledge comes in two facets. The first is knowledge of your organization. Learn how your processes work by taking the Gemba Walk. Talk to the front-line workers and ask them about the processes they work on. Understand why and how you do things in the way you do.

The second facet is gaining a better knowledge about the TLS Continuum tools. Learn how to use them and when. Further utilize the Internet and locate courses, seminars and webinars that can enhance your knowledge of the TLS Continuum. Go to Amazon or Barnes and Noble and research books on process improvement and order and read some of the available titles. (See the Further Reading list at the end of this book for some suggestions.)

Pillar #2: Organizational Alignment

The second pillar, the TLS Continuum Implementation plan, is that of organizational alignment. Every organization has its unique set of mission statements, values and strategies. They are all fed by the unique corporate culture. In order for the implementation plan to be successful, the organization as a whole must buy into the plan. The organization must walk the walk and talk the talk.

Like the voice of the customer pillar, the organizational alignment pillar consists of a series of strategies that help the process on its journey.

Strategy #5: Change Managers to Leaders

Dr. Jeffrey Liker,[1] in his discussions regarding the Toyota Production System, has represented a different focus for corporate management. In this new corporate culture, the role of management is not to occupy that corner office. It is not to turn to the organizational assets and say this is the way we going to do it and there is no room for further discussions. It is time for management to take on a new focus. We are no longer managers but rather leaders of the organization.

We however emphasize that the new role as the corporate leader is grounded in the idea that your role is to be both a problem solver and a guide toward professional development. Your role now is one of leading the cultural change in such a way as to maximize the results of the changes. It is not to be a slave driver of those who report to you. As we stated earlier the command-and-control method is basically obsolete in today's workplace. Your Gen X and Gen Y human capital assets will not tolerate it, to begin with. We are not suggesting that managers have to become buddies of their co-workers, but they must learn how to work as part of an overall team within the organization. They must understand that in the role of the leader they are guides to the improvement process and do not control the ultimate outcomes. The outcomes are determined by the team, and the leader has the responsibility to assist the team in the implementation of those outputs.

The other side of the coin is that our leaders must strive to transform their organizations. This effort is critical to successful process improvement. It does not serve the organization well to just becoming leaders; you must transform the organization.

The vast majority of leaders we have encountered during our consulting practice have been ***transactional leaders***[2] in nature. By this we mean that their efforts are centered on the concept of what they do. There was a time and place when being a transactional leader was the proper and realistic role for the HR professional. It was a time when the reason we were there was to handle the administrative duties of the professional. Our daily lives were centered on the actions we took every day to resolve employee issues. When the employee had a problem with a paycheck or a policy question we were the go-to person for the resolution. This was what we do.

When we transition to ***transformational leadership***, our views of the workplace change. The response becomes one of how what we deliver as Human Resource Professionals fit within the new corporate cultural perspective.

Today's global workplace calls for a renewed focus on our roles. As the organizational strategic initiatives become more critical in the economic market, the HR profession is likewise required to show how what we deliver to the organization is part of those initiatives. We need to be heavily involved in the development of our human capital assets by providing programs to enhance their skills. If we are in fact planning our operations based on perpetuity, we need to develop succession plans for management roles within the organization to ensure that future leaders are where we need them, when we need them and how we need them.

There has much been written over the past couple of years regarding the transformational leader, with a good chance I would be duplicating good work. I suggest you go to Amazon or Barnes and Noble and ask about book titles regarding the term. Barnes and Noble alone bring up 1,294 entries of titles on the topic.

Strategy #6: Educate and Train

While I recognize that in the scientific method and the DMAIC process the solution is arrived at by a series of trial-and-error efforts upon the part of the team members, I will also contend that this change in corporate cultural can't be obtained by a sink or swim attitude. We need to begin the process by ensuring that the entire organization understands what is in it for them (WITFM) from the earliest point in the implementation process. This will come about from a vigorous range of educational programs, which in the very end compare the current and future states of the organization with a concentration on why the change is being made and how it will affect the rank and file of the organization. The education must come from direct communication to all segments of the organization from the corner office to the person in the maintenance department. The communications must be continuous and with a clear message as to the direction we are headed. One of the direct results of this effort will be the identification of those individuals who can't or won't make the required alterations in the way they perform their responsibilities. We fully understand that both members of management and the rank and file are going to feel totally out of place in the new environment of changed corporate culture. This new workspace is not how they were trained to believe organizations functioned. But this is a different world view than what they grew up in. It is not a bad thing if they feel they need to move on.

On the flip side of the coin, we have undertaken the steps of the DMAIC process to resolve a particular problem within your organization. We have looked at the problem and measured how the process is operating. We then analyzed the results for its creditable, verifiable data, which led us to make changes within the process and established a standard of work going forward. The standard of work will quite likely lay out new methods for performing the process within the organization. You are left with two choices—the first is to undertake a management edict as we discussed earlier and let the organization continue to try and reach the goal based on how it has always done things. The other option is to design an employee development program, which takes the new process steps and trains the organization on how the new process looks and behaves. The training program must put the employee base in the position of understanding how the cultural changes and process changes in the long run should make their jobs easier.

Strategy #7: Breakdown Silos

Silos are the bane of our existence. As the global marketplace has evolved everything, we do affect the total organization. As a result, when we start acting from the perspective that it is not our job or that it is someone else's responsibility, then we find ourselves falling into the silo mentality. It is when we fully realize that as John Donne said, "No man is an island," we understand that the reason we implement cross-functional teams is that what we decide to do will affect HR, finance, purchasing, etc. Every part of the organization is directly affected by continuous process improvement efforts. In turn we need to act like we understand that. Don't misunderstand me—I am not saying that functional areas do not have a place in the organization; they definitely do. However, the functional areas are a part of a much bigger picture and in order to implement this we need to encompass the improvement suggestions from across the spectrum of the ideas from employees.

The purpose of the cross-functional team is to take into consideration all the available views regarding organizational issues. When we allow office politics to enter into the picture we are asking for trouble. When we allow a function or an individual to claim their department or job as sacred ground, our improvement efforts fail.

Strategy #8: Avoid Quotas

Many of our organizations tend to quantify their operations base on some hypothetical numbers. Ask your salespeople whether their sales quota is reasonable. Most will tell you it is not. The establishment of arbitrary goals

helps nobody within the organization. Instead let the TLS Continuum methodology set the targets for improvement. The people within the organization
who will recognize if the numerical goals are reasonable are the rank and
file, not the managers per se.

Quotas do not set the data points for problem resolution. Creditable,
verifiable data does. The cross-functional teams will determine what the
appropriate outputs are for the organization. These should be the basis for
the organizational goals and strategic initiatives.

Strategy #9: Coach

In Strategy #6, I discussed that the role of management was to educate
and train the organization on the new processes. Not everything is going
to work the way you plan it; that is just human nature. It is imperative that
your leaders are there to help the organization through the valleys. The leaders need to assist with the exploration of alternatives that will resolve those
issues. The coaching has to be from a beneficial point of view rather than
a punishment. Remember a coach does not create solutions; they assist in
finding the solutions by the questions and observations they make. It is not
the role to be the single source of solutions; nor is it the leader's responsibility to solve the issue by inserting their knowledge or effort.

As a coach, the transformational leader needs to work with the human
capital asset to reinforce what is expected and where they are falling short.
From there the leaser is tasked with helping the employee to understand
what needs to be done to get the employee up to where they need to be.
If there are still problems, then the leader should consider coaching the
employee in the direction of a different career.

Pillar #3: Continuous Process Improvement

The final pillar in the TLS Continuum Implementation plan is that of
continuous process improvement. It is the essence of what we do. Peter
Pande tells us that there is always a better way. The TLS Continuum tells
us that once we identify the system constraint and eliminate it, another
constraint will appear requiring us to start the process once more. Upon
the review of our process improvement efforts, we find that there are
some strategies which will enhance the potential for a successful improvement effort.

Strategy #10: Long-Term Planning to Optimize Your Service Offerings

If we return to the Introduction, we discussed that we were commencing a journey. And while we said that this journey had no end, we still can't begin to embark on the journey without some initial planning. Whether it is your vacation or the road to continuous improvement, we have to begin by planning what we are going to do.

A business colleague told me recently that the goal of every organization is to plan, based on the idea that your organization will survive until the end of time. In this day and age that might seem to be unrealistic, but consider the alternative. Are you going to tell your human assets that "we really appreciate the service you have given to this organization, but we only expect to be around for say three months?" Are you going to tell your customers that we can meet your voice of the customer demands but for only three months, which is when we expect to be out of business? I would have to believe that it is most likely not your method of operations.

This initial journey planning contains multiple facets in order to achieve the successful implementation of TLS Continuum into your organization. These factors include understanding the corporate culture, the value of human capital assets to the organization, the decision-making process and in the long term what do you want the organization to look like.

Your corporate culture is what tells the world who and what your organization is. This corporate culture is the basis for everything we do or say in the name of the organization. The problem is that it is easy to define in its original state, but it is highly difficult to change it once you have established it. To implement a TLS Continuum process within the organization is a necessity. It is not a wish. It is not we will get to it when we can. The change is the very first step in that implementation path.

Corporate culture determines how we approach both our internal assets and our ultimate end users. As we begin the process, we have to start with the understanding that this process will turn the organization on its head. The new corporate culture will have a dramatic effect on the very essence of the organization. Cultural change is required because we are changing the way we approach organizational policies and procedures. In discussions with Kent Linder of Systems Thinking, this change of culture can have both a positive and negative impact on the organization. In the field of mergers and acquisitions it tends to have a negative impact as elements of the corporate culture are lost. It can have a positive effect if the change is created with a participatory direction. By this we mean that the changes are brought about by the involvement of the entire organization.

The new corporate culture reorients the organization from an internal focus to one based on the wants and needs of the customer who purchases our products or services. The change causes us to take a deep review of how we operate and the activities that we undertake, which provide no value to the customer. That is not what they pay us to deliver. The impetus therefore falls on your organization. This cultural change also means that we have to look internally to see how our current values, mission and policies relate to the rest of the internal organization.

In Chapter 2, I defined HR excellence in part by stating that HR excellence means dreaming more than others think practical about the potential for your organization. What is the role of the human capital assets in that definition? It may on the face of it sound like a stupid question, but in reality, it is at the heart of the cultural change we are implementing. Another aspect of this question is, how do you categorize your human capital—expense or asset? Your answer will dictate how effective the corporate cultural implementation will be.

In our breakout session entitled *Who Am I: The Role of Human Capital within the Global Workplace*, we challenge the participants to look at the evolution of these assets from the agriculture period to the knowledge period. Many organizations still function from the belief that we are still in the industrial age. In this period our human capital assets were just a number and as such treated as an item on the balance sheet from the expense column. The direct results are that when we enter difficult economic times, the immediate action is to cut headcount. The human capital assets are disregarded in the long run for their contribution to the organization. The management needs to come to the understanding that in the global marketplace our employees are non-owned, leased corporate assets which are critical to the success of the organization. While the impetus for the change has to come from the top management, it also involves the active role of the entire organization. The best ideas for the critical aspects of this change come not from the top but the front line of the organization. They are the ones who recognize the changes which will make the organization operate more effectively.

Strategy #11: Always a Better Way

At the beginning of this work, we asked you to consider that you were taking a journey. It was a journey but was like none you ever have taken in your lifetime. This journey has a beginning but does not have a set ending. The reason for this is as we implement the TLS process, we uncover system constraints, which impose non-value-added aspects to your processes which slow down the organization. As the process continues, we remove those system constraints and establish a standard of work going forward. We have removed any variations from the process following the roadblock elimination.

The result of the implementation of the TLS process within your organization is that we have found a new method for uncovering the detriments to a well-oiled organization. We have done very well in meeting the demands of the customer based on the voice of the customer surveys we have conducted. But the irony of the process is that once we remove one of the system constraints another one shows up. We then need to recommit the process once again. The rule of thumb is described by Jeffrey Liker in his recent book *Toyota Way to Lean Leadership: Achieving and Sustaining Excellence through Leadership Development*. We talked earlier in the chapter on the TLS Continuum toolbox that our ultimate goal was to create a standard work for each of our processes. The key to discovering problems is that anything that varies from the standard of work is the problem. The result is that as we identify these variations from the standard of work, we find new system constraints that must be removed. Once we identify the new system constraint, we need to start the process over in its entirety including new project charters. The usual time frame is approximately every three to six months. The proponents of the Ultimate Improvement Cycle will tell you that the discovery of the new system constraint happens almost instantaneously.

It is critical that we release that nothing is forever. It means that we need to be ready to change in a heartbeat. That change means that we are improving the total organization going forward.

Strategy #12: Drive for Zero Defects

Allow me to step back in time a little bit and reconsider the improvement and control part of the DMAIC process. We discussed earlier that once we had defined the problem, measured the results and analyzed the creditable and verifiable data, we then turned to establish how we removed the variations in the processes.

Once we established the standard of work for the process at hand, it put in place a system to ensure that there was a smaller opportunity for making errors in the processes. On the factory floor this included such things as a pegboard containing the outlines of all the tools. Thus, the factory workers knew that when they were finished with a tool, we placed it back in its appropriate space. The service end of the spectrum and HR, in particular, can introduce steps to eliminate or drastically reduce the chance for mistakes. Through the use of such tools as Kanban we can ensure that the chance for errors within the HR process is diminished. In the Kanban environment in those instances where you have a supply of parts, the card is placed in the supply bin to alert you when you need to order new ones so there is never the circumstance where you do not have them when needed.

Remember that we stated earlier that one of our responsibilities is to get the service delivery to the customer when they want it, where they want it and how they want it. It does not mean going back to the customer and stating that you know they needed delivery by next Tuesday; however, we made some mistakes in following the orders and the service will be ready for delivery a week later. Rework is a variation from the customer's point of view. Our goal is not to do rework. So to achieve that goal requires us to ensure that we make as few errors as possible.

Strategy #13: Drive Out Fear

How many of you have seen the television commercial in which the speaker is suggesting that the company consider starting a new television channel with VJs and the response is laughter from the executives in the room, with one of them scoffing, what next a weather channel.

Suggestion boxes were started in order to get a handle on the pulse of the employees. It was an attempt to enhance employee engagement through the use of collecting suggestions from employees on how to improve the workplace. The drawback was that the retribution for suggesting something contrary to the management policy could and did result in terminations and in some cases even death. This brings us to the problem present in many of our modern organizations.

In an unscientific poll of some of my fellow HR professionals the consensus was that while all suggestions are considered many are shot down for a wide range of reasons. Any of these sound familiar? That is not the way we do things around here. We tried that; it did not work. Our shareholders would not like it. That is not the way the management wants it done.

The change in corporate culture brought about by the introduction of the Six Sigma methodology relies on the premise that every employee's input has merit. We fully recognize that not everything will work every time and in every place. The difference here is that if we try something and it does not work the recourse is not to tell the employee that you made your suggestion, and it didn't work. It is not to tell the employee that you tried something that never should have been done and it will affect your career. We go back to the define stage and review our plans and see if there is another route, we can go to tackle the problem.

The implementation of the TLS Continuum into your organization is not difficult. With the use of a few logical-thinking-based tools any organization can do so. I would recommend that you order any of Bob Sproull's books, especially his latest *The Secret of Maximum Profitability* in which Bob walks you through the entire process from start to finish. Some of the tools will be seen in Chapter 10.

Notes

1. Beginning with the Toyota Way (2003) and followed with seven subsequent titles, Dr. Liker has laid out the benefits of the Toyota Leadership System, which differs greatly from the Western Management Model. See the Further Reading list for a full list of the titles.
2. Transactional Leadership as discussed at http://en.wikipedia.org/wiki/Transactional_leadership

Chapter 10

The Road to HR Excellence

At this juncture I need to return to Chapter 1 and our discussion about HR excellence. While I discussed HR excellence in general terms, walking the road to HR excellence is not a haphazard journey; it's not something that will happen by chance. I also presented four characteristics of HR excellence. In this final chapter I want to explore the road to achieving HR excellence and the four characteristics more in greater detail.

CARING More about Your Organization Than Others Think Wise

In their 2018 Engagement Research Report, the Gallup Organization found that about half of all the respondents were not engaged with their organizations. They come to work for that paycheck and may be the benefits. They could care less about whether the organization is meeting the needs of the voice of the customer. Their belief is that management is there for its shareholders and how much money the organization can make. The FTEs are basically just a number to the organization. As long as the work gets done, the organization doesn't care about the health of the workforce.

HR excellence means an entirely new way to envision the future. HR excellence means that the entire span of the organization is fully engaged with the management and with the human capital assets that are vital to the success going forward. It means that the human capital assets are engaged in the processes. They feel comfortable expressing their concerns when something is not right. The human capital assets own the various processes within your organization.

Not everyone will be happy with this new focus. You need to recognize that there is a segment of your organization that believes that the organization exists solely for the shareholders. They believe that management's sole view is how much money they can make. They believe that they are just a cog in the system and that their success is of secondary importance in the total picture.

In order to achieve HR excellence in this new normal everyone must equally care for the vitality of the organization. Everyone must be on the same page as to the values, missions, goals and strategies expressed by the organization to their stakeholders. The organization must be founded on the best outcomes for management, human capital assets customers, suppliers and anyone else who contributes to the success of the operations.

RISKING More Than Others Think Safe to Change the Corporate Culture

Understand that the road to HR excellence is a risk issue. The road to HR excellence is not free; there are costs involved. There are financial costs. There are time costs. There are emotional costs. There are cultural costs.

The financial costs come from the monies dispensed to buy equipment. There are funds expensed to train the organization on the new equipment. With that there are the expenditures of time that take parts of the organization away from their regular jobs to be trained on the new processes. Probably the most involved costs come from the tendency of most individuals to prefer the status quo. Why change, everything seems alright. There is a cost when you upset this balance in the organizational life. Until they accept the changes the organization will have a difficult time making the necessary changes.

The final area of costs and risk is that of the cultural realm. Think about your organization for a moment. Is your corporate culture one that that is risk adverse? Does the corporate culture tend toward playing it safe? Thomas Edison tells us that the more we try and fail shows us the way to what works. Management needs to encourage experimentation with new ideas without the human capital assets fearing for their jobs if something does not go right. The organization needs to say yes; we know there is risk involved in what we are trying to undertake. But the expected deliverables are worth the risk. We know the approach that the organization has taken in the past, times are different, and we need to accept the risk of trying to resolve the issues in a new fashion.

DREAMING More Than Others Think Practical about the Potential for Your Organization

How often do you practice stereotyping the individuals within your organization? You claim you don't do it? We all unconsciously do it. We all falsely believe in the potential of each person we hire.

The road to HR excellence is grounded in Napoleon Hill's belief that whatever the mind can conceive and believe it will achieve. The road expects that as an organization you will be open to the possibilities of where your organization can go. There is a wide variety of organizations who have found it beneficial to both the organization's bottom line and the well-being to give the human capital assets time to let their minds run free and see what they can conceive. A good example is the work of Dr. Steven Silver, who while working on some work in the 3M labs, discovered the use of adhesives along one edge of a piece of paper, which became the all-too-familiar Post-it note.

Successful completion of the road to HR excellence requires that your organization acknowledge and encourage the expansion to full-spectrum thinking around what your organization can do.

EXPECTING More Than Others Find Possible from Your Human Capital Assets

The one remaining aspect of the road to HR excellence takes our new-found belief in the power of your organization and applies it to the power of what our individual human capital assets can achieve. HR excellence is founded in the introduction of the diversity of ideas in seeking out solutions to the problems before the organization. HR excellence is founded in the willingness to let go of control and permitting human capital assets to take actions that will help our customers. Whether it is the Toyota Anon tool or just going to get of their way to assist a customer with their issues, the human capital assets must be free to take actions when they are called for.

Even if you accept the four conditions of HR excellence at their face value, there is still the question of how we implement this new philosophy. There are a set of tools that will enable you to make the required changes to your corporate culture to achieve this goal of HR excellence.

The tools described below lay out a roadmap to demonstrate both internally and externally that you are committed to this path. The tools include the logical thinking process's Goal Tree, the self-assessment of your involvement within your organization through the Involvement Questionnaire and the calculation of ideal workload so that you can maintain a level response time to request for assistance from your managers and customers and finally a new way to look at how we handle the determination of costs within your organization.

Employee Involvement Questionnaire

The Employee Involvement Questionnaire (copy of which can be found on Google Drive at (https://drive.google.com/file/d/1wG_S9vv2TnT3z61yYiCz _LMe9Fsocjm8/view?usp=sharing) is a self-assessment of the status of your role in continuous process improvement within your organization. It looks at your involvement from three independent but interdependent focuses.

The first area is that of your own personal involvement. It begins to ask whether your job description adequately describes your role in the organization. Remember part of the HR excellence roadmap is to educate, train and coach. So, at the same time you are analyzing whether your role is described in your job description, there is also in place a development plan to carry you forward into the future with your job responsibilities. Is there room for you to grow? The last two areas that the questionnaire looks at are whether the organization provides you with the various tools that you need and whether as part of the education and training effort the organization has provided you with a basic knowledge of the process improvement methodology.

The combination of the questions in part one provides you with a baseline for the remainder of the calculation of your total involvement.

The second area is that of functional involvement. We began with the personal role in the improvement effort; the second level considers how that role plays out in the role of the HR function, and the first question extends the first section by asking whether you are personally involved in the HR function. I don't mean that you are involved in the role of the organizational fireman. I am referring to whether or not you are involved in the development of the department and organizational strategy. I asked above whether there was a personal development plan in existence; I am now concerned about whether your HR management is involved in that development by truly caring for your well-being within the department. In that same vein we find that there exists a two-edged sword. On one side is that the organization and HR management set clear expectations for the staff regarding the performance levels the organization needs and expects. In the same area, management needs to be open to contributions from you when there is something that is not right. The last area that needs to be reviewed here is whether you have had the opportunity to serve on a cross-functional team. I am not referring to an interdepartmental team but one that is comprised of representatives from departments across the organization—one that looks at problems from many aspects.

The final area takes the personal and functional involvement and carries to the organization as a whole. It looks at how involved you are in the organizational improvement effort. I discussed in the previous chapter the need for the improvement effort to become the corporate mantra. At this juncture the concentration turns to the level of involvement in that corporate mantra. Are you fully involved? Partially involved? Not very involved and, if so, why not? I also touched on the idea that there is always a better way. Part of that is that the cross-functional teams need to look at the problem resolution effort and see if there is something overlooked that would improve the teamwork the next time the team gathers to identify the path to system constraint removal.

Another critical in the continuous improvement process concerns the nature of the data we collect. There is always good data that meets our needs, and then there is data that may be great to have but does not influence the outcomes. It is the responsibility of the teams to lay out the data they need and of management to know what makes good data versus what's nice to have data points.

Each of these options is rated on a scale of 1–5, with 5 being strongly agreeing with the item being evaluated. The resulting scores are then averaged. Any score under a 4 should pen the discussion for ways to improve your involvement going forward.

The ultimate goal of the questionnaire is to lead to HR having a seat at the C-suite table to be an active participant in the design of the strategic efforts behind the corporate alignment to the missions, values and corporate culture changes.

Traffic Intensity

In order to gain an organization that runs smoothly, it is necessary that the level of work in progress (WIP) is kept at an ideal level flowing through the system. The TLS Continuum presents us with two tools to achieve that effort. The first tool is TAKT time, which we discussed on page XXX. TAKT time is a mathematical equation to determine the processing time to complete a process. It is calculated by completing the formula shown below.

$$(TAK\ time) = Net\ available\ time\ to\ work\ divided\ by\ the\ customer\ demand$$

In other words, the time it takes to complete the process is calculated by the amount of time available to work divided by the number of units per day requested by the customer.

The other tool is the use of determining the traffic intensity of the work that is in the system. You can find a copy of the traffic intensity calculator on Google drive at the link shown below: https://dbaiconsulting.com/tools

In TAKT time, we look at the available time in a day divided by the number of demands by the voice of the customer. In the traffic intensity calculator, we take the time available to resolve the issues divided by the number of new requests divided by the number of human capital assets available to solve the problems. The result is a percentage figure of the level of problem traffic. If the resulting percentage is less than 80 percent then the WIP level is manageable and the department can continue to function as it is. In the range from 80% to 100%, there may be some delay in response, but it is still workable. However, if the percentage exceeds 100%, then the problem request level must be changed in order to reduce the intensity levels. Failure to do so will overload the system and create unnecessary waste in the process.

Goal Tree

On page XXX, I presented the Goal Tree as a way to lay out potential system constraints in the use of the TLS Continuum Problem Resolution Guide. Its purpose was to present the process problem along with what might be the cause of the problem and what might be the cause of the cause (Figure 10.1).

The original idea behind the Goal Tree comes from the works of several individuals. Back in 1995 a TOC expert named Oded Cohen, who worked

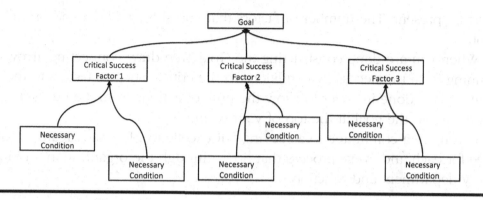

Figure 10.1   The goal tree.

for the Goldratt Institute, conceived of the concept behind the Goal Tree in a tool that he referred to as an Intermediate Objective Map. H. William Dettmer in his book *The Logical Thinking Process* changed the name to a Goal Tree. Bob Sproull in his book *The Ultimate Improvement Cycle* further discussed the use of the Goal Tree in the improvement process.

The Goal Tree simplifies to a point the process of laying out the problem resolution efforts of your organization. The easiest way to demonstrate this is to walk through the construction of a typical Goal Tree.

The process begins by taking a blank sheet of paper or a white board, and after identifying the problem, draw a square at the top. The square is labeled with the number 100 to indicate its location, and then the problem is entered in the box in the form of a full statement with an ultimate goal. For instance, if you are trying to reduce the time to hire, that first box might read at location 100 the problem is stated that "the organization will reduce the time to hire by say 12 days."

On the next level under that graphic, create a series of no more than five (5) identical graphics and number them accordingly to establish their location. These five graphics or boxes represent the critical success factors (CSF). These are statements which state that in order to reduce the time to hire by 12 days these events must take place. It is perfectly acceptable to enter a performance metric in each of these boxes. Again, for instance, one of the CSFs could read that in order to reduce the time to hire by 12 days, the initial interview must be held within 2 days of the receipt of the application. You want to be sure that you place a similar metric in the remaining boxes.

The next and final level of the Goal Tree refers to the necessary conditions in order for the critical factors to exist. Again, represent them by a box and number each. The statement here should describe the conditions that must be present. The number of factors that you show will depend on the problem.

When you are done constructing the Goal Tree draw connecting arrows running from the necessary conditions to the critical success factors to the goal. This is done in order to show the flow of actions from the necessary conditions to the goal at the top of your diagram.

If you are a committee to achieving HR excellence, I would create a Goal Tree for each and every process that flows through the organization and in every department and function.

Throughput Accounting

Part of the process to determine the goal is to change the organizational view of the world. We no longer calculate things based on cost. Our view must transform to a look at system throughput. Costs are not allocated to a particular product or service; rather they are allotted over the entire process. We do this through the implementation of throughput accounting. The formula for calculating the new view is that throughput is the rate of new sales dollars. In other words, it is the total sales dollars minus the total variable costs to produce the end product.

$$Net\ Profit = Throughput\ \ Operating\ Expense$$

$$Return\ on\ Investment = (Throughput - Operating\ Expense)/Investment$$

In order to determine the ROI or net profit we subtract those product costs from the amount of sales. Inventory or investment costs are the funds you have put into machinery and materials to produce your products. The remaining factor is the organization's operating expenses. This provides us with a view of monies traveling through the organization.

While this new approach is usually viewed from a manufacturing view, it can equally be put to use in a service environment like HR. In Figure 10.2, you can see how this can be applied to HR.

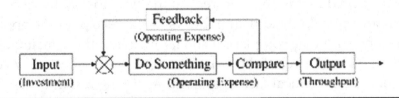

Figure 10.2 Throughout accounting in a service environment.[1]

Every process begins with some sort of input, and in this case, it is an investment in something that is required by the HR process. That investment leads to the expenditure of an operating expense, meaning that HR had to do something (like placing an online ad for an open position). From there you compare your options going forward. At this point you are comparing the process to date to where you thought you would be. If you did not achieve your goal, then you go back to the do something stage and try something else. On the other hand, if you did achieve your goal then you complete the process in the form of an output. The output represents the throughput.

The intent of this book has been to lay out a roadmap for your organization on how to achieve HR excellence using a different, but relatively simple, path to get to the end game. The use of the TLS Continuum methodology toolbox gives you the tools to achieve that prize. If you dedicate yourselves and your organization to the roadmap, you can create that excellent HR function and therefore the excellent organization. It is a journey filled with anticipated and unanticipated twists and turns, but the investment in the time and energy to create HR excellence is well worth the effort to reach the end result.

Note

1. Anderson, David. *Agile Software Management Accounting for Systems.* February 2004. https://www.informit.com/articles/article.aspx?p=169495&seqNum=3

Further Reading

Fleming, John

Human Sigma: Managing the Employee–Customer Encounter. New York: Gallup Press, 2007.

Liker, Jeffrey et al.

The Toyota Way: 14 Management Principles from the World's Greatest Manufacturer. New York: McGraw-Hill, 2003.
The Toyota Way Field book. New York: McGraw-Hill, 2005.
Toyota Talent: Developing Your People the Toyota Way. New York: McGraw-Hill, 2007.
Toyota Culture: The Heart and Soul of the Toyota Way. New York: McGraw-Hill, 2008.
Toyota Way to Lean Leadership: Achieving and Sustaining Excellence through Leadership Development. New York: McGraw-Hill, 2011.
The Toyota Way to Continuous Improvement: Linking Strategy and Operational Excellence to Achieve Superior Performance. New York: McGraw-Hill, 2011.

Sproull, Bob et al.

The Ultimate Improvement Cycle: Maximizing Profits through the Integration of Lean, Six Sigma and the Theory of Constraints. New York: CRC Press, 2009.
Epiphanized: Integrating Lean and Six Sigma. Great Barrington, MA: North River Press, 2012.
Epiphanized: Integrating Lean and Six Sigma, 2nd Edition. Great Barrington, MA: North River Press, 2015.
Focus and Leverage. New York: CRC Press, 2016.

The Problem-Solving, Problem-Prevention, and Decision-Making Guide. New York: Routledge Press, 2018.

Theory of Constraints Lean and Six Sigma Improvement Methodology. New York: Routledge Press, 2019.

The Focus and Leverage Improvement Book. New York: Routledge Press, 2019.

The Secret of Maximizing Profitability. New York: Routledge Press, 2020.

Bibliography

Chapter 1: Organizational Excellence

AZCentral.com. https://yourbusiness.azcentral.com/brief-description-role-managem
ent-organization-22173.html

Ferguson, Richard. *Definition of Excellence.* https://www.fergusonvalues.com/
2018/06/10-best-definitions-of-excellence-in-business/

Kahneman, Daniel. *Thinking Fast and Slow.* New York: Farrar, Straus and Giroux,
2011.

Kokemuller, Neil. Brief Description of the Role of Management in an Organization.
AZCentral.com. https://yourbusiness.azcentral.com/brief-description-role-ma
nagement-organization-22173.html

Merriam-Webster Dictionary. *Definition of Excellence.* 2011. http://www.merriam-w
ebster.com/dictionary/excellence

Spear, Jeffrey. *Definition of Excellence.* n.d. http://studiospear.com/downloads//
DefiningExcellence.pdf

Stark, Peter. *10 Keys to Workplace Excellence.* Jan 24, 2019. https://www.amanet.
org/articles/10-keys-to-workplace-excellence/

Vitale, Joe. https://www.thelawofattraction.com/joe-vitale-quotes/

Vocabulary.com. *Definition of Excellence.* https://www.vocabulary.com/dictionary/
excellence

Chapter 2: The Road to Change

Crosby, Philip B. *Quality without Tears.* New York: McGraw-Hill, 1984.

Dictionary of Oxford Languages. https://languages.oup.com/google-dictionary-en/

General Electric Corporation. *What Is Six Sigma? The Roadmap to Customer Impact.*
GE Document #19991438-1.

Kucera, David. *Quality Circles.* n.d. http://enotes.com/quality-circles--reference/
quality-circles

Lencioni, Patrick. *Silos, Politics and Turf Wars*. San Francisco, CA: Jossey-Bass, 2006.

Total Quality Engineering. n.d. http://www.tqe.com/TQM.html

Toyota Production System. https://global.toyota/en/company/vision-and-philosophy/production-system/

Ulrich David. *GE Workout*. New York: McGraw-Hill, 2002. http://en.wikipedia.org/wiki/ack_Welch. March 3, 2009.19.

US. State Department. *Occupation and Reconstruction of Japan, 1945–52*. https://history.state.gov/milestones.1945-1952/japan-reconstruction

Chapter 3: What the TLS Continuum?

Bloom, Daniel. *Taken from the article "Driving the Relocation 500"*. https://dbaiconsulting.com/Articles/Articale9.pdf

Dictionary.com. *Definition of Sigma*. http://dictionary.reference.com/browse/sigma?s=t. Based on Random House Dictionary.2013

http://focusedperformance.com/articles/tocsigma.html provides us with a clear picture of the tools

Miller, Ken. *We Don't Make Widgets*. Washington, DC: Governing Books, 2010.

Process.st. *Principles of Six Sigma*. http://process.st/six-sigma-principles/

Sproull, Bob and Bruce Nelson. *Epiphanized*, 2nd Edition. New York: CRC Press, 2015, Pages 13–15.

Miller, Lawrence. *Whole-System Architecture A Model for Building the Lean Organization*. https://www.lmmiller.com/wp-content/uploads/2011/06/Whole-System-Architecture-Article1.pdf

The Lean Way. *Principles of Lean*. https://theleanway.net/The-Five-Principles-of-Lean

Chapter 4: Project Design and Team Dynamics

Bahcall, Safi, *Loonshots*. New York: St. Martin's Press, 2019, Pages 199–202.

Bloom, Daniel. *Field Guide to Achieving HR Excellence through Six Sigma*. New York: CRC Press, 2016. Page 124.

Epstein, David. *Range: Why Generalists Triumph in a Specialized World*. New York: Riverhead Books, 2019, Pages 177–178.

Freeman, R. Edward. *The Stakeholder Theory*. http://stakeholdertheory.org/about

Hambleton, Lynne. *Treasure Chest of Six Sigma Growth Methods, Tools, and Best Practices*. New York: Prrentice-Hall, 2008, Page 315.

Heath, Dan. *Upstream*. New York: Avid Reader Press, 2020, Page 26.

Mindtools. *Frederick Taylor and Scientific Management*. https://mindtools.com/pages/article/new/TMM_Taylor.htm33

Phillips, Joseph. *Project Management Professional Study Guide*, 2nd Edition. New York: McGraw-Hill, 2006, Page 9.

Chapter 5: Voice of the Customer

Freeman, R. Edward. *The Stakeholder Theory.* http://stakeholdertheory.org/about
Merriam Webster Dictionary. *Definition of Value.* https://www.merriam-webster. com/dictionary/value
Pearse Trust Blog. *The Role of a Shareholder.* https://www.pearse-trust.ie/blog/ro les-responsibilities-of-company-shareholder#:~:text=The%20shareholders%20a re%20the%20owners,the%20lifetime%20of%20the%20company.&text=By%20 investing%20in%20return%20for,by%20gift%20or%20by%20will

Chapter 6: Organizational Waste

Arthur, Jay. *Free, Now and Perfect.* Denver, CO: Knowledge Ware, 2012, Page 18.
Mikel, Harry and Richard Schroeder. *Six Sigma: The Breakthrough Management Strategy Revolutionizing the World's Top Corporations.* New York: Crown Publishing Group, 2005, Page xii.
Yang, Kai. *Design for Six Sigma for Service.* New York: McGraw Hill, 2005, Pages 42–46.

Chapter 8: HRCI Body of Knowledge

Mathis, Robert L. *Human Resource Management*, 12th Edition. Mason, OH: Thomson Publishing, 2008, Page 61.

Chapter 10: The Road to HR Excellence

Anderson, David. *Agile Software Management Accounting for Systems.* February 2004. https://www.informit.com/articles/article.aspx?p=169495&seqNum=3

Index

Printed in the United States
by Baker & Taylor Publisher Services